# Conrad and Language

# Conrad and Language

Edited by Katherine Isobel Baxter
and Robert Hampson

EDINBURGH
University Press

Edinburgh University Press is one of the leading university presses in the UK. We publish academic books and journals in our selected subject areas across the humanities and social sciences, combining cutting-edge scholarship with high editorial and production values to produce academic works of lasting importance. For more information visit our website: edinburghuniversitypress.com

© editorial matter and organisation Katherine Isobel Baxter and Robert Hampson, 2016
© the chapters their several authors, 2016

Edinburgh University Press Ltd
The Tun – Holyrood Road, 12(2f) Jackson's Entry, Edinburgh EH8 8PJ

Typeset in 10.5/13 Adobe Sabon by
Servis Filmsetting Ltd, Stockport, Cheshire

A CIP record for this book is available from the British Library

ISBN 978 1 4744 0376 4 (hardback)
ISBN 978 1 4744 0377 1 (webready PDF)
ISBN 978 1 4744 0378 8 (epub)

The right of Katherine Isobel Baxter and Robert Hampson to be identified as the editors of this work has been asserted in accordance with the Copyright, Designs and Patents Act 1988, and the Copyright and Related Rights Regulations 2003 (SI No. 2498).

# Contents

| | |
|---|---|
| A Note on Texts | vii |
| Introduction<br>*Katherine Isobel Baxter and Robert Hampson* | 1 |
| 1 Conrad and Nautical Language: Flying Moors and Crimson Barometers<br>*Robert Hampson* | 10 |
| 2 Navigating the 'Terroristic Wilderness': Conrad's Language of Terror<br>*Andrew Glazzard* | 28 |
| 3 Conrad, G. E. Moore and Idealism<br>*John Attridge* | 44 |
| 4 Conrad's Language of Passivity: Unmoving towards Late Modernism<br>*Yael Levin* | 64 |
| 5 The Powers of Speech in Conrad's Fiction<br>*Josiane Paccaud-Huguet* | 82 |
| 6 'Soundless as Shadows': Language and Disability in the Political Novels<br>*Katherine Isobel Baxter* | 99 |
| 7 Conrad and Romanised Print Form: From Tuan Almayer to 'Prince Roman'<br>*Christopher GoGwilt* | 117 |
| 8 Languages in Conrad's Malay Fiction<br>*Andrew Francis* | 132 |

| | | |
|---|---|---|
| 9 | Gallicisms: The Secret Agent in Conrad's Prose<br>*Claude Maisonnat* | 151 |
| 10 | 'The speech of my secret choice': Language and Authorial Identity in *A Personal Record*<br>*Andrew Purssell* | 168 |
| 11 | The Russian Redemption of *The Secret Agent* and *Under Western Eyes*<br>*Ludmilla Voitkovska* | 186 |
| | Afterword<br>*Laurence Davies* | 204 |

Contributors     213
Index     216

## A Note on Texts

The abbreviation *CL* has been used throughout this book for *The Collected Letters of Joseph Conrad* (Cambridge: Cambridge University Press, 1983–2008), unless otherwise stated: Frederick R. Karl and Laurence Davies (eds), *The Collected Letters of Joseph Conrad. Vol. 1: 1886–1897* (1983); *Vol. 2: 1898–1902* (1986); *Vol. 3: 1903–1907* (1988); *Vol. 4: 1908–1911* (1991); *Vol. 5: 1912–1916* (1996); Laurence Davies, Frederick R. Karl and Owen Knowles (eds), *Vol. 6: 1917–1919* (2002); Laurence Davies and J. H. Stape (eds), *The Collected Letters of Joseph Conrad. Vol. 7: 1920–1922* (2005); Laurence Davies and Gene M. Moore (eds), *The Collected Letters of Joseph Conrad. Vol. 8: 1923–1924* (2008); Laurence Davies, Owen Knowles, Gene M. Moore and J. H. Stape (eds), *The Collected Letters of Joseph Conrad. Vol. 9: Uncollected Letters and Indexes* (2008).

The abbreviation *CR* has been used throughout this book for the Cambridge Edition of *The Works of Joseph Conrad: Contemporary Reviews* (Cambridge: Cambridge University Press, 2012) unless otherwise stated: Allan H. Simmons (ed.), *Joseph Conrad: Contemporary Reviews. Vol. 1: Almayer's Folly to Youth*; John G. Peters (ed.), *Joseph Conrad: Contemporary Reviews. Vol. 2: Typhoon to Under Western Eyes*; Richard Niland (ed.), *Joseph Conrad: Contemporary Reviews. Vol. 3: A Personal Record to An Arrow of Gold*; Mary Burgoyne and Katherine Baxter (eds), *Joseph Conrad: Contemporary Reviews. Vol. 4: The Rescue to Last Essays*.

# Introduction

*Katherine Isobel Baxter and Robert Hampson*

Conrad was born in Berdychiv in 1857. Berdychiv, a city and district now in Ukraine, at that time had a population consisting of Ukrainian peasantry and Polish landowners, and a large Jewish community, all legally subjects of the tsar of all the Russias. Conrad's family were *szlachta*, members of the Polish gentry, and like other members of his class, Conrad learned French early. In 1862, his parents (along with the four-year-old Conrad) were exiled to a penal colony in Vologda, 300 miles north-east of Moscow, for their political activities. The following year, the family was allowed to move south to the less harsh conditions of Chernikov, near Kiev, and Conrad and his mother were granted three months' leave for medical treatment. They spent the summer with her family at Nowochastów, where, as *A Personal Record* suggests, Conrad seems to have had his first lessons in French.[1] At this time, Poland, as such, didn't exist: it had been divided, by the Partitions of 1792, 1793 and 1795, between Russia, Prussia and Austria. Until he was naturalised as a British subject and released from his Russian subjecthood in 1886, Conrad travelled on Russian travel documents. In 1865 his mother died, and, in 1867, Conrad and his father, Apollo Korzeniowski, were allowed to move to the Austrian-held part of Poland. In 1869, shortly before his father's death, they moved to Krakow, where Conrad was to stay until 1874. His childhood was thus divided between Russian-controlled Poland and Austrian-controlled Poland.

In October 1874, at the age of sixteen, Conrad left Poland and travelled to Marseilles, where he was based for the next four years, sailing on French merchant ships. His travels at this stage took him to the Caribbean and, possibly, to South America. In 1878, he joined the British steamer the *Mavis*, and made his first sustained contact with English people and the English language. After this, he joined the British Merchant Navy, based himself in London, and began to learn English. His sea-voyages also brought him into contact with other languages.

In the first place, British ships were multinational, multilingual communities.[2] In addition, his voyages necessarily involved periods in other countries. He sailed twice to Australia. He also visited Madras, Bombay, Calcutta and Mauritius and made frequent visits to Singapore. Most importantly, he spent ten weeks as first mate of the *Vidar* making four trading trips between Singapore and various small ports on Borneo and Celebes (Sulawesi), where he picked up some Malay. In 1890, when he was in the Congo, notes in his Congo Diary show that he was also trying to learn some Kikongo.

Before he went to sea, Conrad was bilingual in Polish and French. In addition, he had some schoolboy Latin as well as some knowledge of two other languages, Russian and German, the languages of Poland's colonising powers. While he claimed not to know these latter two languages, biographical incidents suggest he had greater facility in them than he purported to. In 1893, for example, when he returned home after nearly twenty years' absence, his uncle, Tadeusz Bobrowski, advised him: 'From Brześć telegraph for horses, but in Russian, for Oratów doesn't receive or accept messages in an "alien" language.'[3] This suggests Conrad had some degree of competence in Russian. Two decades later, in October 1914, when Conrad and his family were struggling to get back from an ill-timed visit to Poland, his son Borys records his surprise at hearing his father apparently speaking fluent German at a border.[4] From the evidence of his letters and fiction, he also had some smattering of Dutch, Italian and Spanish.

If Conrad's own biography predisposed him to a sensitivity to language and the implications of how words are deployed, this can only have been reinforced by the intellectual milieu in which he published. For this period saw a flourishing of philosophical interest in language on the continent and in the British Isles. In the nineteenth century, European scholarship had focused much of its attention on philological and exegetical investigations of language. Biblical scholars uncovered the polyglot nature of the texts of the Old and New Testaments and consequently began to investigate the haphazard history of their canonisation. This scholarship was enriched by the methodologies of comparative linguistics whereby languages were compared in order to create genealogies or *Stammbaum* (family trees). These *Stammbaum* sought to trace the origins of specific languages (such as Sanskrit and Latin) back to a limited number of proto-languages (such as Proto-Indo-European). This scholarship was not undertaken in isolation, however, and both philology and comparative linguistics were influenced by and influential on some of the most important arenas of intellectual thought in the nineteenth century, from theology and science to colonial and imperial endeavour. Biblical philology and comparative linguistics were heavily informed by Orientalist scholarship in particular, and thus the languages they investigated were primarily Asian and European as opposed to those from the Pacific and the Americas. Moreover, their theories developed in tandem with those in the natural sciences, most clearly observed in the mutual influence between Charles Darwin and the comparative linguist August Schleicher, who had invented the genealogical model of the *Stammbaum*.[5] Taken as a whole this linguistic scholarship created an apparently objective apparatus for understanding language and its evolution; yet, in doing so, it also drew attention to the historical instability of language and its susceptibility to the influences of social migration and societal change.

The linguists' recognition of the historical instability of language was augmented in the late nineteenth and early twentieth centuries by developments in logical philosophy that investigated the insufficiencies of language in relation to truth. Philosophers such as Gottlob Frege demonstrated the lack of direct equivalence between words and their objects, and the necessity of taking the 'sense' of a word into consideration in order to understand its role in a statement.[6] Frege recognised that words that shared a literal referent do not automatically carry the same meaning. For example, the name Jósef Teodor Konrad Korzeniowski and the name Joseph Conrad refer to the same person, and yet the two statements 'Joseph Conrad = Joseph Conrad' and 'Joseph Conrad = Jósef Teodor Konrad Korzeniowski' are not equivalent. The former statement is self evident (a = a); the latter requires investigation for us to verify its truth (a = b). In Frege's terms, whilst Joseph Conrad and Jósef Teodor Konrad Korzeniowski *denote* the same person, the *sense* of the two names differs. Thus, to an Anglophone audience Joseph Conrad might be the name applied to the author of nineteen novels and novellas whose influence on English letters continues to this day, whilst Jósef Teodor Konrad Korzeniowski would connote a man born in Berdychiv who pursued an international maritime career before settling in Britain as a writer. What Frege draws our attention to, therefore, is the contextual nature of language, even at its semantic level.

While Frege's observations grew out of his training in mathematics, they were paralleled by those of his peer, Ferdinand de Saussure, who had grown up in the philological tradition outlined above. Saussure's contention was that language is intrinsically arbitrary, and this underpinned his larger claim for the similarity of semantic functions across languages, a claim whose roots in comparative linguistics are evident. The implications of arbitrariness for semantic theory, however, were at least as influential as Saussure's claims for universal structures across languages. Like Frege, Saussure drew attention to the contextual nature of words as signs and emphasised the way in which meaning is derived from the relation of words to each other through their functional rather than instrinsic values.

These theories, Frege's developed in Jena and Saussure's in Geneva, found their way into British intellectual life through the circulation of both books and people during the first decades of the twentieth century. Frege's ideas, for example, were picked up by Bertrand Russell, who corresponded with Frege in the first decade of the new century and in due course mentored Ludwig Wittgenstein, to whom he had been recommended by Frege. In turn, Wittgenstein's own early philosophy was developed out of Frege's theories in conversation with Russell, G. E. Moore and Maynard Keynes, all members of the Cambridge Apostles and associates of the Bloomsbury group.[7] Thus through the exchanges of university scholarship, artistic associations, and an increasingly dynamic international publishing industry, these philosophical engagements with the structure, history and function of language began to permeate the intellectual life of English letters more broadly. We can observe this influence in Eliot's 1920 article on Swinburne in the *Athenaeum*, where the vocabulary of philosophical logic and linguistics mediates his literary criticism. Eliot begins with the assertion that 'Language in a healthy state presents the object, is so close to the object that the two are identified.' He uses Swinburne as an example of this identification: 'They are identified in the verse of Swinburne solely because the object has ceased to exist, because the meaning is merely hallucination of meaning, because language, uprooted, has adapted itself to an independent life of atmospheric nourishment.' However, he goes on, 'the language which is more important to us is that which is struggling to digest and express new objects, new groups of objects, new feelings, new aspects, as, for instance, the prose of Mr. James Joyce or the earlier Conrad'.[8]

While Conrad may not have thought of his own writing practice in this quasi-scientific way, nonetheless his own assessment of language in the world echoes in an existential vein the same concerns for the precarious and arbitrary condition of language expressed by Frege, Wittgenstein and Saussure. In his famous correspondence with Cunninghame Graham in the 1890s Conrad perceives the logical result of language's radical instability: 'Half the words we use have no meaning whatever and of the other half each man understands each word after the fashion of his own folly and conceit . . . words, once pronounced, die.'[9]

Although Conrad's distinctive writing style had attracted interest and comment from the start of his writing career, serious academic attention to Conrad and language did not begin until the late 1970s. In 1966

René Rapin made a pioneering study of Conrad's knowledge of French (or, at least, his knowledge of French as evidenced in one set of letters) in the Introduction to his edition of Conrad's letters to Marguerite Poradowska.[10] From the evidence of these letters, Rapin concluded that Conrad made frequent and at times quite serious mistakes in French, but what struck him, beyond these faults, was the natural ease – indeed, what he saw as Conrad's extraordinary aptitude – for expressing himself in a language which was neither his mother tongue nor the language environment in which he lived during his forty-six years as a seaman and later as an English writer.

Rapin's pioneering work was followed up by Yves Hervouet in the late 1970s in a two-part essay 'Joseph Conrad and the French Language'.[11] Hervouet began by attending to Conrad's use of French in conversations as well as in his correspondence and other writing. On the basis of this evidence, he noted Conrad's tendency to switch to French, both in speech and in writing, when dealing with cultural, political and emotional matters. Hervouet's major contribution, however, was in showing how French vocabulary, idiomatic phrases and grammar impacted on the English of Conrad's literary texts. Hervouet's monograph *The French Face of Joseph Conrad*, which was published posthumously in 1990, also documented the part played in Conrad's fiction by his memories (and, perhaps, even translations) of a range of French texts.[12]

This aspect of Conrad's relation to language was picked up by comparative linguists, and the study of gallicisms in Conrad's fiction was closely followed by studies of his polonisms. For example, in 1974, Irmina Pulc published her essay 'The Imprint of Polish on Conrad's Prose'.[13] However, it wasn't until 1994 that Mary Morzinski published the first book-length treatment of the subject, *Linguistic Influence of Polish on Joseph Conrad's English*.[14] Conrad's work also invited attention from linguists working in the area of stylistics. In 1980, Werner Senn's monograph *Conrad's Narrative Voice* provided an extensive analysis of stylistic aspects of Conrad's writing, beginning with adjectival style and negation.[15] However, Senn's approach is not rigorously stylistic: he includes a chapter on 'Eyes, Faces, Looks' and concludes with a chapter on free indirect style which draws on Seymour Chatman's work on narratology. This trajectory from stylistics to narratology anticipated one direction Conrad studies was to take subsequently.

In the previous year, Jeremy Hawthorn had published *Joseph Conrad: Language and Fictional Self-Consciousness*.[16] In his Introduction, Hawthorn notes how the critical treatment of Conrad's interest in language to date had tended to focus on the argument 'about the extent to which he "chose" to write in English' or 'the extent to which his other languages influenced his English'.[17] Hawthorn drew on Conrad's plurilingual background to focus, instead, on Conrad's 'more than commonly developed consciousness of language', by which Hawthorn meant not pedantry about grammar but rather 'an awakened philosophical curiosity about language'.[18] He argues that Conrad's fiction concerned itself with 'the nature of language, the status of fiction, and ... the whole question of self-consciousness', and the monograph traces 'a movement from an early fascination with language, both spoken and written, through to a concern with the relation between "mental" and "real" events, culminating in a concern with fiction and self-consciousness'.[19]

In 1983, Martin Ray addressed himself to Conrad's languages in 'The Gift of Tongues: The Languages of Joseph Conrad'.[20] Ray begins with Conrad's choice of English, but the latter part of his essay explores the contradiction between Conrad's aesthetic commitment to *le mot juste* and his acute knowledge, derived from his multilingual experience, that 'languages were nothing but approximate and provisional representations of the world'.[21] The following year Ray published a second essay, 'Language and Silence in the Novels of Joseph Conrad', which teases at this problem from another perspective.[22] In this essay, Ray considers Conrad's essay 'Outside Literature', where 'he contrasts the futile indulgence of his literary career with the practical consolations of his former life as a sailor'.[23] Ray fixes (as does Conrad) on the way the two occupations require 'different approaches to language': 'The artist seeks words which will capture the fleeting and evanescent impressions of an imaginatively apprehended reality', while for the sailor, 'language is a precise and practical tool, a medium which can be perfectly adequate for its task, since the demands upon it are finite and utilitarian'.[24] The writer of the 'Notices to Mariners' must avoid the imaginative and the ambiguous: 'indeed, the author of such Notices must exhibit a rigorous concern for the precision of his style comparable to the literary artist's regard for *le mot juste*' in order to produce what Conrad calls 'the most trusted kind of printed prose'.[25] The technical language of the sea, with its 'ideal of perfect accuracy', represents the perfect adaptation of words to things and actions, whereas imaginative writing, as Conrad was forced to recognise on a daily basis, was a confrontation with the elusiveness of language.[26]

The chapters in this volume follow in the tradition initiated by Hawthorn and Ray. They approach the topic of 'Conrad and Language' not from the perspective of comparative linguistics or stylistics, but rather in terms of that 'more than commonly developed consciousness of language', which produced 'an awakened philosophical curiosity about language' that included a questioning of the relation of words and things and a recognition of language's approximate representation of reality. We open with Hampson's exploration of Conrad's nautical language, which expands upon Ray's earlier investigations to consider how that language was shaped for contemporary readers and how it was received by his reviewers. The following chapter, by Andrew Glazzard, pursues a different kind of technical language, that of political terror: Glazzard draws out the varied ways in which Conrad deploys the language of terrorism across *The Rover*, *The Secret Agent* and *Under Western Eyes* in order to re-evaluate how we in turn use that language today.

In the next set of chapters, John Attridge turns our attention to the intriguing parallels between G. E. Moore's philosophical investigations of Idealism and Conrad's own scepticism about idealistic abstraction, while Yael Levin introduces a different kind of philosophical consideration in relation to Conrad's fiction: the relationship between language, subjectivity and (in)action in narrative voice, character and plot. Levin compares the scenes of narration in *Lord Jim* to the narrative strategies of Beckett's fiction, in order to trace a particular paradigm of modernist lateness in both author's works. Josiane Paccaud-Huguet likewise attends to Marlovian narration, applying J. L. Austin's concept of the perlocutionary speech act to an analysis of *Chance*. In the following chapter, Baxter unpacks the connections between disability, language and silence in Conrad's political novels through an engagement with critical paradigms in disability studies.

Turning to the question of specific languages and their textual appearances, Christopher GoGwilt considers the complex relationship between the non-English speech of many of Conrad's characters and the way in which that speech, particularly Malay and Russian, is translated and transliterated on the page. Picking up on GoGwilt's engagement with Malay, Andrew Francis explores in detail the colonial linguistic context of Conrad's representations of the Malay Archipelago. Claude Maisonnat then returns us to *The Rover* in order to trace the gallicisms that haunt this late novel, arguing that as much as Conrad may have misremembered his French in later years, 'his French ... never forgot him'. Andrew Purssell's chapter provides a useful counterpoint to Maisonnat's, delineating Conrad's conscious self-fashioning as an English author, rather than simply an author in English, in his account of his literary origins in *A Personal Record*. Ludmilla Voitkovska brings us back to the present, with an analysis of the recent publication of two full Russian translations of *The Secret Agent* and *Under Western Eyes*. Engaging with the problems posed to Conrad in attempting to present 'things Russian' to Western readers, and the different problems posed to Russian translators when the 'style russe' is translated into Russian,

Voitkovska argues that the appearance of these new translations marks a shift in the Russian reception of Conrad's work. Finally, Laurence Davies, in his afterword, draws together these various approaches to Conrad's existence within and between multiple languages, showing how they are in dialogue with current debates in relation to cosmopolitanism, transnationalism and migrant culture and how they demonstrate Conrad's own importance for such debates.

## Notes

1. Joseph Conrad, *A Personal Record* (London: J. M. Dent and Sons, 1923), p. 65. Conrad's father, Apollo Korzeniowski, in addition to his political activities, was also a poet, a dramatist and a translator. He had mastered four languages (English, French, German and Russian) and translated into Polish works by Alfred de Vigny, Victor Hugo, Charles Dickens and William Shakespeare.
2. See Robert Hampson, '"Under the folds of the Union Jack": Conrad and the multinational world of ships', Plenary Lecture, International Joseph Conrad Conference, Roma Tre, June 2013.
3. Tadeusz Bobrowski to Józef Korzeniowski, 22 May 1893, quoted in Zdzisław Najder, *Joseph Conrad: A Life*, trans. Halina Najder (Rochester, NY: Camden House, 2007), p. 184.
4. 'My Father had always insisted that he could only speak a few words of German, however, in this emergency, it seemed to me that he spoke at considerable length and with great fluency'. Borys Conrad, *My Father: Joseph Conrad* (London: Calder and Boyars, 1970), p. 97.
5. See Robert J. Richards, 'The Linguistic Creation of Man: Charles Darwin, August Schleicher, Ernst Haeckel, and the Missing Link in Nineteenth-Century Evolutionary Theory', in Matthias Dörries (ed.), *Experimenting Tongues: Studies in Science and Language* (Stanford: Stanford University Press, 2002), pp. 21–48.
6. Frege began his studies at the University of Jena, where Schleicher had been an honorary professor, the year after Schleicher's death.
7. Wittgenstein was nominally a member of the Apostles too but does not seem to have attended with any regularity.
8. T. S. Eliot, 'Swinburne as Poet', in *The Sacred Wood* (London: Methuen, 1964), pp. 149–50. First published as 'Swinburne', *Athenaeum* 4681 (16 January 1920), pp. 72–3.
9. Joseph Conrad to R. B. Cunninghame Graham, 14 January 1898. CL2 17.
10. René Rapin (ed.), *Lettres de Joseph Conrad à Marguerite Poradowska* (Geneva: Droz, 1966), p. 53. The following passage derives from this page.
11. Yves Hervouet, 'Joseph Conrad and the French Language', *Conradiana* 11.3 (1979), pp. 229–51 and *Conradiana* 14.1 (1982), pp. 23–49.
12. Yves Hervouet, *The French Face of Joseph Conrad* (Cambridge: Cambridge University Press, 1990).
13. Irmina P. Pulc, 'The Imprint of Polish on Conrad's Prose', in Wołodymyr

T. Zyla and Wendell M. Aycock (eds), *Joseph Conrad: Theory and World Fiction* (Lubbock: Texas Tech University Press, 1974), pp. 117–40.
14. Mary Morzinski, *Linguistic Influence of Polish on Joseph Conrad's English* (Lublin: Maria Curie-Skłodowska University, 1994).
15. Werner Senn, *Conrad's Narrative Voice: Stylistic Aspects of his Fiction* (Bern: Francke, 1980).
16. Jeremy Hawthorn, *Joseph Conrad: Language and Fictional Self-Consciousness* (London: Edward Arnold, 1979).
17. Ibid. p. x.
18. Ibid. p. xi.
19. Ibid. p. 2.
20. Martin Ray, 'The Gift of Tongues: The Languages of Joseph Conrad', *Conradiana* 15.2 (1983), pp. 83–109.
21. Ibid. p. 101.
22. Martin Ray, 'Language and Silence in the Novels of Joseph Conrad', *Conradiana* 16.1 (1984), pp. 19–40.
23. Joseph Conrad, 'Outside Literature', in *Last Essays* (London: J. M. Dent and Sons, 1926), pp. 59–65. Ray, 'Language and Silence', p. 28.
24. Ray, 'Language and Silence', p. 28.
25. Ibid. p. 28; Conrad, 'Outside Literature', p. 65.
26. Conrad, 'Outside Literature', p. 65.

# Chapter 1

# Conrad and Nautical Language: Flying Moors and Crimson Barometers

*Robert Hampson*

At the very start of his writing career, when Conrad first submitted the typescript of *Almayer's Folly* to Fisher Unwin for consideration for their Pseudonym Library, it bore the name 'Kamudi', the Malay word for 'rudder'. This foreshadowed his subsequent pseudonymous entry into professional writing; it provided a linguistic context for the novel's opening words ('Kaspar! Makan!') and for the smattering of Malay words in the opening chapters ('godowns', 'rattan', 'prau'). To begin with, many of the Malay words used in the novel are transparent: they have acquired the status of loan words, part of the verbal traffic of British colonial trade. Subsequent Malay words – Rajah Laut, Tuan, Orang Blanda, Mem Putih – will become familiar in the course of Conrad's Malay fiction; others (chelakka, bitchara, Tannah Mirrah) are more recherché.[1] Nevertheless, as one reviewer noted, the 'few Malay words sprinkled about his pages set up none of the feeble irritation that most foreign tongues, used as local colour, are apt to do: they have the piquancy of capsicums in a curry'.[2] What is missing from this novel (and from Conrad's Malay fiction generally), however, is the Malay language for working a ship, some of which Conrad presumably knew, since he was familiar with the word 'kamudi'. Instead, we find in Conrad's Malay fiction the usual British nautical language: brig, roadstead, supercargo, bulwarks, fore-deck, poop.

Nautical language had entered English prose writing with the early accounts of voyages of exploration. Swift had satirised this language – and the obscurity of precise technical terms to the general reader – in *Gulliver's Travels*. At the start of Book II, there is a long paragraph in which Gulliver describes how the crew of the *Adventure* responded to a storm. It begins: 'Finding it was like to overblow, we took in our spritsail, and stood by to hand the foresail; but making foul weather, we looked the guns were all fast, and handed the missen.' It concludes, after numerous such sentences: 'We got the starboard tacks aboard, we cast off our weatherbraces and lifts; we set in the lee braces, and hauled forward by the weather bowlings, and hauled them tight, and belayed them, and hauled over the missen tack to windward, and kept her full and by as near as she would lie.'[3] Although, as Starkman notes, this is taken almost verbatim from Samuel Sturmy's *Mariners Magazine* (1679), the passage exceeds realism and turns into parody through recontextualisation.

In 'Heart of Darkness', Marlow's discovery of a copy of *An Inquiry into Some Points of Seamanship* famously leads him to see in its words 'a singleness of intention, an honest concern for the right way of going to work'.[4] This chapter will explore Conrad's handling of nautical language in such works as *The Nigger of the 'Narcissus'*, *Lord Jim*, 'Typhoon' and 'The End of the Tether'. It will explore Conrad's negotiation of precision and clarity – and the kind of contract he establishes with his readers. It will also explore Conrad's engagement with 'nautical language' in another sense: the problem of representing the kind of language used by ship's crews. The second engineer in 'Typhoon', for example, emerges from the stokehold complaining: 'did the condemned sailors think you could keep steam up in the God-forsaken boilers simply by knocking the blanked stokers about?'[5] How did Conrad address this problem elsewhere in his fiction? What solutions did he find, and how was this aspect of his work regarded by contemporary readers?

## Flying Moors

*The Nigger of the 'Narcissus'* (1898) begins by establishing some of the spaces of the ship: 'Mr Baker, chief mate of the ship *Narcissus*, stepped in one stride out of his lighted cabin into the darkness of the quarter deck. Above his head, on the break of the poop, the night-watchman rang a double stroke.'[6] The passage sets up a set of easily comprehended spatial relations, and suggests certain hierarchical relations, while sustaining the title's contrast of lightness and darkness. The precise meanings of quarter deck and poop – the latter referring to the raised deck at the stern of the ship, the former to the deck between the poop and the mainmast – might evade the casual reader, but this does not prevent engagement with the narrative. Mr Baker's order ('Tell the boatswain to send all hands aft' [*NN* 3]) is not too obscure: most readers would be familiar with the distinction between fore and aft. Even the final preparations for sailing – 'The carpenter had driven in the last wedge of the main-hatch battens ... the windlass oiled and made ready to heave up the anchor' (*NN* 3–4) – are fully comprehensible for readers without much nautical knowledge. There are also comparatively few nautical terms in the rest of this first chapter: just a reference, towards the end of the chapter, to 'the slack of the chain-cable between the windlass and the hawse-pipe' rising off the deck and 'the handle of the screw-brake' moving 'in slight jerks' (*NN* 19), which call Singleton into action. Without knowing the various components named, readers accept the necessity for his intervention. Perhaps the most important nautical term so far, however, is contained in the subtitle: 'A Tale of the Forecastle'. The 'forecastle', the crew's living quarters at the front of the ship, stand in contrast to that 'lighted cabin' to the rear from which the mate emerged. With this subtitle, Conrad indicated that his tale was primarily concerned with the crew of the *Narcissus* rather than its officers.

The second chapter, where the *Narcissus* goes to sea, necessarily involves an increased use of nautical language. When the tug has left it, 'the ship moved ahead slowly under lower topsails', and then 'the sheets were hauled home, the yards hoisted' (*NN* 21) and the voyage begins. Similarly, in chapter 3, when the storm hits the ship, there has to be some technical description of their response: 'orders were given to furl the fore and mizzen top-sails', and, next morning, 'the main topsail had to be goose-winged' (*NN* 41).[7] In chapter 4, when the ship is righted, there again has to be a certain amount of technical language to explain the manoeuvre. In response to Captain Allistoun's command to 'Wear ship', the crew reappear, as if resurrected, on the forecastle head: 'hanging on to the rails; clambering over the anchors, embracing the cross-head of the windlass, or hugging the fore-capstan' (*NN* 63). Under Allistoun's leadership, they then go through a series of actions: 'casting the lee main braces off the pins', squaring 'the main yard' and hauling 'the main brace' (*NN* 63). As a result, the *Narcissus* 'went off slowly', 'paid off very gradually' and 'brought the wind abaft the beam' (*NN* 64). In chapter 5, Conrad presents the 'hard and unceasing' toil that maintains the ship's progress: from the boatswain, 'climbing up with marlinspikes and bunches of spunyard rovings, or kneeling on the yard and ready to take a turn with the midship stop' (*NN* 69), to Baker's orders to the crew to 'Set the topmost stunsail' and 'Fetch the sail along; bend the down-haul clear' (*NN* 76). In the final chapters, there are fewer nautical terms. Once again, as in the example just cited, even if the exact meaning is not clear to the reader, the use of technical terms serves to signify the restoration of order in the face of the tumult of the sea and the mutinous stirrings of the ship's crew.

Neil Munro, in the *Glasgow Evening News*, praised Conrad's 'confident but not pedantic handling of marine material' in *The Nigger of the 'Narcissus'*.[8] The anonymous reviewer for the *Manchester Courier* (22

December 1897) similarly praised Conrad's 'intimate knowledge' and 'intense enthusiasm for sea, ships and sailors' (*CR1* 163). However, the reviewer for the *Illustrated London News* (8 January 1898), while praising Conrad's description of the storm, thought it was both 'at too great length' and 'in language too technical' [*CR1* XXX]. The reviewer for the *Army and Navy Gazette* (26 February 1898) praised the 'masterly manner' in which Conrad presented 'the inner life of the merchant service as viewed from the seaman's viewpoint' and singled out for particular commendation the depiction of the *Narcissus* 'lying over upon her beam ends in a gale off the Cape' and the account of 'the successful effort made by the captain at dawn to wear the ship and right her'. However, after this informed praise, the reviewer expresses his concern: 'These and most of the descriptions are so technical that we should doubt whether the book can be properly appreciated by the landsman.' Nevertheless, he notes, the book 'seems to have made a distinct hit' (*CR1* 185) with the general reader. In North America, George Hamlin Fitch, in the *San Francisco Chronicle* (3 April 1898), praised the book's 'pictures of the sea and of the *Narcissus*' for being 'technically correct and at the same time full of dramatic force' (*CR1* 201). The reviewer in the *New York Tribune* (3 April 1898) similarly praised Conrad for being 'accurate as only one writer out of ten thousand is accurate' (*CR1* 216). By comparison, the reviewer in the *Springfield Sunday Republican* (3 April 1898), while praising it as 'one of the best sea stories of recent years', expressed the concern that 'probably many readers will be repelled by the prolixity of the descriptions and the multiplicity of the nautical terms' (*CR1* 218). However, this perhaps tells us more about the reviewer's anxieties about the Springfield readership than it does about the novel.

Most of the negative reviews were more concerned with the absence of 'plot' than with the technical nautical language. The hostile review in the *Daily Mail* (7 December 1897), for example, shows what Conrad had left out: 'There is no plot, no villainy, no heroism, and apart from a storm and the death and burial, no incident' (*CR1* 150). 'The Old Sea Salt', reviewing the work for the *Daily Chronicle* (22 December 1897), is even clearer about his expectations: 'There is no pirate in it, no wreck, no desert island, no treasure trove' (*CR1* 161). The reviewer in the *Glasgow Herald* (9 December 1897), who has nothing but praise for Conrad's fiction ('there is no novelist of the day who is more original in his methods than Mr Conrad'), reveals, with appropriate wryness, another component of the contemporary popular sea-novel which Conrad omits: 'the introduction in mid-ocean of beautiful but athletic young ladies who have been yachting with their papa' and suffered 'some extraordinary ill-fortune at the whim of Father Neptune' (*CR1* 154). These reviews help us to understand the expectations underlying the contemporary criticisms of the novel's lack of plot, but they also remind us of a history of sea-fiction and the degree of familiarity with nautical language that these works engendered in the common reader. Reviews regularly refer to a tradition of nautical fiction 'from Smollett to Cooper and Michael Scott, from Marryat to Mr Clark Russell' (*CR*1 190), including neglected writers such as Hermann Melville and contemporaries such as Pierre Loti and Kipling's recently published *Captains Courageous*.

It is these readers of sea-fiction that 'Youth' (1898) also addressed. The opening paragraph recalls 'the good old days when mail-boats were square-rigged at least on two masts and used to come down the China Sea before a fair monsoon with stun'-sails set alow and aloft' (*Y* 3). Marlow's account of the doomed voyage of the *Judea* maintains this level of light, precise technical language. Thus he recounts their first encounter with a gale in the Yarmouth Roads: 'We were flying light, and you may imagine how bad it was when I tell you we had smashed bulwarks and a flooded deck' (*Y* 6). The collision with a steamer before they can leave the Tyne is described with similar economy and simplicity: 'the steamer struck a glancing blow with the bluff of her bow about our fore-rigging' (*Y* 8). The 'piecemeal' dismantling of the ship by the second gale, which they encounter in the Atlantic, maintains this balance of technical language and comprehensibility: 'the bulwarks went, the stanchions were torn out, the ventilators smashed, the cabin-door burst in' (*Y* 11). Similarly, after the explosion, when the *Judea* is being towed by a steamer, Marlow recounts how the crew 'went aloft to furl the sails': 'We coughed on the yards, and were careful about the bunts' (*Y* 28). Conrad, through Marlow, provides enough technical language to sound authoritative, but not so much that the reader is overwhelmed.

The same can be said of *Lord Jim* (1900). Thus, in the omniscient narrator's account of Jim's experiences on the training ship, we are told that he learned 'a little trigonometry and how to cross top-gallant yards', but no knowledge of either is required of the reader.[9] The significance of Jim's station 'in the foretop' is clear enough without a precise knowledge of ship's masts: 'from there he looked down, with the contempt of a man destined to shine in dangers' (*LJ* 6). The rescue makes more demands on the reader: the mob of boys 'clustered around the davits'; Jim is pushed and staggers 'against the mizzen mast'; and the order is given to 'clear the falls' (*LJ* 7). However, the narrative is so fast-paced that the precise meaning of the technical terms does not need to be understood to gain an impression of the action, although the precision itself gives authority to the narrative. Similarly, on board the *Patna*, the heaviest use of technical language precedes the moment of collision: the narrator describes the 'patent-log on the taffrail' periodically ringing 'a single tinkling stroke for every mile traversed' (*LJ* 19); two Malay crewmen are described 'one on each side of the wheel, whose brass rim shone fragmentarily in the oval of light thrown out by the binnacle' (*LJ* 19); 'the links of wheel-chains ground heavily in the grooves of the barrel' (*LJ* 19); and 'the ash-buckets racketed, clanking up and down the stoke-hold ventilators' (*LJ* 20). Even if we are not quite certain of the function of all these parts of the ship, Conrad presents vividly certain visual impressions, while also suggesting the soundscape of the steamer. When Marlow takes over the narration, the authority of his technical understanding of ships is underlined. Thus, when he describes his response to Jim's misleadingly 'promising appearance', he recalls 'the skipper of an Italian barque' dancing on his hat in mortification 'because his duffer of a mate got into a mess with his anchors when making a flying moor in a roadstead full of ships' (*LJ* 40–1). Here the difficulty of the technical language serves to emphasise the various professional judgements that are being made: the skipper's angry and critical response to his mate and Marlow's precise professional judgement on Jim. Marlow decodes this nautical story subsequently: 'I would have trusted the deck to that youngster on the strength of a single glance . . . and, by Jove! it wouldn't have been safe' (*LJ* 45).

Jim, too, uses technical language when he recounts his memories of events leading up to his jump from the *Patna*. This is appropriate enough, given that his addressee is a ship's captain. He begins with his experience on the lower deck, and his sense that the bulkhead was bulging under his hand. Marlow imaginatively supplements Jim's account, picturing him 'in the peopled gloom of the cavernous place, with the light of the bulk-lamp falling on a small portion of the bulkhead that had the weight of the ocean on the other side' (*LJ* 84–5). Jim then recounts his experience 'on the foredeck' with another 'sleeping crowd', amid a 'confusion of boxes, steam-winches, ventilators' (*LJ* 85), who exerted their own pressure on him. Jim's account of the jump itself begins with a careful piece of scene setting: 'The *Patna* had a long bridge, and all the boats were up there, four on one side and three on the other – the smallest of them on the port-side and nearly abreast of the steering gear' (*LJ* 89). While economically signalling the inadequate number of lifeboats for the number of people on board, this passage also presents the stage on which the action in the next two chapters will be played out, from Jim being struck with 'a boat-stretcher' by the chief engineer when he reached the bridge (*LJ* 91) through the frustration of the four Europeans, who have managed to get 'the sliding bolt of the foremost boat-chock jammed' (*LJ* 95–6), to 'the grinding surge of the heavy davits swinging out at last' and 'the boat-falls' ripping 'through the blocks' (*LJ* 108) as one of the lifeboats is finally freed. This is all the technical language in these two chapters. The drama of the freeing of the lifeboat and the abandonment of the ship by the European officers and crew is largely conveyed in non-technical language, with Jim's narration supplemented by Marlow's imaginings: 'It must have been a pretty sight, the fierce industry of these beggars toiling on a motionless ship that floated quietly in the silence of a world asleep' (*LJ* 96).

## Crimson barometers

In chapter 1 of *Liza of Lambeth* (1897), Liza responds to the organ grinder playing the Intermezzo from 'Cavalleria': 'Oh, I sy . . . this is too bloomin' slow; it gives me the sick.'[10] The narrator then observes:

> That is not precisely what she said, but it is impossible always to give the exact unexpurgated words of Liza and the other personages of the story; the reader is therefore entreated with his thoughts to piece out the necessary imperfections of the dialogue.[11]

In *The Nigger of the 'Narcissus'*, Conrad faces a comparable problem. As the crew assemble in the forecastle at the start of the voyage, the narrator observes: 'All were speaking together, swearing at every second word.' Later, when Craik nearly goes over the side, he consigns the crew 'with abominable words to the "divvle"' and is reproached by Mr Baker for being 'a foul-mouthed beggar'. Podmore the cook complains too about young Charley's swearing (*NN* 22), and Donkin is described as not admitting 'of any hereafter, except for purposes of blasphemy' (*NN* 107). Even the second mate, young Mr Creighton, has 'a gentlemanly way of damning us up and down the deck' (*NN* 46). The pervasiveness of bad language in the crew's exchanges creates a problem of verisimilitude which Conrad addresses through a variety of strategies. On some occasions he uses mild swear words. Donkin grumbles about 'perishin' with cold . . . in bloomin' wet rags' (*NN* 41). Later, he praises his shipmates as a 'bloomin' condemned lot of good men' (*NN* 74). On some occasions, Conrad uses stronger swear words. Thus Donkin complains to Wait: 'You put no more weight on a rope than a bloody sparrer' (*NN* 33). At the crisis of the storm, when there is an argument about cutting the masts, the crew all wanted to see 'them damn bloody sticks go overboard' (*NN* 44). And when the crew suddenly remember Wait after the ship has been overturned by the storm, Donkin's curt response is 'Damn him' (*NN* 47). Sometimes Conrad uses substitutes. When Donkin introduces himself as 'a sailor like you', he gets the response: 'Blamme me if you don't look a dam sight worse than a broken down fireman' (*NN* 9). When the crew work to break through the bulkhead to rescue the trapped Wait, Belfast curses 'the Clyde shipwrights . . . all North Britain, the rest of the earth, the sea – and all his companions', ending with the vow never to associate with any fool who does not 'know his knee from his elbow' (*NN* 51). Wait's ungrateful response is similarly bowdlerised: 'I began to think the whole smart lot of you had been washed overboard' (*NN* 52). As well as 'Blamme', 'blamed' and 'blanked' are frequently resorted to. Thus Donkin inquires 'What kind of blamed ship is this?' (*NN* 9), and he calls the Finn a 'blanked deaf and dumb fool' (*NN* 10). Wait similarly rejects Belfast's reproach about the stolen pie: 'Blow your blamed pie' (*NN* 29). And Singleton chides Wait 'don't raise a blamed fuss with us' (*NN* 32) about his dying. Sometimes Conrad simply leaves a blank. Thus one of the crew in the forecastle complains about the conditions on board the *Narcissus* that 'they get their money's worth out of poor Jack, by —!' (*NN* 7). Similarly, Belfast's tale about his quarrel with an officer on another ship has the officer challenging him 'What do you say, you —!' At other times Conrad is more inventive. Belfast is supposed to have responded by calling the officer a 'nosing, skipper-licking, useless, sooperfloos bridge-stanchion' (*NN* 7), where 'nosing' suggests 'brown-nosing', 'skipper-licking' suggests 'arse-licking', but 'bridge-stanchion' has me floored.[12]

The text I have been quoting from is the serial text. Conrad came under pressure from his publisher to make changes for the book publication. In a letter to Edward Garnett (11 October 1897), he observed: 'Heinemann objects to the *bloody's* in the book. . . . So I struck 3 or 4 *bloody's* out. I am sure there is a couple left yet, but damn it, I am not going to hunt 'em up' (*CL2* 395). In later texts, the vehement reference to 'them damned bloody sticks' became the less forceful 'them damned sticks' and Wait's response to Donkin, 'You are a bloody fool' (*NN* 86), became the less convincing 'You are a crazy fool.'[13] The rest remain untouched. The anonymous reviewer in the *Daily Mail* (7 December 1897) praised Conrad's representation of sailors' language: 'Their talk and their swearing, especially the latter, is absolutely natural' (*CR1* 150), while the anonymous reviewer for the *Spectator* described the story as providing 'a picture of rough seafaring life, frank yet never offensively realistic' (*CR1* 165). However, W. L. Courtney, reviewing the book in the *Daily Telegraph* (8 December 1897), snagged on those remaining 'bloody's' and began his review with the question of swearing (*CR1* 150–4). After commenting on the ugliness of the title, he turns his attention to the language of sailors. He notes that 'some excellent persons have objected to Captain Marryat's stories of the sea, because his heroes and heroines use somewhat rough and explicit language, and swear a good deal'. However, Marryat's 'realism' is 'not a patch on Mr Conrad's': 'Captain Marryat was sometimes inclined to invest a spade with the literary distinction of being an agricultural implement', but Conrad 'remorselessly refers to it as a shovel, with a singularly effective and sanguinary adjective attached' (CR1 150–1). Courtney, like other reviewers, clearly sees here the influence of 'naturalism' from across the Channel. The anonymous reviewer of the *Court Journal* (11 December 1897), for example, begins the review by remarking 'One must commonly pay for realism, as it is generally understood, with occasional shocks to one's sense of propriety', before noting 'some passages or words' which could have been left out of what is, otherwise, 'a remarkably able piece of work' (CR1 155). With this health warning about an occasional 'lack of reserve', the review is generally appreciative of Conrad's 'audacious, uncompromising naturalism' (CR1 155). The reviewer for the *Literary World* (28 January 1898) similarly praised the novel for its 'freshness, vigour and strength', while criticising it for 'a want of restraint and a too realistic rendering of forecastle dialogue' (CR1 179). It is 'a wonderful and fascinating piece of workmanship', which is also 'brutal, and in many places absolutely repellent by reason of the robustness of the adjectives employed' (CR1 178). The reviewer for the *Des Moines Daily News* was less fazed by Conrad's lexical choices: 'The story . . . is replete with sprightly conversations in nautical language so strongly flavoured that one sees the picture of the sea' (CR1 207). The reviewer in the Baltimore *Sun* (3 April 1898), after mentioning the 'swearing sailors', observes: 'The picture, so coarse in places as to be disgusting, is yet so strong that we lose sight of our disgust in honest admiration' (CR1 220). Similarly, the reviewer in the *Advance* (5 May 1898) praises the work for portraying 'with great vividness the swearing, quarrelling, polyglot lot which forms the crew of a sailing vessel' (CR1 223). In short, American reviewers were much more accepting of Conrad's rendering of the language of sailors than were their English equivalents.

As this suggests, some of the early reviewers objected to the bad language in *The Nigger of the 'Narcissus'*. However, there is one piece of language use in this work which stands out for modern readers. Wait objects at one point: 'You wouldn't call me nigger if I wasn't half-dead' (NN 59), so clearly Conrad knew this was a sensitive word. However, none of the British reviewers objected to the use of the word in the text, and many of them quite happily used it themselves in their reviews, as is evident in the reviews in the *Scotsman*, the *Daily Telegraph*, the *Irish*

*Daily Independent*, the *Manchester Guardian* (and many more) across a range of readerships and political affiliations. Some, like the *Glasgow Herald*, the *Christian World* and the *Literary World*, use the term in quotation marks, as if to distance themselves from it, but none actually complains about its repeated use in the novel. The title was changed for the American edition to *The Children of the Sea* – according to British reviewers, because the original title was 'considered too ungainly'.[14] American reviewers offered a different version. The reviewer in the *Brooklyn Daily Eagle* (9 April 1898), for example, suggested that the original title 'from the view point of the British reader contained nothing offensive', but welcomed the new title as better fitting 'public taste in this country' (*CR1* 204). The reviewer in the *Literary World* (Boston) observed that 'Our British brethren have a way of calling a negro a "nigger"' and described the change of title as evidence of 'our superior refinement' (*CR1* 210). It is perhaps significant that both these reviewers were from the North East. Mary Brent Read, in the *Atlanta Constitution*, and Paul Pry, in the *Age-Herald* (Birmingham, Alabama), both note the change of title in their positive reviews of the novella, but make no comment on the change (or on James Wait) (*CR1* 206, 212).

If the geographical location of the reader and the reviewer was a factor in the reception of the novel, the kind of journal in which the fiction appeared also had an impact on what Conrad was able to say. *The Nigger of the 'Narcissus'* first appeared in the coterie-based literary magazine the *New Review*, which had a masculinist agenda aimed primarily at the educated, male reader. 'Typhoon', by contrast, was first published in *Pall Mall Magazine*, an illustrated literary magazine for a general, family readership.[15] I have already cited the bowdlerised violent language of the engineer of the becalmed *Nan-Shan*, when he emerges on deck from the engine-room, where the temperature has 'gone up to a hundred and seventeen degrees' (*T* 22). When Jukes, the mate, mentions that the barometer is falling, the engineer tells him to 'shove the unmentionable instrument down his gory throat': 'Who cared for his crimson barometer?' (*T* 24). As with his earlier statement, where he wished that he might be 'everlastingly blanked for a swab-headed deckhand' (*T* 23), many of the substitutions that Conrad has made are quite transparent. Conrad, in effect, offers a double-voiced text: an irreproachable text for the delicate or juvenile reader and a readily translatable text for those with stronger nerves. Interestingly, the engineer is presented as differing in his linguistic habits from the other Europeans on board, namely the ship's officers. The captain describes him as a 'profane man' and observes to Jukes that he will have to 'get rid of him' if this goes on (*T* 25). With a surge of anger, the captain then exclaims: 'Damme! I'll fire him out of the ship if he don't look out' (*T* 25). Does this mean that 'Damme' is more acceptable than the words used by the engineer, or is this Conrad undermining MacWhirr's response to the engineer's profanities by giving him this profanity of his own? The former seems to be the case, since MacWhirr uses 'dam' again, when he subsequently imagines the interrogation he would face if he tried to dodge the bad weather: 'It must've been dam' bad' (*T* 34).

Ships' engineers, perhaps because of their working conditions, seem to have been particularly profane. In *Lord Jim*, the second engineer of the *Patna* makes his first appearance at the head of the bridge ladder with the 'tale of his complaints' liberally sprinkled with foul language. Conrad's representation of that speech, however, has toned down the profanities:

> He was more than half-cooked, he expected; but anyway, now, he did not mind how much he sinned, because these last three days he had passed through a fine course of training for the place where the bad boys go when they die – b'gosh he had – besides being made jolly well deaf by the blasted racket below. The durned, compound, surface-condensing, rotten scrap-heap rattled and banged down there like an old deck-winch. (*LJ* 22)

As in *The Nigger of the 'Narcissus'*, Conrad uses milder expletives ('jolly', 'blasted') as well as standard substitutions: 'b'gosh' for 'by God', 'durned' for 'damned'. In addition we have that coy and elaborate periphrasis for 'hell', which seems to mock the process of substitution that Conrad is engaged in; the word 'compound', which seems to stand in for a compound swear word, which it invites us to supply; and the compound adjective 'surface-condensing', which seems more like a technical term than a swear word. The captain of the *Patna* is also foul-mouthed. The narrator introduces him as someone who habitually lets loose 'a torrent of foamy, abusive jargon that came like a gush from a sewer' (*LJ* 22). In his case, this is clearly also a judgement upon him as a captain. Thus, just as Jim is thinking that the skipper 'did not belong to the world of heroic adventure', the captain shows that this is an understatement by venting 'a cloudy trickle of filthy expressions' (*LJ* 24), where the metaphor again suggests the cloacal nature of his language. The gap between Jim's romantic dream and the reality of the *Patna* is starkly revealed in this moment. When Conrad represents the captain's brief conversation with Marlow, the captain's foul language is suggested (and concealed) through phonetic transcriptions and German curses. Thus, after complaining about 'damned Englishmen' (*LJ* 41), he criticises the 'Gottam fuss' made by Captain Elliott, the Master Attendant, and then exclaims: 'A man like me don't want your verfluchte certificate'

(*LJ* 42). Brierly's mate, Mr Jones, is also prone to cursing – though not in the same league as the captain. When he is told that he will not succeed to the command of Brierly's ship, he responds: 'Don't you mind old Jones, sir; damn his soul, he's used to it' (*LJ* 63). He then realises that he has 'shocked' the 'delicate ear' of the new captain, who tells him that he is 'known for an old ruffian' (*LJ* 63). However, he is clearly unrepentant, because he tells Marlow that 'the damned bottle-washers stood about listening' to this exchange (*LJ* 63). In this case, Jones's language, unlike the captain's, is presented as part of his character as 'a first-rate sailor' (*LJ* 59), while the new captain's 'delicate' response is represented as part of his characterisation as a 'popinjay' (*LJ* 63).

It is difficult to work out the status of the word 'damned' to which the new captain objected. Here the word is used in full both to the new captain and in conversation with Marlow. However, later, when Brown is telling Marlow about his exchanges with Jim, the text represents him as swearing 'God d-n it!' and as asking Jim 'what is it that you have found here that is so d-d precious?' (*LJ* 381). Yet at the end of the chapter, when Marlow reports Brown's mate's story of Brown running off with a dying woman, the mate concludes with the observation that she had a 'Dam' bad sort of fever' (*LJ* 384). In *Lord Jim*, as in other works, the representation of swearing is inconsistent. Thus Brown can swear by 'God', but 'd-n it!' has to be censored, while the German captain repeatedly exclaims 'Mein Gott!' Perhaps Brown gets a dash as a sign of his moral offensiveness, while 'Mein Gott!' gets by because it is in a foreign language. We might compare this with the deputy assistant resident's use of the Dutch '*vordamte*' and his more restrained exclamation 'Almighty!' (*LJ* 279).

Jim complains that his companions in the open boat called him 'horrible names', but the only examples he gives – 'it's that blasted mate' and 'too much of a bloomin' gentleman' – hardly justify the complaint (*LJ* 116–17). Jim himself is given to very polite expletives. When Marlow visits him in Patusan and outlines his success, he observes: 'Jove! I told you I would hang on. . . . Jove! Only think what it is to me' (*LJ* 246–7). Marlow is equally polite in response: 'Confound your delicacy!' (*LJ* 247). Jim's account of his imprisonment similarly invokes 'Jove!', damns his jailers with the politer 'confound them!', and refers to his revolver as a 'bally thing' (*LJ* 249). His account of his escape includes his reflection 'how beastly it would be to get a jab with a bally long spear' (*LJ* 251). Similarly, his response to the legend that is circulating about him among the local people is: 'what can you do with such silly beggars? They will sit up half the night talking bally rot' (*LJ* 266). And he describes one of the cases he has to solve as 'a dashed conundrum': the marital problem involves 'a confounded story about some brass pots' and solving the problem was 'the dashedest nuisance' (*LJ* 268). He goes on: 'There was the making of a sanguinary shindy in the thing. Every bally idiot took sides with one family or the other ... Honour bright! No joke!' (*LJ* 269). As has been observed by others, Jim speaks like the schoolboy hero of a boys' book. Jim's distinctive idiom sets him apart from his more realistically represented *Patna* colleagues and from Brown.

Conrad had already negotiated the issue of appropriate language with his first representation of shipboard life in 'Youth', first published in *Blackwood's Magazine*. Mild expletives were clearly acceptable in this journal. When Captain Beard is found adrift in the middle of the dock, Marlow expresses the crew's surprise with the exclamation: 'How the devil did he get there?' (*Y* 9). The mate, Mahon, describes the problem of pumping the *Judea* during the first gale: 'By God! It's no child's play' (*Y* 11). Similarly, after the explosion, Mahon exclaims: 'Good God! Don't you see the deck's blown out of her?' (*Y* 24). The young Marlow, however, is given even milder language: 'By Jove, this is the deuce of an adventure!' (*Y* 12). The ship's crew have their language neutered: they were not going to sail 'in a something hooker' (*Y* 14). Marlow's welcome to the East by the 'Western voice' on the steamer he approaches is even more heavily censored: 'The voice swore and cursed violently; it riddled the solemn peace of the bay by a volley of abuse. It began by calling me Pig, and from that went crescendo into unmentionable adjectives – in English' (*Y* 39). The subsequent exchange, after Marlow identifies himself, traces the limits of the expressible. The voice begins apologetically: 'Oh, my goodness! I say' (*Y* 39). He then runs through a succession of permissible adjectives: 'this infernal lazy scoundrel of a caretaker has gone to sleep again ... I nearly ran foul of the end of this damned jetty' (*Y* 40). The voice's crescendo of vituperation ends with the unrepeatable: 'I'll get the Assistant Resident to give him the sack, by ... !' (*Y* 40). Marlow concludes, ironically, 'I had faced the silence of the East. I had heard some of its language' (*Y* 40), but he is not able to represent all that language for his audience.

## Compass cards, steam gauges and scrap iron

I want to conclude by considering two perfect sea-stories, 'Typhoon' and 'The End of the Tether' (both 1902), and a more problematic sea-story, 'The Partner' (1911). As he did with the *Narcissus*, Conrad introduces the *Nan-Shan* in 'Typhoon' through a mapping of her dimensions. First, there is a reference to 'her flat bottom, rolling chocks on bilges, and great breadth of beam' that make her 'an exceptionally steady ship in a seaway' (*T* 7). This is obviously important for the typhoon she will have to face later. Next, the account of MacWhirr's first sight of his command guides the reader's eye 'from stem to stern, and from her keelson to the trucks of her two stumpy pole-masts' (*T* 8). Even if not all of the terms are familiar to us, the tracking of the eye's movement suggests their meaning. Similarly, when the cargo is loaded, not all the terminology will be familiar, but Conrad's onomatopoeic evocation of the soundscape carries the reader over the gaps in precise referentiality: 'The cargo chains groaned in the gins, clinked on coamings, rattled over the side' (*T* 12). During the typhoon, the ship is presented to us through fragmentary glimpses. At times these are literally the momentary perceptions of individual characters: 'Captain MacWhirr could catch a desolate glimpse of a few tiny specks black as ebony, the tops of the hatches, the battened companions, the heads of the covered winches, the foot of a mast' (*T* 43). At other times, the narratorial perspective similarly picks out discrete details. For example, the account of the *Nan-Shan* being 'looted by the storm' operates through an assemblage of disassembled technical details: 'trysails torn out of the extra gaskets, double-lashed awnings blown away, bridge swept clean, weather-cloths burst, rails twisted, light-screens smashed' (*T* 44). The non-specialist reader can readily understand the significance of the 'bridge swept clean' and 'rails twisted'; the more technical details add up to a picture of destruction without the reader being required to assign precise meanings to them. Indeed, the reader's own limited understanding might strengthen the impression of confusion. Conrad presents not just an impressionistic account of the experience of being caught in a typhoon, but also, through his shifting focalisation, an embodied and, effectively, a phenomenological account of that experience.

In chapter 4, Conrad sets against this experience of chaos and turmoil a succession of scenes involving focus and concentration. Thus, when Captain MacWhirr struggles against the gale into the wheel-house, a detailed description of the wheel-house is followed by a description of the helmsman attending to the job of steering: 'The steam gear clattered, stopped, clattered again; and the helmsman's eyeballs seemed to project out of a hungry face as if the compass card behind the binnacle glass had been meat' (*T* 64). Similarly, Conrad offers a detailed description of the engine-room:

> the iron walls of the engine-room . . . rose high into the dusk of the skylight, sloping like a roof; and the whole lofty space resembled the interior of a monument, divided by floors of iron grating, with lights flickering at different levels, and a mass of gloom lingering in the middle, within the columnar stir of machinery under the motionless swelling of the cylinders. (*T* 68)

This evocation of the enclosed space of the engine-room is also brought to focus on the 'purposeful industry' of a single human, the engineer Mr Rout: 'when he stood still, holding the guard-rail in front of the starting-gear, he would keep glancing to the right at the steam-gauge, at the water-gauge, fixed upon the white wall in the light of a swaying lamp' (*T* 69). Finally, in chapter 5, when MacWhirr returns to the chart-room and surveys the destruction wrought by the storm, he strikes a match and peers at the barometer 'whose glittering top of glass and metals nodded at him continuously' – and realises, from the extremely low reading, that 'the worst was to come' (*T* 84). In each of these scenes, Conrad describes in detail a precise shipboard location. The evocation of the spaces of the ship is then brought to focus on a specific individual and their concentrated engagement with a specific piece of nautical technology: the compass-card, the steam- and water-gauges, the barometer. The drama of the storm, in which 'purposeful industry' and specialised technology are set against the power of wind and waves, is played out through this series of scenes.

'The End of the Tether', which was published in *Blackwood's Magazine*, uses a similar technique of a few familiar nautical terms combined with precisely chosen, tightly focused technical detail. Thus, in the first two sections, the steamer the *Sofala*, the barque the *Fair Maid*, and the clipper the *Condor* are economically evoked through references to 'the head' of the ship, 'the helm', 'the bridge' (*Y* 165), 'the cabin', 'the stateroom', 'the sails' and 'the poop-deck' (*Y* 171–2). Within this minimalist mode, focus falls first on navigation: 'Her compasses were never out ... She made her landfalls to a degree of the bearing' (*Y* 166). As with the compass-card, the steam-gauge and the barometer in 'Typhoon', focus falls on a specific technical detail, one which, in 'The End of the Tether', will prove crucial to the narrative. In section VII, again as in 'Typhoon', shipboard experience is presented through a soundscape: 'the deadened beat of the engines ... and the slight grinding of the steering-chains' (*Y* 219). This is repeated in section XI, when Massy, in his cabin, hears somebody dragging 'a heavy box past his door', 'the autocratic clang of the engine-room gong', and the propeller 'beating slowly: one, two, three; one, two, three' (*Y* 273). Focalisation through Massy produces a phenomenological engagement with sense impressions that pre-empts a precise understanding of technical processes. An odd exception to the economical evocation of shipboard life is the mention, in section XIII, of a canvas tent 'used for the storing of nautical objects' and the detailed itemisation of its contents: 'a shabby steering-wheel, a battered brass binnacle on a stout mahogany stand, two dingy life-buoys, an old cork fender lying in a corner, dilapidated deck-lockers with loops of tin rope instead of door-handles' (*Y* 294). None of these carefully described items has any significance in the narrative, although the agglomeration of jumble anticipates another storage space, 'a storeroom with iron sides', containing 'all sorts of rubbish', including 'a mound of scrap-iron' (*Y* 321), from which Massy selects the iron he uses to deflect the needle of the ship's compass.

As with 'Typhoon', the swearing in 'The End of the Tether' has been muted. Captain Elliott exclaims 'confound his cheek' (*Y* 208), when narrating how Massy banged the door of his office; Massy, in turn, later calls Sterne 'a confounded fool' (*Y* 217); and Van Wyk calls Massy 'a confounded fool' (*Y* 284) – but that is about it. Massy is 'eager to shake his fist and roar abuse in bad Malay at the poor carpenter' (*Y* 267), but there is no account of him actually doing this.[16] When he finally swears at the second engineer, 'Dam' you and the ship! I wish she were at the bottom of the sea!' (*Y* 275), the curse also marks the introduction of a new idea into Massy's head for a solution to his problems. When he later loses his temper at the second engineer's drunkenness, the language remains comparatively restrained: 'you confounded swilling pig, you . . . you beast!' (*Y* 310) He calls him 'a tippling old rascal' and complains about him talking 'infernal rot', to which the second mildly responds that he is 'sick of the dam' boilers' (*Y* 317). On a different tack, Sterne's mildly blasphemous reflection, 'You could not find another man like this one in the whole round world – thank God' (*Y* 254), is recuperated by Captain Whalley's fervent 'God forbid!', 'God knows', 'thank God', which are not blasphemy, but rather the expression of his religious belief (*Y* 291–3).

In his later sea-fiction, 'Typhoon' and 'The End of the Tether', Conrad found various ways of negotiating both kinds of nautical language. First, he developed techniques for handling the technical language of the sea in such a way as to combine authority with comprehensibility for a non-specialist readership. For example, the tracking eye of the narrative produces a spatial context for technical language. At other times, the narrative focuses on a particular piece of ship's equipment. He also found various solutions to the problem of representing the language of sailors for a general readership. In 'Typhoon', this is through inventive substitutions and the production of a double-voiced text; in 'The End of the Tether', the sailors' language has been neutered. In both cases, Conrad was producing stories that were first published in family magazines. 'The Partner' is an interesting text to consider briefly in this context, since its narrator writes stories for magazines, and the story plays with the way in which 'raw material' is 'cooked' for magazine consumption.[17] 'The Partner', which was published in *Harper's Magazine*, has almost no technical nautical language. Stafford observes that, as chief mate, he will have opportunities 'to manipulate the chains and anchors', which is vague enough. He is then depicted 'whittling away the forelock of the forty-five-fathom shackle-pin', but the reader is not required to understand what exactly has been done, since the implication is immediately spelt out: 'of course that cable wasn't safe any more', and so it proves.[18] When the ship is wrecked, there is a brief moment of technical impenetrability as 'the lifeboat drops on a grapnel abreast the fore-rigging' (*WT* 117), but, when two sailors then drop Cloete into the lifeboat, it is clear enough what is happening. The obscurity of the technical language here can be read as a badge of authenticity or an awkward textual excrescence. Similarly, the fact that the swearing is neutered is appropriate given that the primary narrator is a writer of popular magazine fiction. Thus the retired stevedore, 'an imposing old ruffian', is represented as showing a surprising classical restraint, when he responds to his interlocutor with the testy 'To Hades with your connections' (*WT* 92). While the ex-stevedore is allowed the single curse, 'Damn boatmen' (*WT* 95), Cloete, in the story he narrates, merely 'lets out a horrid cuss-word' (*WT* 105), which is left unspecified, and George fails to tell him to 'go to the devil' (*WT* 107). The magazine writer shows similar restraint, exclaiming 'By Jove!' at one of the story's climactic moments. Such restraint was a lesson that Conrad had also clearly learned.

### Notes

1. For a fuller account of Malay in Conrad's fiction, see Andrew Francis's chapter in this volume.
2. 'White Man and Brown', *Daily Chronicle* (11 May 1895). Rpt. *CR1* 18.
3. Jonathan Swift, *Gulliver's Travels and Other Writings*, ed. Miriam Kosh Starkman (London: Bantam Books, 1962), p. 93.
4. Joseph Conrad, *Youth, Heart of Darkness, The End of the Tether: Three Stories* (London: J. M. Dent and Sons, 1946), p. 99. Subsequent references are cited in the text as *Y*.
5. Joseph Conrad, *Typhoon and Other Tales* (London: J. M. Dent and Sons, 1923), p. 23. Subsequent references are cited in the text as *T*.
6. Joseph Conrad, *The Nigger of the 'Narcissus'*, ed. Allan Simmons (London: Everyman, 1997), p. 3. Subsequent references are cited in the text as *NN*.
7. That is, with the mainsail set to leeward and the jib set to windward.
8. Neil Munro, 'Joseph Conrad's Latest', *Glasgow Evening News* (5 August 1897). Rpt. *CR1* 147. Munro was a Glasgow-based journalist and novelist, mainly remembered as the author of a series of stories about a Clyde steamboat.
9. Joseph Conrad, *Lord Jim* (London: J. M. Dent and Sons, 1923), pp. 5–6. Subsequent references are cited in the text as *LJ*.

10. W. Somerset Maugham, *Liza of Lambeth* (London: T. Fisher Unwin, 1897), p. 11.
11. Ibid. p. 12.
12. Compare Donkin's description of his shipmates as 'bloomin' backlickers' (*NN* 112).
13. Joseph Conrad, *The Nigger of the 'Narcissus'* (London: J. M. Dent and Sons, 1923), p. 59 and p. 117.
14. These are the words of the reviewer in the *Academy* (12 March 1898). Rpt. *CR1* 189.
15. For Conrad and the *New Review*, see Peter D. McDonald, *British Literary Culture and Publishing Practice, 1880–1914* (Cambridge: Cambridge University Press, 1997); for Conrad and *Pall Mall Magazine*, see Linda Dryden, '"The times indeed are changed": Conrad, "Typhoon" and *Pall Mall Magazine*', *Conradiana* 41.2–3 (Fall/Winter 2009), pp. 133–52.
16. Interestingly, the carpenter is Chinese. See Andrew Francis's chapter in this volume.
17. For a discussion of this aspect of the story, see Robert Hampson, 'Storytellers and Storytelling in "The Partner", "The Informer", "The Lesson of the Master" and *The Sacred Fount*', in K. Carabine, O. Knowles and P. Armstrong (eds), *Conrad, James and other Relations* (Boulder, CO: East European Monographs, 1998), pp. 123–46.
18. Joseph Conrad, *Within the Tides* (London: J. M. Dent and Sons, 1923), p. 108. Subsequent references are cited in the text as *WT*.

Chapter 2

# Navigating the 'Terroristic Wilderness': Conrad's Language of Terror
*Andrew Glazzard*

Of all the words from the political lexicon in current and frequent use, 'terrorist' is one of the most familiar and also one of the most problematic. On one level, the connection between word and concept is straightforward enough: we can recognise an act of terrorism (a hijacking, a suicide bombing, a beheading) as easily as we can recognise any other manifestation of human activity. But if we seek to define the word objectively, to strip away the layers of pejorative meaning that have accumulated around it, we quickly find ourselves in a wilderness of mirrors – or, to use a metaphor favoured by one terrorism expert, in a linguistic 'Bermuda Triangle'.[1] The scale of the problem becomes clear if we consider that a directory of the various definitions of 'terrorism' used by academics, governments and international bodies runs to over 250 entries. The definitional problem has been judged to be of sufficient seriousness to require the attentions of several committees of the United Nations – which, despite starting work on a definition in 1972, have still not achieved an agreed result. A recently proposed 'academic' definition, designed to be sufficiently inclusive and exclusive to command expert consensus, contains twelve points and runs to a page of closely written text.[2]

Why is this so difficult? As the UN committees have discovered, agreement is elusive because of the well-worn antithesis of 'terrorism' and 'freedom fighting': some UN member states insist that national liberation struggles should be omitted from the definition's scope, while others insist that violence by states should be specifically excluded. This shows that the linguistic problem is not simply an academic one. Definitions of 'terrorism' are politically contested because so much hangs on them – such as whether a country can be said to be in a state of war, whether violence can be justified pre-emptively or in response to the violence of others, or whether an act of violence is political and therefore should fall outside the boundaries of ordinary criminal law (or indeed whether the criminal law should apply at all). In short, the word may define who, in politics, are the heroes and who are the villains. As a result, while the word has only gained in currency since international terrorism became a feature of the daily news from the late 1960s, its utility and the ethics of its use have come under increasingly sceptical scrutiny. For some, the word's function is not descriptive but purely pejorative: 'Conveying criminality, illegitimacy, and even madness, the application of *terrorist* shuts the door to discussion *about* the stigmatised group or *with* them, while reinforcing the righteousness of the labellers, justifying their agendas and mobilizing their resources.'[3] Those who pursue the new academic discipline of critical terrorism studies go further, and charge that the word is not merely used tactically to legitimise and delegitimise, but is actually fundamental to a political project aiming to shape our perceptions in such a profound way as to create 'a new and unquestioned reality':

> the language of the 'war on terrorism' is not simply an objective or neutral reflection of reality. ... Rather, it is a deliberately and meticulously composed set of words, assumptions, metaphors, grammatical forms, myths and forms of knowledge – it is a carefully constructed *discourse* – that is designed to achieve a number of key political goals.[4]

Anyone who is sceptical about the relevance to the 'real world' of language and the study of language would do well to consider the use (or perhaps abuse) of 'terrorism'.

Literary critics should have a lot to say about this debate. The medium we study is language, and language is evidently one of the subject's many battlegrounds – and not merely in the debate over definitions. Terrorism is a form of communication that requires mediation to achieve its social effects, and while mass media representation has been the focus of most research into terrorism in communications studies, terrorism self-evidently depends on words as well as images – in manifestos, claims of responsibility and even how groups choose to name themselves.[5] Conrad was more interested in politics and its lexicon than most authors, so examining his contribution may be instructive. Can Conrad's fiction help us navigate the treacherous waters of this linguistic 'Bermuda Triangle'? And what might the contentiousness of defining terrorism tell us about Conrad's use of language? This chapter will seek to answer these questions with reference not only to two of the major political novels, *The Secret Agent* (1907) and *Under Western Eyes* (1911), but also to a late novel, *The Rover* (1923), in which the backstory of the French Revolution provides an important additional dimension to Conrad's examination of terrorism. More specifically, I shall seek to identify what political phenomena Conrad labels with the word 'terrorism', how these are represented linguistically, and what this might tell us about both the phenomena and the label.

## Terror and trauma: *The Rover*

Historians may argue about when the phenomenon of terrorism was first recorded – whether, for instance, the *sicarii* Zealots who violently opposed the Roman occupation of Judea in the first century CE were terrorists *avant la lettre*[6] – but it seems clear the word entered the English language from French at the end of the eighteenth century. Significantly, it originated from political attempts to implement and justify a radical transformation of civil society, and can be traced to Maximilien Robespierre's policy of making terror 'the order of the day', encapsulated in his notorious speech to the Convention on 5 February 1794, in which he used the word 'terror' both to label his enemies pejoratively, and to proclaim a new approach to dealing with them. Counter-revolutionaries, Robespierre proclaimed, had 'spread terror among the people', but in a state of emergency the Republic should have a monopoly of terror and should be free to terrorise its enemies:

> virtue, without which terror is fatal; terror, without which virtue is impotent. Terror is nothing but prompt, severe, inflexible justice; it is therefore an emanation of virtue. It is less a special principle than a consequence of the general principle of democracy applied to our country's most pressing needs.[7]

Following the coup of June–July 1794, Robespierre was himself charged with *terrorisme* – meaning the cruel and arbitrary abuse of power – and it was in this sense that the word entered the English language. One of the first recorded uses in the *Oxford English Dictionary* (*OED*) of 'terrorist' is by Edmund Burke in 1795, for whom the Jacobins were 'Hell Hounds called Terrorists' who had been 'let loose on the people'.[8] 'Terrorism' thus acquired its pejorative sense, its instrumental utility, and its flexibility of use from the outset. In its earliest appearances, it was also applied to the policy of a state rather than the techniques of a state's enemies. Moreover, at this time political 'terror' was not confined to the French revolutionary state: in a telling usage, William Godwin explained in 1795 why he had withdrawn the incendiary preface from his political thriller *Caleb Williams* in the previous year with a comment clearly modelled on Robespierre's proclamation: in Pitt's England, 'Terror was the order of the day; and it was feared that even the humble novelist might be shown to be constructively a traitor.'[9]

The first terrorists to be labelled as such were, then, states not groups. Nevertheless, it is striking that the word was applied to insurgent groups less than a decade after it entered the English language. Francis Plowden described Irish insurgents as 'sanguinary terrorists' in his 1805–6 history of Ireland.[10] From then until the mid-twentieth century, it could be applied to either groups or states – usually, but not exclusively, as a pejorative label. Two of the exceptions are relevant to the novels under discussion here. Conrad would have been familiar with the Russian Nihilist group Narodnaya Volya, not least from reading *Underground Russia* (1883), a polemical memoir by the revolutionary terrorist Stepniak (Sergei Kravchinsky), a copy of which Conrad owned: this features an idealised portrait of the Russian 'Terrorist' who combines 'the two sublimities of human grandeur: the martyr and the hero'.[11] The German-American anarchist Johann Most, the model for Karl Yundt in *The Secret Agent*, published a series of articles entitled 'Advice for Terrorists' in his anarchist newspaper *Der Freiheit* in 1882.[12] By the 1970s, when insurgent and revolutionary violence had supplanted that of totalitarian states in political discourse, the word had lost its original meaning of a state policy of violence – itself an illustration of the effect of political power upon language.

Given the word's historical origins, it is significant that 'terrorist' appears frequently in *The Rover* – a novel deeply concerned with the political and psychological legacy of the French Revolution. Scevola Bron, a former Jacobin revolutionary, is allocated numerous political labels, from the ironically double-edged 'patriot' to the highly pejorative 'blood-drinker' and '*sans-culotte*' (the latter pejorative in the post-revolutionary period at least). 'Terrorist' is similarly political and even more pejorative and is used to designate Scevola eight times (three times in the compound 'ex-terrorist'). The first usage, by Réal during his discussion with Peyrol in chapter IV, is dismissive and insulting: 'Could you hear the fall of a leaf – and with that terrorist cur trumpeting right above my head?'[13] The next six instances are more interesting, all occurring in chapter VII, alongside an additional and significant reference to the 'spirit of terrorism' (*Ro* 79). To appreciate the significance of this labelling, we need to register the context of each occurrence in the chapter.

Chapter VII begins with a midday meal in the kitchen of the Escampobar Farm. Peyrol, watching Scevola eat, 'let his gaze rest on the ex-terrorist' (*Ro* 79). This prompts a significant meditation from Peyrol, who had not previously 'concerned himself very much with the mental states of the people with whom he lived' (*Ro* 79). Knowing that major events are beginning to occur around the sleepy world of the farm, Peyrol has become attentive and curious: 'Now, however, he wondered to himself what could be the thoughts of the ex-terrorist patriot, that sanguinary and extremely poor creature occupying the position of master of the Escampobar Farm' (*Ro* 79). Scevola is sanguinary in a double sense – as we have been told, he is judged to be bloodthirsty, but also at this point his face is flushed: his 'aspect was more feverish than usual' (*Ro* 79), perhaps because of the red wine that accompanies the meal.

Strictly speaking it is the narrator who labels Scevola as the 'ex-terrorist', but this passage is focalised through Peyrol, so we might assume that Peyrol mentally applies the epithet. Either way, two points are significant. The first is that 'ex-terrorist' clearly suggests that Scevola's employment of revolutionary violence lies thoroughly in the past, that events have removed any cause or motive for more bloodletting, and that the epithet therefore designates nothing more than a political role that he once played. The second point is the conjunction between the epithet and what Peyrol is seeking to do – understand Scevola's mental state. The significance of both points emerges as we read on. In passages of free indirect discourse and reported speech, Scevola curses the post-revolutionary settlement, before uttering a prediction whose sinister tone is undermined by the dramatic irony available to the historically knowledgeable reader: 'Some day tyranny will stumble and then it will be time to pull it down again. We will come out in our thousands and – *ça ira*!' (*Ro* 81). It is this outburst that prompts the narrator to comment that Peyrol's lack of response depressed 'the feebly struggling spirit of terrorism in the lonely breast of Citizen Scevola' (*Ro* 81). Unlike Peyrol, the narrator is able to penetrate Scevola's mental state and reveal that 'ex-terrorist' is misleading: in fact, Scevola yearns for an opportunity to exercise his sanguinary instincts once more. This passage thus becomes important validation of Scevola's local reputation for bloodthirstiness. Furthermore, by drawing attention to his loneliness, the narrator begins to offer an explanation for Scevola's conduct. The more we learn about Scevola's past, the more we infer that his attraction to political violence is as much pathological as it is ideological. Catherine, for example, recalls that prior to the Revolution Scevola 'was the butt of all the girls' and that 'all the countryside knew about him' (*Ro* 92). What was known is left unsaid, but it is clear that, in his youth, Scevola's behaviour and personality were abnormal. His excitement at the massacre in Toulon – recalled by Catherine just prior to this comment – is presumably therefore a symptom of his abnormality, or, we might say today, his psychopathy.

Despite the use of political epithets to describe Scevola, *The Rover* – in contrast with *Nostromo* (1904) – is concerned less with the politics of revolution and more with its psychology and psychopathology. Scevola can be seen as a case study of how and why individuals become involved in acts of extreme cruelty: just as Peyrol seeks to understand the mental state of the individual before him in the farmhouse, so does the reader. Indeed, this nod towards psychological investigation is one manifestation of the novel's sustained interest in mental illness. Recent work has refocused our attention on this late novel as a trauma narrative, with Robert Hampson's analysis of Arlette suggesting that the novel was part of Conrad's complex response to the First World War and the traumatic experiences of his son Borys on the Western Front.[14] But what matters here is the close thematic and linguistic connections in chapter VII between Scevola's terrorism and the trauma of the Revolution, which come together in the story of the tartane.

While reconnoitering the coastline, Peyrol discovers an abandoned tartane (a small Mediterranean fishing ship) and is told it belongs to the Escampobar Farm, to which Peyrol returns and where he interviews Scevola. The latter is initially hesitant, but then tells the tartane's story: during the Revolution it was a scene of mass murder. Peyrol suspects that Scevola was himself a participant; the latter goes as far as to admit that he and an accomplice threw many corpses into the sea, and that the tartane was never cleaned and was therefore abandoned. (Peyrol finds it to be bloodstained and containing nothing but 'a wisp of long hair and a woman's earring' [Ro 87].) In the course of the interview, the narrator labels Scevola as 'the terrorist' three times.

Up to this point, the novel has used 'terrorist' in what could be seen as a precise and historical sense of 'participant in the Reign of Terror' – the word's original sense with which Conrad, steeped in French history of the period, would presumably have been familiar. The tartane, however, helps us to recover the word's psychological as well as its historical/political meaning. As the location of a scene of extreme revolutionary violence, the 'tragic craft' which also took Arlette's parents to their deaths and brought Arlette and Scevola back from the massacre in Toulon, it is an emblem of the Revolution's trauma. Its discovery by Peyrol prompts the narrator to recall Catherine's anguished wait for the return of her family 'while she listened to the booming of guns about Toulon and with an almost greater but different terror to the dead silence which ensued' (Ro 85). The next day, Catherine tells Peyrol: 'Don't talk to me about the tartane! She took my brother away for ever. I stood on the shore watching her sails grow smaller and smaller' (Ro 90). This prompts her to tell Peyrol 'of the days and nights of waiting' during the fighting and massacres in Toulon (a recollection which, incidentally, lends weight to the thesis that this is a disguised First World War narrative):

> Then came a night as if the world were coming to an end. All the sky was lighted up, the earth shook to its foundations, and she felt the house rock, so that jumping up from the bench she screamed with fear. . . . Nearly a week later she was dozing by the fire when voices outside woke her up, and she beheld standing in the middle of the salle, pale like a corpse out of a grave, with a blood-soaked blanket over her shoulders and a red cap on her head, a ghastly-looking young girl in whom she suddenly recognized her niece. She screamed in her terror: 'François, François!' This was her brother's name, and she thought he was outside. Her scream scared the girl, who ran out of the door. All was still outside. Once more she screamed 'François!' and, tottering as far as the door, she saw her niece clinging to a strange man in a red cap and with a sabre by his side, who yelled excitedly: 'You won't see François again. Vive la Republique!' (Ro 90–1)

Catherine's recollections include the word 'terror', and this word's proximity to the repeated labelling of Scevola with the cognate word 'terrorist' underlines an association that is not only linguistic but also conceptual. The word 'trauma' is, unsurprisingly enough, absent from a novel published only three years after Freud conceptualised 'traumatic neurosis' in *Beyond the Pleasure Principle* (1920). But what we understand today as trauma is at least partly evoked in these passages by 'terror', a word freighted in the novel with heavy psychological significance. The word is first used in chapter III when the narrator relates Peyrol's upbringing: the death of his mother touches him with 'the panic of the supernatural' (Ro 24) but at the age of twelve he experiences 'another kind of terror' (Ro 24) among the chaos of Marseilles. However, when he is initiated into seamanship, Peyrol adapts himself to 'the new and inexplicable conditions of life in something like twenty-four hours' (Ro 25): he becomes so inured to shock, confusion, threat, violence and fear that even bloodshed and the threat of starvation have little or no effect on him psychologically. This explains why the tartane has no adverse psychological effect on him: he has been hardened, not traumatised, by his experiences, and so can 'without very strong emotion figure to himself the little place choked with corpses' (Ro 87).

The principal victim of the trauma of the Revolution is Arlette, and again the keyword is 'terror'. Even before the revelations of chapter VII we infer she is suffering, as when in chapter IV we are told that her eyes

> had been smitten on the very verge of womanhood by such sights of bloodshed and terror as to leave in her a fear of looking steadily in any direction for long, lest she should see coming through the empty air some mutilated vision of the dead. (Ro 48–9)

It is only when she confesses her complicity in the revolutionary killings – running with the sans-culottes and 'yelling . . . the very same words' (*Ro* 154) – that she is able to cope with the memory of her experiences.[15]

*The Rover* thus does more than restore to our idea of terrorism its historically grounded original sense of a policy of state violence. It reminds us that violence on this scale and intensity – whatever its motivations and however it is perpetrated – works on the mind as much as in the physical world. This, of course, is central to the very purpose of terrorism: however it is defined, it is at its core the use of violence or the threat of violence to inspire fear. But the novel's psychologically damaged victims, as well as its psychopathic perpetrator, expand our understanding of the effects of political violence: it produces trauma as well. Most importantly, its labelling of Scevola as 'terrorist', when combined with its insistence on the psychopathological effects of (state) terrorism on individuals, takes 'terrorism' from the discourse of politics and makes it a phenomenon with real and observable psychological effects. In the process, *The Rover* prefigures the terrorist novel which flourished in the 1970s, the 1990s and early 2000s and which has predominantly focused on victims of terrorism rather than its politics. As one important study of the terrorist novel puts it, 'it is not the terrorism that is fully present in the novel, but terrorism's effects'; novels in this period 'foreground the wounds of terrorism: to identify and construct the innocence of the innocent and the wounds of the wounded'.[16] *The Rover* foregrounds the wounds, but is rather more complex in what it says about guilt and innocence.

## Flowers of the terroristic wilderness: *The Secret Agent* and *Under Western Eyes*

*The Secret Agent* also examines a victim of terrorism from a psychopathological perspective: Winnie's response to the death of her brother as a result of an elaborate terrorist plot that miscarries conjures up a violent reaction determined by her biological inheritance and the environment of her youth: 'Into that plunging blow . . . Mrs Verloc had put all the inheritance of her immemorial and obscure descent, the simple ferocity of the age of caverns, and the unbalanced nervous fury of the age of bar-rooms.'[17] Significantly, 'terror' is again a word used repeatedly to evoke Winnie's feelings after she has killed her husband, as with the 'abstract terror' she feels when imagining the scene of her hanging. Yet what is more interesting about this novel's use of the language of terror is the identity of the only character consistently designated with the epithet 'terrorist'. This is not Verloc, the immediate perpetrator of the attempted terrorist attack in Greenwich, nor Vladimir, the act's instigator. Nor, most revealingly, is it the Professor, whose utopian project of regenerating the world through acts of spectacular violence prefigures the utopian objectives of more recent terrorist groups such as Al Qaida[18] – although one reason for his fear of the multitude is the possibility that it is 'impervious to sentiment, to logic, to terror, too, perhaps' (SA 82). The epithet is reserved instead for the skeletal and sepulchral revolutionary agitator Karl Yundt, and is applied seven times. In six instances the noun is qualified by the adjective 'old', as when he is described sitting in the chair normally reserved for Winnie's mother: 'The terrorist, as he called himself, was old and bald, with a narrow, snow-white wisp of a goatee hanging limply from his chin. An extraordinary expression of underhand malevolence survived in his extinguished eyes' (SA 42). This repeated conjunction of age and political descriptor is clearly significant. As with Scevola, we might consider that Yundt is an ex-terrorist, that his political career – like that of Johann Most – comprised agitation, propaganda and incitement to extreme physical violence, but that this lies in the past.[19]

Norman Sherry notes, but does not explain, a curious but important feature of Yundt's presentation, his incongruity: 'He is malevolent but extinguished, a "moribund murderer"' (SA 253).[20] In fact, he is even more incongruous – or rather contradictory – than Sherry suggests. Contradictions – oxymorons – seem to be his essence: his 'passion' is 'worn-out', his 'fierceness' is 'impotent', he is a 'senile sensualist'. The phrase 'moribund murderer' appears in a vivid and comic simile ('the thrusting forward of a skinny groping hand deformed by gouty swellings suggested the effort of a moribund murderer summoning all his remaining strength for a last stab' [SA 42]). This is important as the narrator makes clear that Yundt has not killed anyone:

> The all but moribund veteran of dynamite wars had been a great actor in his time – actor on platforms, in secret assemblies, in private interviews. The famous terrorist had never in his life raised personally as much as his little finger against the social edifice. (SA 48)

In this respect, it is also important that 'terrorist' is a self-appellation. It is the role that he performs, despite never having committed an act of political violence. Yundt is indeed a peculiarly contradictory terrorist or war veteran. His wars, it is clear, are of the purely propagandising variety, but he is a role-player rather than an ideologue: 'He was no man of action; he was not even an orator of torrential eloquence, sweeping the masses along in the rushing noise and foam of a great enthusiasm' (SA 48). He once possessed, however, an 'evil gift', the 'shadow' of which 'clung to him yet like the smell of a deadly drug in an old vial of poison' (*SA* 48). This gift is an ability to perform the role of a corrupter of society:

> he took the part of an insolent and venomous evoker of sinister impulses which lurk in the blind envy and exasperated vanity of ignorance, in the suffering and misery of poverty, in all the hopeful and noble illusions of righteous anger, pity, and revolt. (*SA* 48)

The narrator's insistence that Yundt's radicalism is a performance denies him any political legitimacy, and yet his rhetoric has had a real-world effect. Yundt is therefore not a genuine ideologue, but is paradoxically a strongly ideological figure: he represents a kind of malign political mischief-making that has very real and damaging political and social consequences.

Yundt is, then, one of the large cast of Conrad's characters whose eloquence is malign and socially damaging (compare Kurtz's 'unbounded power of eloquence – of words – of burning noble words'[21]). So, while on one level his self-appellation of 'terrorist' might seem ironic, on another it is entirely apt: he creates terror with words. We see this occur in the novel, when his gruesome imagery of cannibalistic capitalism – a 'terrifying statement' – creates a state of distress in Stevie (*SA* 51). Clearly, Yundt's malign eloquence has in times past influenced more widely the credulous elements in society. This gift seems remarkable in one whose 'enunciation would have been almost totally unintelligible to a stranger' (*SA* 42–3), but this becomes yet another of his contradictions. The important point, though, is that through these contradictions, which simultaneously attribute political agency to his character and deny it, his 'evil gift' of eloquence is itself a political statement: eloquence does not persuade simply through rational processes, but affects us emotionally. As a result, words have power and force as much as bombs and bullets.

In contrast with Yundt, the three 'terrorists' of *Under Western Eyes* are practical and effective activists, 'propagandists of the deed' in Mikhail Bakunin's famous formulation.[22] Each in a different way undermines the simple correspondence between word and concept that is assumed by the narrator when he mentions Mme de S—'s 'mystically bad-tempered' book which, amongst its 'declamatory, and frightfully disconnected' statements, seeks to shift the blame for the assassination of Tsar Alexander II (1881) from 'the terrorists' to palace intriguers.[23] The first to be described as a 'terrorist' is Haldin, who uses the word as a self-appellation immediately after he has revealed to Razumov his part in Mr de P—'s assassination, but in doing so challenges its normative assumptions: 'You suppose that I am a terrorist, now – a destructor of what is' (*UWE* 19). Here, though, Haldin – perhaps following Stepniak, on whom he is partly based[24] – is not so much accepting the label as problematising it, suggesting that its application and use in society are determined by political power, while pointing out that it is those who wield that power who really deserve the label: 'But consider that the true destroyers are they who destroy the spirit of progress and truth, not the avengers who merely kill the bodies of the persecutors of human dignity' (*UWE* 19). Here, then, is a classic instance of the violent oppositionist's manifesto: the 'freedom fighter' resists the label of terrorist and applies it to his enemies; he insists on the moral justification for violence that responds to the violence of the state, which is illegitimate because it is used in order to perpetuate tyranny; he justifies his own violence by the righteousness of its cause.

The second 'terrorist' is a more minor character, Yakovlitch, first glimpsed by Razumov arriving at the Chateau Borel for a meeting with Peter Ivanovitch, and then seen by the narrator in a conspiratorial tableau in the Hotel Cosmopolitan along with Peter Ivanovitch, Nikita and Sophia Antonovna. It is during this second appearance that he is labelled as 'the veteran of ancient terrorist campaigns' (*UWE* 330). Sophia Antonovna has already supplied an explanation for 'ancient': Yakovlitch has found safe haven in America after undertaking a revolutionary 'mission' at 'a time of activity' fifteen years previously (*UWE* 241). The suggestion of antiquity reminds us of Yundt, but it is clear that Yakovlitch is a more potent and significant figure, with a genuinely violent past and possessing some kind of knowledge or expertise required by the conspirators in their plans, believed by the narrator to involve dispatching 'a steamer with a cargo of arms and conspirators to invade the Baltic provinces' (*UWE* 330).

The third 'terrorist' is perhaps the novel's most repugnant character and therefore, we might feel, most deserving of the label. Nikita is not designated as 'terrorist' until the novel's violent climax in Part Fourth, when he attacks Razumov in the Hotel Cosmopolitan, but from his introduction in Part Third we are left in no doubt as to the 'sinister aptness' of his more frequent, alliterative appellation, Nikita Necator: 'He was supposed to have killed more gendarmes and police agents than any revolutionist living . . . the Necator of bureaucrats, of provincial governors, of obscure informers' (*UWE* 266–7). Indeed, his apparently habitual recourse to violence, and the fact that he evidently enjoys it – preparing to attack Razumov, he directs his accomplices with 'an excited, gleeful squeak' (*UWE* 369) – suggests a pathological condition. More grotesque than Scevola, Nikita's psychopathology is also demonstrated in the narrated action rather than through the recollections of other characters: it is more vivid and explicit, and crucially has none of the insight into the possible aetiology of his condition that the narrator of *The Rover* supplies. Indeed, the grotesqueness of Nikita's terrorism receives a notable acknowledgement in Conrad's 1920 'Author's Note', alongside a highly suggestive note of anxiety:

> As to Nikita – nicknamed Necator – he is the perfect flower of the terroristic wilderness. What troubled me most in dealing with him was not his monstrosity but his banality. He has been exhibited to the public eye for years in so-called 'disclosures' in newspaper articles, in secret histories, in sensational novels. (*UWE* xxxii)[25]

Conrad appears to fear that he may have derived Nikita from popular-cultural constructions of terrorism, which would mean that he is a simple villain rather than either a realistic portrait of a political actor or a psychological case study. Conrad thus recognises the immense cultural baggage that a pejorative and political word such as 'terrorist' might bring with it: Nikita may be as much a cliché from political-cultural discourse as a representation of an idea, a movement or a person.

These three very different applications of 'terrorist' in *Under Western Eyes* themselves prove a point: the word is multivalent, contingent in meaning, capable of indicating a range of political positions and behavioural characteristics. Haldin begins to problematise the word, and in doing so initiates a process that continues by implication in each subsequent usage. In each case, the 'terrorist' is shown to favour violence, but for different purposes: Haldin seeks to purify the land by removing agents of persecution, Yakovlitch is working to bring about an insurrection, and Nikita appears to be dedicated to eliminating informers while actually indulging a taste for violence and protecting the security of his own position – one of the novel's final disclosures, reported by Sophia Antonovna from a conversation with the spymaster Mikulin, is that Nikita was himself a police agent all along. While in the twenty-first century we might assume terrorism to possess essential characteristics, and the word itself to signify a stable and defined category of phenomena, *Under Western Eyes* inscribes a fundamental scepticism about the reliability of the label and the stability of the category. The implications for the novel's politics are important: far from being a conservative text which satirises its grotesque revolutionaries in order to condemn them, the multivalence of one of its political keywords encourages us to look beyond the superficial negativity and question conventional labels. Moreover, Conrad's later paratextual reference to Nikita as 'the perfect flower of the terroristic wilderness' raises a further, even more fundamental question. This 'wilderness' is of course not a real place but a metaphor – and one that features in a passage that explicitly acknowledges the concept of terrorism to be at least in part culturally constructed by journalism and popular fiction. In other words, not only is the 'terrorism' label relative, but our conception of what it means is shaped and may even be determined by figurative language. The 'Author's Note' thus further problematises the idea of terrorism by invoking suggestions that seem to me to be strikingly modern in anticipating some of the main claims of the proponents of critical terrorism studies: terrorism is as much an idea in the minds of observers and cultural producers as it is a behaviour exhibited by its perpetrators.

## Conclusion: 'It suited me to label him in that way'

When we extend our view to encompass all three novels we can see that the word 'terrorism' encompasses a remarkable range of characters, philosophies and histories. We also see how, in *The Rover*, its meaning is initially located in a specific historical and political context but is then extended beyond this into psychology and a study of victimisation. This diversity tells us something more fundamental than the simple and familiar point that the word's meaning depends on who is using it and why (crucial though that is). It tells us that political language is by its nature plastic and multidimensional, simply because it is required to mediate contention. This is evidently an important point in Conrad's fiction, and is made explicit by the narrators of two further texts, 'Heart of Darkness' (1899) and 'An Anarchist' (1906). In the former, the Russian tells Marlow that the human heads on stakes in Kurtz's compound are the heads of rebels, and Marlow furiously glosses this for his listeners on the *Nellie*: 'Rebels! What would be the next definition I was to hear? There had been enemies, criminals, workers – and these were rebels. Those rebellious heads looked very subdued to me on their sticks' (*HD* 132). The disillusioned Marlow recognises this is an instance of the instrumental use of a 'definition' from the political lexicon to legitimise oppression and delegitimise victims. Furthermore, the hierarchies of both the Company's operations and Kurtz's rogue state rest on the linguistic practices of definition and labelling ('enemies, criminals, workers'). 'An Anarchist' makes a similar point about instrumentality and the political lexicon – the narrator is careful to put 'anarchist' in quotation marks after he has heard Paul's story – and similarly links this with economic exploitation. The manager of the cattle estate, Harry Gee, expresses and maintains his and the company's political and economic power through his instrumental use of language (and has learned to do so in French as well as English). Asked by the narrator if

Paul is 'really an anarchist', Gee replies: 'I don't care a hang what he is ... I gave him the name because it suited me to label him in that way. It's good for the company.'[26] Gee's purpose is to ensure that Paul is unemployable elsewhere, and the political label is like a linguistic fetter attached to 'the slave of the Marañon estate'. Evidently, what Marlow calls 'burning, noble words' can have real and immediate social effects.

Conrad's insistence that words are not merely neutral carriers of objective meaning but can be used instrumentally and politically helps us to take a view of political language that is broader than that expressed in probably the most famous work on the subject, George Orwell's 'Politics and the English Language' (1945). Orwell's essay rests on an assumption that a stable relationship between words and things is possible, but the essay argues that this is deliberately perverted by political writers who seize particularly on abstractions, as they are more vulnerable to manipulation than concrete words. To deal with this problem of linguistic deception Orwell recommends a different approach to thinking:

> When you think of something abstract you are more inclined to use words from the start, and unless you make a conscious effort to prevent it, the existing dialect will come rushing in and do the job for you, at the expense of blurring or even changing your meaning. Probably it is better to put off using words as long as possible and get one's meaning as clear as one can through pictures and sensations.[27]

In this case, if we were to follow Orwell's advice we might think of terrorism not in terms of definitions but in terms of its physical characteristics or effects. But this is impossible without making ideological assumptions: if we think of a bomb, or an explosion, or a man in a balaclava (as opposed to, say, a poster displaying a 'freedom fighter' or 'martyr') we betray our political orientation. What, instead, we might learn from Conrad's examination of the word is that a stable relationship is unachievable. This should not, however, place Conrad with those thinkers, condemned by Orwell, who hold 'that all abstract words are meaningless, and have used this as a pretext for advocating a kind of political quietism'.[28] Indeed, the opposite is the case: Conrad's examination of political language implies a need for scepticism, vigilance and an awareness of context and contingency, underpinned by an acceptance that if language has power, that power may be used for a variety of purposes.

With this realisation, the diplomats of the UN committees labouring apparently in vain, and the political scientists and terrorism experts who deplore their inability to reach consensus on a definition of terrorism, might be better served by accepting the multivalency of political language and by recognising the centrality of language to the phenomena they seek to understand. Words are weapons, used by 'terrorists' and by their opponents. Conrad's fiction helps us to understand this by showing us how this might happen and what might be its effects. Scepticism, but not quietism, is the best approach for navigating the terroristic wilderness.

## Notes

1. Brian Jenkins, head of terrorism research at the RAND Corporation, quoted in Lisa Stampnitzky, *Disciplining Terror: How the Experts Invented 'Terrorism'* (New York: Cambridge University Press, 2013), p. 4.
2. See Alex P. Schmid, 'The Definition of Terrorism', in Alex P. Schmid (ed.), *The Routledge Handbook of Terrorism Research* (London and New York: Routledge, 2011), pp. 39–98.
3. Philip Herbst, *Talking Terrorism: A Dictionary of the Loaded Language of Political Violence* (London: Greenwood Press, 2003), pp. 163–4.
4. Richard Jackson, *Writing the War on Terror: Language, Politics and Counter-Terrorism* (Manchester: Manchester University Press, 2005), p. 2.
5. There are many studies of terrorism as a form of communication. A representative example is Brigitte Lebens Nacos, *Mass-Mediated Terrorism: The Central Role of the Media in Terrorism and Counter-Terrorism* (London: Rowman and Littlefield, 2007).
6. Walter Laqueur, *Terrorism* (London: Sphere Books, 1978), pp. 18–19.
7. Maximilien Robespierre, *Report on the Principles of Political Morality* (5 February 1794). Rpt. in Keith Michael Baker (ed.), *University of Chicago Readings in Western Civilization. Vol. 7: The Old Regime and the French Revolution* (Chicago: University of Chicago Press, 1987), pp. 368–84 at p. 374.
8. Edmund Burke, *Letters on a Regicide Peace* (1795), cited under 'terrorist' in OED.
9. William Godwin, *Caleb Williams* (London: Penguin, 1988), p. 4. The quotation comes from Godwin's second preface (dated 1795), published in the 1796 edition alongside the suppressed 1794 preface.
10. *An historical review of the state of Ireland, from the invasion of that country under Henry II to its union with Great Britain on the first of January 1801*. Cited under 'terrorist' in OED.
11. Stepniak, *Underground Russia: Revolutionary Profiles and Sketches from Life* (London: Smith, Elder, 1883), pp. 3–4. Stepniak was an exile in London from the early 1880s until his death in 1895, and was lionized by left-wing intellectuals including, among Conrad's close circle, the famously Russophile Garnett family. For the book's presence in Conrad's library, see Hans van Marle, 'A Novelist's Dukedom: From Joseph Conrad's Library', *Conradian* 16.1 (1991), pp. 55–78 at p. 73.
12. See Martha Crenshaw (ed.), *Terrorism in Context* (University Park: Pennsylvania State University Press, 2007), p. 44. Most printed *Der Freiheit*

in London until he was imprisoned for praising in its pages the assassination of Tsar Alexander II. He resumed its publication in the United States, where his glorification of political violence became even stronger.
13. Joseph Conrad, *The Rover* (London: J. M. Dent and Sons, 1948), p. 44. Subsequent references are cited in the text as *Ro*.
14. See Robert Hampson, *Conrad's Secrets* (London: Palgrave Macmillan, 2012), pp. 172–5.
15. Hampson infers from her confession that Arlette had actually participated in some of the killings. Ibid. p. 174.
16. See Robert Appelbaum and Alexis Paknadel, 'Terrorism and the Novel, 1970–2001', *Poetics Today* 29.3 (Fall 2008), pp. 387–436 at pp. 415, 425–6. Appelbaum and Paknadel's study is based on a sample of more than a thousand works of fiction, from which a smaller sample of twenty-five novels was then analysed in depth. The study notes that narrative point of view is crucial – and fictions are rarely narrated by or focalized through the 'terrorist' (victims, law enforcement officers, bystanders or unwitting collaborators are common narrators or focalizers).
17. Joseph Conrad, *The Secret Agent* (London: J. M. Dent and Sons, 1947), p. 263. Subsequent references are cited in the text as *SA*.
18. For a discussion of the Professor's resemblance to twenty-first-century utopian terrorists, see John Gray, 'Joseph Conrad, Our Contemporary', in *Heresies: Against Progress and Other Illusions* (London: Granta, 2004), pp. 100–9.
19. See Norman Sherry, *Conrad's Western World* (Cambridge: Cambridge University Press, 1971), pp. 253–9. Sherry notes that Most died shortly after Conrad began work on 'Verloc', and was widely vilified in obituaries.
20. Ibid. p. x.
21. Joseph Conrad, *Youth, Heart of Darkness, The End of the Tether: Three Stories* (London: J. M. Dent and Sons, 1946), p. 118. Subsequent references are cited in the text as *HD*.
22. 'Letters to a Frenchman on the Present Crisis', 1870. Available at <https://www.marxists.org/reference/archive/bakunin/works/1870/letter-frenchman.htm> (last accessed 19 September 2015).
23. Joseph Conrad, *Under Western Eyes* (London: J. M. Dent and Sons, 1947), p. 163. Subsequent references are cited in the text as *UWE*.
24. See Cedric Watts, 'Stepniak and *Under Western Eyes*', *Notes and Queries* (November 1966), pp. 410–11.
25. One of the 'secret histories' Conrad clearly had in mind was 'The Azeff Scandal' in the *English Review* by 'D.S.' (Ford Madox Ford's brother-in-law David Soskice), which Conrad must have read while in the later stages of working on *Under Western Eyes*: the terrorist murderer Erno Azeff is also a double agent, using his Machiavellian brand of extreme violence against the tsarist state and his fellow revolutionaries as needs dictate.
26. Joseph Conrad, *A Set of Six* (London: J. M. Dent and Sons, 1954), pp. 139–40.
27. In *The Complete Works of George Orwell. Vol. 17: I Belong to the Left: 1945*, ed. Peter Davison (London: Secker and Warburg, 1999), p. 429.
28. Ibid. p. 432.

Chapter 3

# Conrad, G. E. Moore and Idealism
*John Attridge*

In this chapter, I want to compare certain aspects of Conrad's attitude to language with contemporary developments in English philosophy. In particular, I want to consider how far G. E. Moore's watershed 1903 essay 'The Refutation of Idealism' and Conrad's less technical but, on the whole, equally sceptical views on 'idealism' and 'ideals' can be seen to address similar problems and to express a common mood or structure of feeling. It is not my purpose here to argue that Conrad shared Moore's philosophical position with regard to Idealism, although I will suggest that the tension between such opposing terms as 'abstract ideas' and 'material advantage' in Conrad's work does bear some relation to the more properly metaphysical questions in Moore's essay.[1] As well as this loose correspondence at the level of content, however, I want to suggest that Moore's modernist intervention in the discourse of philosophy and Conrad's modernist literary sensibility share meaningful affinities at the level of medium – at the level, that is, of language. A large part of what made Moore's philosophy recognisably new was his rigorous analysis of the meaning of inherited philosophical terms and his own deployment of a novel philosophical idiom. Moore's rebellion against Idealism – arguably the dominant philosophical school in Victorian Britain – was a linguistic, as well as a substantive rebellion. Thus, I suggest below, Moore's sense that the Idealist vocabulary of Victorian philosophy produced confusion paralleled Conrad's scepticism about some of the misleadingly abstract 'ideals' that had regulated nineteenth-century political discourse, as well as his desire to refurbish this faded vocabulary using the sensory concreteness of impressionist style.

In his introduction to a 1956 essay collection entitled *The Revolution in Philosophy*, based on a series of BBC Third Programme Lectures, Gilbert Ryle looked back on the change that had come over British philosophy between mid-Victorian figures like J. S. Mill and Leslie Stephen and the younger generation of G. E. Moore and Bertrand Russell. Due to specialist journals such as *Mind* and the *Proceedings of the Aristotelian Society* rather than in generalist quarterlies and monthlies, philosophy had increasingly become the 'professional practice of submitting problems and arguments to the expert criticism of fellow craftsmen', with the result that 'eloquence' was now less sought after than 'ratiocinative rigour'.[2] Moore was a key figure in this shift. The chapter on Moore by G. A. Paul develops Ryle's point about the move away from 'eloquence', emphasising Moore's 'direct, simple, conversational language' and his avoidance of the 'tired-out words of the subject'.[3] This 'care about words' translated into a scrupulous vigilance against ambiguities and obscurities in the received formulae of conventional metaphysics.[4]

Moore was the principal exponent of a movement in British philosophy known as 'the New Realism'.[5] Along with Personal Idealists like Henry Sturt and Pragmatists like William James, Moore's Realism challenged the doctrines of Absolute Idealism, a school of thought whose most influential British adherent in Moore's day was F. H. Bradley. As J. A. Passmore observes in a retrospective essay written for the centenary of the journal *Mind*, Moore's Realism was distinct from both Pragmatism and Personal Idealism in its deployment of 'a new style of argument', in which 'the making of careful distinctions' was paramount.[6] This 'style of argument', Passmore concludes, '*was* destructive to Idealism, which could not endure so minute an examination'.[7] Unlike other, competing positions in the intellectual marketplace, that is, Moore's philosophy was distinguished by a 'new style' of rigorous linguistic precision. Recalling his own experience of Moore's influence on the undergraduate atmosphere at Cambridge, and especially on the members of the Apostles, J. M. Keynes likewise emphasised Moore's rigorous attention to the meaning of words. 'Moore's method', he recalled in *Two Memoirs* (1949),

> was a method of discovery by the instrument of impeccable grammar and an unambiguous dictionary. 'What *exactly* do you mean?' was the phrase most frequently on our lips. If it appeared under cross-examination that you did not mean *exactly* anything, you lay under a strong suspicion of meaning nothing whatever.[8]

Keynes goes on to elaborate the importance of Moore's *Principia Ethica* (1903), with its exaltation of aesthetic contemplation and personal affection as supreme goods, for the aesthetic and social milieu of the Bloomsbury group. But even apart from these actual teachings, it is clear from Keynes's recollection that Moore's impact on him and other young Cambridge intellectuals consisted also in his sensitivity to subtle shades of meaning – his insistence on knowing 'What *exactly* do you mean?'

Both Moore's linguistic fastidiousness and his readiness to apply this analytic rigour to the supposed obscurities of Idealist philosophy are apparent in *Principia Ethica*. One of the book's central arguments, for instance, concerning the 'naturalistic fallacy', proposes that almost all philosophers have fallen prey to a basic linguistic confusion. With the exception of Henry Sidgwick, Moore argues, ethical writers have mistakenly collapsed the adjective 'good' with the substantive it is supposed to modify, so that 'good' is identified with 'natural objects' such as 'pleasure'.[9] In order for ethical discussion to be meaningful, however, 'good' must be 'indefinable', in the sense that it cannot be analysed into constituent parts or equated with any 'natural object'.[10] The key claim of Moore's 'naturalistic fallacy', in other words, is not that ethicists have been wrong about what 'good' is, but that they have made a logico-grammatical blunder – they have 'attempted to define the good, without recognising what such an attempt must mean'.[11] Moore's general approach to the critique of Idealism can be inferred from his remarks in *Principia Ethica* on the important concept of an 'organic whole'. This idea proves to be a key tool in Moore's own ethical theory, but in order to serve this purpose, Moore says, it must first 'be divorced from its present unfortunate usage. Philosophers, especially those who profess to have derived great benefit from the writings of Hegel, have latterly made much use of the terms '"organic whole", "organic unity", "organic relation"'.[12] These usages, however, 'have no distinct sense and, on the contrary, both imply and propagate errors of confusion'.[13] Clearly in Moore's sights here are Oxford Idealists like T. E. Green, whose collectivist social theory depended on a fervently organicist conception of society. Moore may also be assumed to have Idealism in mind when he rebukes, in the final pages of *Principia Ethica*, the 'common' expectation that philosophical discoveries should display 'symmetry': 'To search for "unity" and "system", at the expense of truth, is not, I take it, the proper business of philosophy.'[14] As Henry Jones complained in an 1893 article, the current revolt against Idealism was typified by a denigration of overarching theories: 'They suggest that system-making is not consistent with sobriety of thought, and they confine themselves to analysis, the exposition of difficulties and polemic.'[15] Moore's blithe admission, in *Principia Ethica*, that his ethical philosophy displays neither 'symmetry' nor 'unity' is thus a shot across the bows of the Idealist orthodoxy.

As W. R. Sorley pointed out in a semicentennial *Mind* essay, Moore's 'New Realist' critique of Absolute Idealism began with his 1899 article 'The Nature of Judgement', which argues that the 'concepts' used in thought exist independently of the minds that think them.[16] For the purposes of this chapter, however, I want to focus on Moore's 1903 essay 'The Refutation of Idealism', both because it is probably the most influential of Moore's attacks on Absolute Idealism, and because it foregrounds matters of sensation and perception that are also important to Conrad. Moore's readiness to take the Idealist tradition to task for its logical and terminological slackness is central to 'The Refutation of Idealism'. The essay's main objective is to challenge the Idealist doctrine that *esse* is *percipi* – to challenge, that is, the claim that whatever exists is wholly mental. As with *Principia Ethica*, the essay's implicit premise is that philosophers in general, and Idealists in particular, have been insufficiently rigorous in examining the stock concepts of philosophical debate. Moore's grievance with the Idealist shibboleth of 'organic unities' recurs in 'The Refutation of Idealism', where it is given an even more ironic inflection:

> In this, as in other matters, Hegel's main service to philosophy has consisted in giving a name to, and erecting into a principle, a type of fallacy to which experience has shown philosophers ... to be addicted. No wonder he has followers and admirers.[17]

The essay's central argument is that mental entities like sensations are not altogether reducible to mental states. Under analysis, sensations are seen to entail both a perceiving consciousness and another element, the 'object' of the sensation, and this object must itself be distinct from subjective conscious experience. In the perception of blue, for instance, Moore holds that the experience of seeing blue must be separable from something called 'blue', which would be the 'object' of this perception.[18] The failure of philosophers to notice this distinction is due in part to the inadequacies of language: 'language offers us no means of referring to such objects as "blue" and "green" and "sweet," except by calling them sensations'.[19] Here, Moore proceeds according to the method of painstaking linguistic precision evoked by Keynes. But there is also a phenomenological axis to Moore's argument, which involves awakening his reader to an easily overlooked feature of conscious experience. The failure to separate consciousness from its objects is due not only to 'mere negligence of expression', but also to the introspective elusiveness of consciousness itself. '[T]he moment we try to fix our attention upon consciousness and see *what*, distinctly, it is, it seems to vanish: it seems as if we had before us a mere emptiness.'[20] Rendering this 'transparent' and 'diaphanous' medium perceptible is thus the explicit purpose of this phenomenological phase of Moore's argument. 'My main object in this paragraph has been to try to make the reader *see* it.'[21]

It is doubtless easy to overestimate the significance of this echo of Conrad's phraseology in the 1897 'Preface' to *The Nigger of the 'Narcissus'*: 'My task which I am trying to achieve is, by the power of the written word, to make you hear, to make you feel – it is, before all, to make you *see*.'[22] Nonetheless, it is worth pausing to consider how far this coincidence of phrasing reflects a real analogy between the aims and methods outlined in the two essays. Moore's article, to be sure, makes its 'appeal' primarily in the manner of 'the thinker or the scientist' that Conrad evokes at the beginning of the 'Preface', and not via the artist's route of 'an impression conveyed through the senses' (*NN* ix). But Conrad's famous ambition of rejuvenating the 'old, old words, worn thin, defaced by ages of careless usage' bears comparison with Moore's efforts, in 'The Refutation of Idealism', *Principia Ethica* and elsewhere, to scrutinise and debunk the stock terms and formulae of philosophy – to renew the 'tired-out words of the subject', as Paul put it (*NN* ix). Moore's interrogation of the common practice of referring to sensory qualities as the 'content' of a perception, rather than its 'object', is one instance of this project of terminological renewal.[23] And while Moore's dismantling of unreflected axioms sometimes proceeds by way of logical analysis, in the passage referred to above his method is very close to Conrad's own: the success or failure of Moore's argument at this juncture turns on his ability to present an accurate picture of conscious experience, convincing enough to dislodge conventional misperceptions. Moore's attempt to 'make the reader *see*' may seem anaemic by comparison with Conrad's lavish impressionism, but terms like 'diaphanous' and 'transparent' connote a quasi-literary desire to describe an elusive quality of experience. Both Conrad and Moore use a jolt of phenomenology to defibrillate the 'old, old words'. Within the very different frames of reference of their respective crafts, both writers shared a desire to uproot cliché and turn back the tide of 'careless usage'.

One might, of course, object that Moore's 'new style' of language, for all its common-sense vocabulary, is confined to a technical and esoteric domain, whereas Conrad makes an explicit link between the aesthetic objectives of the 'Preface' and an ethos of 'solidarity' with common human experience (*NN* viii). However, Conrad's own affection for professional nautical idioms suggests that the principle, at least, of a rigorously exact technical language was not alien to his literary practice. As Martin Ray points out, 'technical words' appealed to Conrad because they 'enjoy a direct correspondence with the objects which they describe'.[24] Conrad's most explicit consideration of this topic is the second chapter of his memoir *The Mirror of the Sea* (1906), which castigates newspaper writers for mangling proper nautical usage in their references to nautical events. Whereas journalists invariably refer to an anchor's being cast, Conrad points out that 'the anchor ready for its work is already overboard, and is not thrown over, but simply allowed to fall'.[25] An anchor, that is, 'is never cast, and to take a liberty with technical language is a crime against the clearness, precision, and beauty of perfected speech' (*MS* 13). The example of the anchor is a happy rhetorical choice, first, because it allows Conrad to present the journalist's mistake as empirically, and not just formally unsound. Technical language is no mere arbitrary jargon, but rather possesses a referential aptness that anyone familiar with the sea can appreciate. Secondly, this example allows Conrad to enlist the anchor as a metaphor for technical language itself, to great effect. 'An anchor is a forged piece of iron, admirably adapted to its end, and technical language is an instrument wrought into perfection by ages of experience, a flawless thing for its purpose' (*MS* 13). With this analogy in place, Conrad's praise for the anchor comes to sound like an oblique eulogy to technical language. It too, after all, is conceived as a tool 'forged and fashioned for faithfulness' (*MS* 14). When Conrad describes how the anchor will 'bite' the 'ground' and 'hold till the cable parts', it is hard not to imagine the referential grip of technical language, faithfully catching hold of objects in the physical world (*MS* 14).

Ray suggests that Conrad imagines technical language as a system of abstract 'counters', but in *The Mirror of the Sea* he seems intent on attributing sensory thickness to the professional language of sailors.[26] This is already intimated in the criticism of journalistic abuses, and is made explicit in Conrad's discussion of a related example, 'the growth of the cable' (*MS* 21). This image, he writes, 'has all the force, precision, and imagery of technical language that, created by simple men with keen eyes for the real aspect of the things they see in their trade, achieves the just expression seizing upon the essential' (*MS* 21). Conrad explicitly likens this goal to 'the ambition of the artist in words' (*MS* 21), and hammers home the point by characterising the master's question 'How does the cable grow?' as an 'impressionistic phrase' (*MS* 21). Conrad offers a similar specimen of nautical language some five years later in 'The Silence of the Sea' (1909), his article on the missing steamship *Waratah* and the general subject of ships lost at sea. Having assured the reader that his views on this topic derive from 'the testimony of his senses', Conrad further authenticates his remarks by glossing a piece of specialised terminology: whereas laypeople might speak of a ship's being endangered by 'waves', Conrad and other sailors habitually use the expression 'seas'.[27] The landsman's word 'does not come glib to a seaman's tongue', and even writing it is difficult for Conrad when he is mentally immersed in 'a time far removed from the modes of thought and speech common to the shore' ('Silence' 173). This distinction between the 'modes of thought and speech' proper to sea and land life continues with the 'sailor's phrase' that seamen are accustomed to use when referring to big 'seas': 'they come at one like a wall' ('Silence' 173). Here again, as with the captain's 'impressionistic phrase' in *The Mirror of the Sea*, the special language of nautical life is endowed with a decidedly literary quality. As a metaphor, the comparison between a wave and a wall, like the image of the cable's 'growth', seems designed to achieve precisely the aim of sensory concreteness outlined in the 'Preface' to *The Nigger of the 'Narcissus'*. Although these are, surely, stock phrases, Conrad implies that such nautical idioms transcribe an especially acute apprehension of the visible world.

The virtues of precision that Conrad praises in 'technical language' are similar to the qualities that distinguished Moore's 'new style of argument'. And correspondingly, the negligent use of language that Conrad imputes to journalists is comparable to the confused and inexact terminology that Moore abominates in Idealism. Both Moore and Conrad propose a rigorous linguistic regimen as a corrective to the abuses practised in another sphere of discourse. What did Conrad dislike so much about newspaper writing? As Stephen Donovan has shown, Conrad's attitude towards the press can be traced with considerable precision to the particular conditions of a burgeoning mass media industry. One such condition was the mass newspaper's cultivation of 'shock' as an integral part of modern news consumption.[28] Donovan also argues convincingly that Conrad's contempt for journalistic cliché would have been shaped by other fictional representations of newspaper reporting.[29] In a more general sense, though, Conrad's hostility towards journalism tends to be directed at the medium's supposed untruthfulness. He was giving voice to a long and dearly held belief when he told J. M. Dent in 1917 that 'journalists can't speak the truth – nor even *see* it as other men do' (*CL6* 56). Small chance, then, of their making a reader *see* it. There were, as Donovan shows, many features of journalistic discourse that made it an uncongenial environment for truth in Conrad's eyes. An over-reliance on certain abstract nouns is, perhaps, a less pervasive ill than the quest for 'shock' and the alleged addiction to cliché. Nonetheless, I want to suggest that a tendency to rely on rhetorical abstractions was one of the things that Conrad had in mind when he contrasted journalism with 'technical language' in *The Mirror of the Sea*, and that, in this way, journalism exemplifies a much broader category of untrustworthy uses of language.

The figure in Conrad's fiction who most obviously combines his hostility to modern journalism with his distrust of rhetorical abstractions is Kurtz. Matthew Rubery has shown that the rapidly changing late Victorian newspaper industry was a vitally important context for 'Heart of Darkness', a work which Conrad described in a letter to his translator Henri-Durand Davray as the 'wild story of a journalist' (*CL2* 407). Kurtz is repeatedly associated in Marlow's narrative with 'eloquence', a quality ascribed both to his written report for the International Society for the Suppression of Savage Customs and to the oral discourse he delivers to Marlow during their journey downriver.[30] Although this aspect of Kurtz's personality is not exclusively identified with his status as a journalist, we are surely to understand that his newspaper writing would have expressed the same euphuistic sensibility as his 'report' and his speeches. As a correspondent rather than a reporter, Rubery points out, 'Kurtz's primary concern is with persuasion, explaining why he disregards surrounding living conditions while cultivating his rhetoric.'[31] And although Kurtz's colleague opines at the end of the novel that he 'really couldn't write a bit', his acceptance of Kurtz's report when it is offered to him for publication by Marlow suggests that, on the contrary, Kurtz's 'high-strung' writing is perfectly serviceable copy (*HD* 181, 155). The 'eloquence' of Kurtz's pamphlet doubtless consists in a general tone of moral fervour, typical of imperialist manifestos like Leopold II's address to the 1876 Brussels Geographical Conference, but a particular feature of such writing is the penchant for abstractions. The prevalence of this device in Kurtz's pamphlet is suggested by Marlow's recollection of its contents, which is confined to a vague duo of personifications: 'an exotic Immensity ruled by an august Benevolence' (*HD* 155). The pamphlet's abstractness is also underlined by the complete absence of 'practical hints': Kurtz's 'noble words' soar above concrete practicalities (*HD* 155). Another suggestion that Kurtz's writing favours such abstractions is the testimony of the Russian harlequin, who first apprises Marlow of Kurtz's gift for oratory. Marlow, again, gives only a dismissively vague précis of these reported monologues, which are reduced to a list of abstract nouns: 'love, justice, conduct of life – or what not' (*HD* 165). The tone of Marlow's reference to the 'Immensity' and the 'Benevolence' of the pamphlet is less overtly scornful than this 'what not', but in both cases Conrad's shorthand for Kurtz's 'eloquence' is a sequence of morally charged abstractions – or what we might call, ideals.

In one of his exuberantly pessimistic letters to R. B. Cunninghame Graham, Conrad facetiously harangued his correspondent about his faith in 'ideals':

You with your ideals of sincerity, courage, and truth are strangely out of place in this epoch of material preoccupations. What does it bring? What's the profit? What do we get by it? These questions are at the root of every moral, intelligence or political movement. Alas! What you want to reform are not institutions – it is human nature. (*CL2* 25)

Even allowing for the somewhat febrile raillery of Conrad's correspondence with Cunninghame Graham, the cynicism expressed here does reflect at least one side of Conrad's attitude towards 'ideals'. Cunninghame Graham, to be sure, is not accused of succumbing to newspaper cant or demagoguery, like Kurtz's 'love' and 'justice'. Nonetheless, the list of abstract nouns – 'sincerity, courage, and truth' – affiliates these 'ideals' with the hackneyed topics of Kurtz's discourse to the Russian harlequin, or his report on civilising the Congo. And as with the violent contrast between the high-minded rhetoric of Kurtz's report and its one, horrifyingly 'practical' prescription – 'Exterminate all the brutes!' – Conrad derides Cunninghame Graham's espousal of such ideals as quixotic, radically at odds with the 'material preoccupations' of the age. Conrad would present essentially the same cynical political analysis in 'Autocracy and War', his 1905 essay on the 'bottomless abyss' of Russia and the bellicose geopolitics of modern Europe (*NLL* 134). In the modern era, he concludes, 'No war will be fought for an idea' (*NLL* 141). 'Industrialism and commercialism', disguised by 'high-sounding names', have replaced older ideologies, and modern democracy 'has elected to pin its faith to the supremacy of material interests' (*NLL* 142). As in the letter to Cunninghame Graham, these conditions leave little hope for the efficacy of ideals: 'the conscience of but very few men amongst us, and of no single Western nation as yet, will brook the restraint of abstract ideas as against the fascination of a material advantage' (*NLL* 148). The letter's antithesis of 'ideals' and 'material preoccupations' reappears here as 'abstract ideas' and 'material advantage'.

It is sometimes observed that sensitivity to the 'visible world' in Conrad's fiction is combined with another, more abstract register. In *Poets of Reality*, for instance, J. Hillis Miller suggests that Conrad's 'attempt to render the exact appearances of things is not an end in itself', but serves rather as a means of revealing 'the truth of life'. For Conrad, Miller argues, this 'truth' consists in an underlying 'darkness' – a 'metaphysical entity' that is 'incompatible with language'.[32] Ian Watt's discussion of 'the convergence of the symbolist and impressionist traditions' in Conrad's work also distinguishes between concrete and abstract tendencies in Conrad's use of language. The device that Watt famously dubbed 'delayed decoding' – 'the verbal equivalent of the impressionist painter's attempt to render visual sensations directly' – is accompanied in 'Heart of Darkness' by other, more symbolic modes of signification, often 'conceived at a rather high level of abstraction'.[33] Another variation on this dualist reading is proposed by Michael Levenson, for whom the 'Preface' to *The Nigger of the 'Narcissus'* displays a 'tension' between 'the sensory apprehension of life's surfaces' and a countervailing interest in 'inwardness and depth', corresponding to the broader Conradian problem of 'the dissociation of fact and subjectivity'.[34] Although pursuing widely divergent critical projects, Miller, Watt and Levenson all point towards a dualism in Conrad's stylistic imagination between the 'fidelity to the truth of my sensations' proclaimed in the 'Author's Note' to *Within the Tides* and a more abstract order of experience.[35]

I would like to suggest that Conrad's pessimistic juxtaposition of material interests with ineffectual ideals corresponds to the same dualism, so that what is at stake is not only self-interest versus principled moral action, but a more basic opposition between the material and the metaphysical worlds. In *Under Western Eyes* (1911), there are signs that the bogus political philosophies of Peter Ivanovitch and Mme de S— are guilty of a fatuous disregard, not only for 'material interests', but for materiality itself, in the sense of concrete physical existence. Mark Wollaeger articulates this slippage well: Conrad's depiction of Ivanovitch drives a 'wedge' between 'the human individual, characterized chiefly in terms of his baser drives, and more sublimated manifestations of human consciousness, which are made to seem weaker and less authentic'.[36] This tension is embodied in the image of Ivanovitch as a shackled fugitive from the tsarist state, degenerating to a bestial condition in order to survive. In his person are combined both

> The civilized man, the enthusiast of advanced humanitarian ideals thirsting for the triumph of spiritual love and political liberty; and the stealthy, primeval savage, pitilessly cunning in the preservation of his freedom from day to day, like a tracked wild beast.[37]

Ivanovitch's 'ideals' are implicitly undercut by this resurgence of his brute nature, which is felt to be irreconcilably disjunct from the uplifting content of his 'humanitarian' writings. A similar scepticism seems to be at play when Conrad has Ivanovitch's patron Mme de S— profess to be a political 'supernaturalist', whose revolutionary slogan is 'spiritualize the discontent' (*UWE* 221–2). Such reckless disregard for the material world puts Mme de S—'s mystical utopianism beyond the pale of credible political philosophies, which must come to terms with the physical manifestations of power and disempowerment.

In a much-quoted 1902 letter expounding his artistic philosophy to William Blackwood, Conrad assured his editor and publisher that he was much more concerned with fact than subjectivity. Rather than occupying himself with the 'endless analysis of affected sentiments', the 'essence' of his work is

> nothing but action – action observed, felt and interpreted with an absolute truth to my sensations (which are the basis of art in literature) – action of human beings that will bleed to a prick, and are moving in a visible world. (CL2 418)

As well as reprising the impressionist dictum of 'scrupulous fidelity to the truth of my own sensations' that he would proclaim in the 'Author's Note' to *Within the Tides* and elsewhere, this statement of artistic intent certainly seems to foreground Conrad's determination to represent a corporeal world, peopled by embodied agents whose 'sentiments' – and, presumably, ideals – are secondary to their flesh and blood materiality.[38] Nothing, we might imagine, could be further from the prosopopoetic protagonists of Kurtz's report, the 'exotic Immensity' and the 'august Benevolence'. In a statement like this, Conrad seems to define his own discursive bearings in contradistinction to the 'humanitarian ideals' that suffuse Ivanovitch's memoir or the 'abstract ideas' of more credulous political dispensations. Such a style of writing recalls the virtues attributed to the 'technical language' of sailors, coined by observers with 'keen eyes for the real aspect of the things they see' (*MS* 21). Just as sailors naturally avoid the abuses committed by journalists, so too this physically concrete aesthetic is more trustworthy, less treacherous than a discourse of abstract ideals.

The tension evoked in the letter to Cunninghame Graham and 'Autocracy and War' between political ideals and 'material preoccupations', 'material interests' or 'material advantage' is a central motif in *Nostromo* (1904). As Richard Niland observes, all of Conrad's political novels address 'the "descent" of political ideas into the arena of practical political application', but what makes *Nostromo* especially pertinent in the context of Conrad's attitude to language is the way that this conflict between ideals and realpolitik intersects with the idea of 'eloquence'.[39] The phrase 'material interests', used in 'Autocracy and War' to label the temperament of the democratic age, rings like a refrain through *Nostromo*, where it expresses Charles Gould's hope that capitalist investment will civilise the chaotic political environment of Conrad's fictional Latin American nation, Costaguana.[40] This apparently hard-headed faith in 'material interests' is given a linguistic inflection through the motif of Gould's hyperbolically English taciturnity. 'Anyone can declaim', he tells his wife, 'but I pin my faith to material interests. Only let the material interests once get a firm footing, and they are bound to impose the conditions on which alone they can continue to exist' (*N* 84). As is often pointed out, Gould's irrefrangible reserve is thrown into relief by several examples of the 'eloquence of one sort or another produced in both Americas', from the relatively benign 'loquacity' of Don José Avellanos, to the 'provincial Excellency' in Sulaco who authorises the reopening of the San Tomé mine, the Nationalist leader Pedro Montero, who delivers an energetic but scarcely audible address to the crowd gathered to observe his arrival in Sulaco, and the Monterist flunkey Sotillo, who, 'Like most of his countrymen, . . . was carried away by the sound of fine words, especially if uttered by himself' (*N* 83, 112, 90, 390, 285). A slightly less prominent counterpoint to Gould's reserve is the emotional letters addressed to him by his father, original recipient of the 'perpetual concession of the San Tomé mine' (*N* 53). 'His poor father could be eloquent too', Gould recalls, reminding his wife of a particularly purple passage from his correspondence (*N* 83). Gould's father was also, we know, prone to romanticise the material fact of the mine with imagery of 'the Old Man of the Sea, vampires, and ghouls' (*N* 58). Gould's taciturnity separates him, not only from the indigenous Costaguanans, but also from an earlier, more superstitious, more verbose generation. By contrast with his father's Victorian bombast, Charles Gould renounces all 'eloquence' and proposes to approach the mine as a material thing, a source of wealth and nothing more. Allergic to rhetoric and resolutely rooted in the physical world, Gould seems to be, not only a product, but an allegorical embodiment of Conrad's aesthetic of 'action' and the depiction of 'human beings . . . moving in a visible world'. Even when courting his wife, he did not 'open his heart . . . in any set speeches' but rather 'simply went on acting and thinking in her sight. This is the true method of sincerity' (*N* 60).

Whereas Gould's uncle had defended the principle of 'rational liberty', Gould seeks to erect a *cordon sanitaire* of silence against the political ideals and programmes that flourish so copiously in Costaguana (*N* 64). Like Kurtz's report and Ivanovitch's 'humanitarian' writings, all such high-minded programmes appear in an ironic light in the novel, seeming pitifully out of touch with the 'puerile and bloodthirsty game' of Costaguanan politics (*N* 49). Avellanos's humiliation at the hands of Guzmán Bento, indeed, prefigures the image of Ivanovitch's abjection in *Under Western Eyes*. '[C]lanking his chains' in Bento's travelling entourage of captives, he 'seemed only to exist in order to prove how much hunger, pain, degradation, and cruel torture a human body can stand' (*N* 137). This piercing vision of unaccommodated man contrasts ironically with Avellanos's continued commitment to 'eloquence' and 'Ideals', filtered through to the reader in the form of sonorous excerpts from his 'famous' speeches and the manuscript of 'Fifty Years of Misrule' (N 136, 112). While Avellanos attempts to find 'new Ideals' for the current political situation, the idealistic politics of Giorgio Viola, the novel's 'old Garibaldino', are frankly nostalgic (N 136, 124). Viola's fanatical veneration of Garibaldi and proud attachment to 'liberty' as a political ideal have little purchase on the Costaguanan political scene. He himself feels 'contempt' for the 'non-political nature of the riot' triggered in Sulaco by the Monterist coup: 'They were not a people striving for justice, but thieves' (N 16, 20). The bathetic diminishment of his catch-cry at the end of the novel into a half-hearted joke about marriage – 'Liberty, liberty. There's more than one kind!' – aptly sums up the contemporary relevance of Viola's nineteenth-century liberal politics (N 543). As Gould says bitterly to Dr Monygham, the abstract nouns from which political discourse is composed are changed utterly by contact with the Costaguanan climate: 'Liberals! The words one knows so well have a nightmarish meaning in this country. Liberty, democracy, patriotism, government – all of them have a flavour of folly and murder' (N 408). Far better, seemingly, to put one's faith in 'material interests' than in 'abstract ideas' like these.

As it turns out, of course, the picture of Gould as a fully exteriorised man of 'action', and his belief that he has successfully disenchanted the San Tomé mine, eluding the spell that ruined his father, are ironic. Charles Gould's technical knowledge about the mine is one of the characteristics that seem to differentiate him from earlier generations of his family: his investors are aware that he 'knew everything that could be known of it' (N 75). This scientific understanding of the mine would seem to bolster his attempt to grasp it solely in its 'material' aspect. Even before Gould resumes the San Tomé concession, however, Conrad reveals that he is prone to romanticise the objects of his technical knowledge. Although 'he had pursued his studies in Belgium and France with the idea of qualifying for a mining engineer . . . this scientific aspect of his labours remained vague and imperfect in his mind' (N 59). Rather, Gould is beguiled by the 'dramatic interest' of mines, studying them 'as one would study the varied characters of men' (N 59). As his wife realises, Gould's fascination with mines is not scientific, but expresses instead a 'profoundly sensible, almost voiceless attitude . . . towards the world of material things' (N 59). This early sign that Gould's resolute focus on 'material things' conceals a latent anthropomorphism foreshadows his later attitude to the San Tomé mine, which is likewise corrupted by retrograde romantic notions. The most forceful exposition of this view of Gould's character is delivered by Martin Decoud, who, refuting Emilia Gould's initial intuition of Gould's magnificent 'unsentimentalism', vehemently insists that Gould is both an 'idealist' and a 'sentimentalist' (*N* 50, 214, 218). As Decoud says, the obtrusive presence of the San Tomé mine, 'the greatest fact in the whole of South America', makes such a reading of Gould's character wildly counter-intuitive (*N* 214). Nonetheless, Gould is every bit as susceptible to sentimentalism and superstition as his father: 'he cannot act or exist without idealising every simple feeling, desire, or achievement. He could not believe his own motives if he did not make them first part of some fairy tale' (*N* 215). Just as he has anthropomorphised famous mines in Germany, Spain and Cornwall, Gould has 'idealised' this most intractable of all Costaguanan facts. Key elements of this character analysis will be confirmed with greater authority later, in a passage that shifts between Gould's reported thoughts and the narrator's commentary. Whereas Decoud is an 'imaginative materialist', Gould is both 'too severely practical' and 'too idealistic' to observe the fate of the mine with detachment (*N* 364). Reflecting bitterly on his misguided decision to back the Ribierist cause, he recognises that the mine had 'insidiously corrupted his judgement' (*N* 364). Believing himself to be following the dictates of 'good business', he has become entangled in the political turmoil that consumed his uncle. Thinking himself a disenchanted modern capitalist, he is in fact a romantic 'adventurer' like his forebears, inheritor of his father's 'imaginative weakness' (*N* 365).

Niland suggests that the sceptical depiction of progress in *Nostromo* 'resonates with [Max] Weber's notion of the disenchantment of modernity', although noting that the stereotype of a pre-capitalist utopia is 'ironized'.[41] With respect to the theme of idealism and idealisation, however, it would appear that Conrad's irony goes even further, questioning the Weberian narrative of disenchantment itself. As we have seen, Gould's attempt to cultivate a purely instrumental relation to the San Tomé concession founders on his own 'sentimentalis[m]', first foreshadowed in his tendency to treat mines like people. In spite of himself, Gould does invest the 'material' process of mining with ideal value. Neither Charles nor Emilia Gould's first impressions of the rehabilitated San Tomé mine suggest an attitude of disenchantment. The 'growling mutter' of the stamps speaks directly to Gould's 'heart' with 'the peculiar force of a proclamation', realising a sound which he had 'heard ... in his imagination' on his first visit to 'the jungle-grown solitude of the gorge' (*N* 105). It is not the untouched natural world but the functioning mine that is invested here with romantic energy, while the vocal imagery of the 'mutter' and the 'proclamation' ironically assimilates this mute fact to the 'eloquence' of Costaguanan political life. As a character in whom 'the most legitimate touch of materialism was wanting', it is perhaps not surprising that Emilia Gould also invests the matter of the mine with ideal significance (*N* 75). Nonetheless, her response to the first processed products of the mine serves as a vivid example of a wider pattern in the novel. Touching a freshly minted ingot with trembling hands, 'she endowed that lump of metal with a justificative conception, as though it were not a mere fact, but something far-reaching and impalpable, like the true expression of an emotion or the emergence of a principle' (*N* 107). Charles and Emilia Gould's supposedly modern, disenchanted sensibility is not, in the end, so different from the feeling of the Indios, who 'invested [the mine] with a protecting and invincible virtue as though it were a fetish made by their own hands' (*N* 398). Europeans and indigenous Americans alike feel compelled to attach ideal significance to the fact of the mine. *Nostromo* depicts a system of production in the age of Weberian disenchantment, but it also suggests that the tendency towards re-enchantment is persistent and incorrigible.

The duality of the silver as both physical object and cathectic vessel persists into the novel's coda, where Nostromo falls victim to its phantasmal magnetism. As with Charles Gould's 'subtle conjugal infidelity', Nostromo's fixation on the hidden treasure is figured in erotic and, in his case, uncomfortably patriarchal terms (*N* 365). He 'yearned to clasp, embrace, absorb, subjugate in unquestioned possession this treasure', an image that is recalled in a literally romantic context when he declares his love for Giselle Viola: 'Masterful and tender, he was entering slowly upon the fullness of his possession' (*N* 529, 538). This imagery of the silver as an alternative object of desire becomes more overt as the secret romance plot progresses, taking not a triangular but a quadrilateral shape in which the silver is the fourth term. Nostromo is distracted from the 'woman he desired' by 'the shining spectre of the treasure ... claiming his allegiance'; later, finding himself unable to reveal the location of the treasure to his lover, he has a vision of the silver as a jealous succubus: 'The spectre of the unlawful treasure arose, standing by her side like a figure of silver, pitiless and secret with a finger on its pale lips' (*N* 531, 542). The cycle of Gould Senior's dreams of 'vampires' and Charles Gould's transformation of the San Tomé mine into a 'fairy tale' is closed in the novel's final section with this gothic imagery (*N* 56, 215). Charles and Emilia Gould's idealisation of the silver may be less garish than this ghostly personification, but Conrad nonetheless implies an equivalence between ideals and spectres, both spiritual emanations that give a double life to 'the world of material things'.

Charles Gould's quarrel with the ghost of his father is presented as, at once, a rejection of 'eloquence' and a rejection of idealism: Gould will avoid the mistakes of the past by resolutely observing the logic of 'material interests'. This programme is also supposed to insulate him from the 'eloquence' of Costaguanan politics, and this, too, is a flight from idealism. Don José Avellanos's political philosophy is idealistic in the sense that it trusts naively to high-minded principles. His earnest allusion to the 'comity of civilized nations' could not be more different from the war of each against all sketched sardonically in 'Autocracy and War': Avellanos is an anachronistic advocate of idealpolitik in the age of Bismarck (*N* 140). But taciturnity combined with a strict groundedness in 'the world of material things' is also a rejection of *linguistic* idealism: the reliance on abstract nouns that sustains Avellanos's political vision. Gould renounces the emotive rhetorical abstractions associated with Kurtz's report and Cunninghame Graham's politics, and with Avellanos and Viola in *Nostromo*. In this respect, Gould's attempt to 'pin [his] faith' to material things is like a practical application of Conrad's doctrine of verbal concreteness. We have seen that Gould embodies the values of Conrad's letter to Blackwood, preferring sincere action in Emilia's 'sight' (the 'visible world' of the letter) to the mere profession of sentiments. And if Conrad's writing eschews the abstract realm of ideals in favour of close attention to physical reality, then here too Gould's taciturnity and his choice of 'material interests' over ideals accord with Conrad's impressionism. Gould, who combines 'technical knowledge' of the mine with a sensitivity to 'material things', might be expected to appreciate the eulogy to 'technical language' in *The Mirror of the Sea*, with its celebration of 'simple men with keen eyes for the real aspect of the things'. But if *The Mirror of the Sea* expresses unreserved admiration for this form of 'perfected speech', the vision of *Nostromo* is more complicated. Gould may set out to place his faith in 'material things' and thereby avoid the travesties and fatuities of Avellanos's 'new Ideals', but his attempt to separate 'the greatest fact in the whole of South America' from all ideal associations is unsuccessful.

I have suggested that Moore's attempt to renovate the language of philosophy can be compared to Conrad's own preoccupation with style – his sense that the 'old, old words' were in need of renewal. Correspondingly, Moore's sense that existing philosophical idioms were insufficiently rigorous parallels Conrad's vituperation of verbal slackness and ineptitude: Moore, too, might have appreciated the description of 'technical language' offered in *The Mirror of the Sea*. This analogy between Moore and Conrad can, I suggest, be further refined by considering Conrad's attitude towards rhetorical abstractions and, specifically, 'ideals'. The doctrine of sensory concreteness that Conrad propounded in the 'Preface' and elsewhere is implicitly opposed to the various cant discourses that he satirises throughout his fiction. The rhetorical signature of such discourses is, frequently, their reliance on emotive abstractions, like the 'Benevolence' and 'Immensity' of Kurtz's pamphlet, or José Avellanos's sonorous appeal to 'peace, prosperity and ... an honourable place in the comity of civilized nations' (N 140). In *Chance*, de Barral relies on a similar species of empty rhetoric to promote his speculative financial enterprises, which carry names like 'the "Orb" Deposit Bank' and 'the "Thrift and Independence" Association'.[42] Abstraction facilitates humbug – and worse; conversely, rigorous attention to the 'real aspect of things' precludes the unscrupulous use of vague emotive terms. Such 'ideals' occupy much the same place in Conrad's linguistic ethos that loose philosophical usages like 'sensation' and 'organic unity' do in Moore's philosophy. Moore's insistence that philosophical words and sentences should have a sharply defined *meaning* is comparable to Conrad's preference for words that have an authentic *reference* – albeit a reference to the speaker's 'own sensations'. Moore's hitting upon Conrad's famous phrase as a way of describing his own rhetorical agenda is thus not mere coincidence, but aptly captures a real affinity between their respective projects. His aim of making the reader *see* involves drawing back the veil of conventional usage, just as Conrad's linguistic regimen prescribes an avoidance of lazy or fraudulent abstractions.

Of course, Moore means to oppose something more specific than what Conrad called 'abstract ideas' when he takes up the cudgels against Idealism: Conrad's pessimism about the valency of 'ideals' in a world governed by 'material interests' is of a different order from Moore's refutation of the claim that *esse* is *percipi*. Nonetheless, it is something more than a play on words to suggest that Conrad and Moore both express doubts about 'idealism'. I have noted that the emphasis in Conrad's allusions to 'material interests' or 'material advantage' sometimes seems to fall suggestively on the qualifier, reaching beyond the prosaic meaning of self-interest to imply an orientation towards the material world. And the depiction of the 'materialist' Decoud in *Nostromo* makes clear that disenchantment with political idealism can be continuous with more properly philosophical beliefs about the nature of the universe. 'It is through Decoud', as Wollaeger puts it, 'that scepticism first enters Conrad's fiction as an explicit theme.'[43] As Wollaeger and others have noted, a kind of abstraction invades Conrad's own writing in the working out of Decoud's story, which operates at times like a philosophical allegory about the dangers of scepticism. As a 'materialist' who lacks 'faith in anything except the truth of his own sensations', Decoud has no defence against the implacable material presence of the Golfo Placido: his 'individuality' is literally engulfed by 'the world of cloud and water, of natural forces and forms of nature' (*N* 229, 497). Whether or not we are convinced by the logic of Decoud's suicide, the presence of this bona fide 'materialist' in *Nostromo* does illustrate how Conrad's scepticism about political or 'humanitarian' ideals can have a philosophical dimension. My main concern in this chapter has been with Conrad's aversion to the rhetorical abstractions which he sometimes called 'ideals', but this kind of 'idealism' is not categorically distinct from the Idealism that Moore sought to oppose. The way that Conrad's aesthetic formula – 'fidelity to the truth of my own sensations' – is used to express Decoud's philosophical position underlines the possibility of slippage between these two levels: between the commitment to physical reality as a principle of style and a more metaphysical version of this commitment.

*Nostromo* shows that various reservations and equivocations attend Conrad's dubiety about 'ideals' and admiration for physically concrete language. Gould's unsuccessful attempt to purge all idealism from his attitude to the San Tomé mine suggests that the strict adherence to 'the real aspect of things' prescribed in *The Mirror of the Sea* is, in practice, elusive. Conrad is evidently attracted to Gould's taciturnity and his distaste for 'eloquence', but, equally clearly, Gould's total suppression of 'eloquence' is shown to be a failure – despite his determination to think in 'material' terms, an ideal conception infiltrates his attitude towards the 'fact' of the mine.

Conrad returned to the theme of nautical language in the 1922 essay 'Outside Literature', which deals with the 'Notices to Mariners' issued by the Admiralty to the merchant fleet. In some ways the later essay recalls the fond depiction of 'technical language' in *The Mirror of the Sea*, but where Conrad's purpose in 1906 had been to draw an analogy between nautical and literary discourses, 'Outside Literature' makes a distinction. Although the essay affects a rueful nostalgia for the 'Perfect Accuracy' of these communications, this accuracy is deemed to be alien to the concerns of literature. Whereas the 'Preface' to *The Nigger of the 'Narcissus'* had identified 'the light of magic suggestiveness' as a distinguishing characteristic of literary writing, 'Notices to Mariners' convey 'not suggestion but information of an ideal accuracy' (*NN* ix).[44] Lacking suggestiveness, this perfectly exact nautical idiom is also prohibited from making any appeal to 'man's spiritual side', and 'all suggestion of Love, of Adventure, of Romance, of Speculation, of all that decorates and ennobles life, except Responsibility, is barred' (*LE* 39–40). 'Notices to Mariners', in other words, would appear to purchase their 'Perfect Accuracy' at the expense of any claim upon the discourse of ideals, and it is this limitation that excludes them from the realm of literature. This distinction is consistent with the vision of *Nostromo*, which recognises ideals as stubborn social and psychological facts, objects of representation in their own right. Moore's articles could aspire to the condition of 'technical language' because they were addressed to 'a special public, limited to a very definite special subject', as Conrad puts it in 'Outside Literature' (*LE* 40). Because ideals in all their treacherous vagueness form part of the subject matter of literary representation, however, 'Perfect Accuracy' is not a condition to which literature can reasonably attain.

## Notes

1. Joseph Conrad, *Notes on Life and Letters* (London: J. M. Dent and Sons, 1921), p. 148. Subsequent references are cited in the text as *NLL*.
2. Gilbert Ryle, 'Introduction', in A. J. Ayer et al. (eds), *The Revolution in Philosophy* (London: Macmillan, 1956), pp. 1–11 at p. 3.
3. G. A. Paul, 'G. E. Moore: Analysis, Common Usage, and Common Sense', in Ayer et al., *Revolution in Philosophy*, pp. 56–69 at pp. 68–9.
4. Ibid. p. 61.
5. The 'New Realism' was a label coined in J. S. Mackenzie, 'The New Realism and the Old Idealism', *Mind* 15.59 (1906), pp. 308–28.
6. J. A. Passmore, 'G. F. Stout's Editorship of *Mind* (1892–1920)', *Mind* 85.337 (1976), pp. 17–36 at p. 32.
7. Ibid. p. 32.
8. S. P. Rosenbaum, *The Bloomsbury Group: A Collection of Memoirs, Commentary and Criticism* (Toronto: University of Toronto Press, 1975), p. 89.
9. G. E. Moore, *Principia Ethica* (Cambridge: Cambridge University Press, 1959), pp. 59, 13.
10. Ibid. p. 8.
11. Ibid. p. 15.
12. Ibid. p. 30.
13. Ibid. p. 31.
14. Ibid. p. 222.
15. Henry Jones, 'Idealism and Epistemology', *Mind* 2.7 (1893), p. 28.
16. W. R. Sorley, 'Fifty Years of *Mind*', *Mind* 35.140 (1926), pp. 409–18 at p. 415.
17. G. E. Moore, 'The Refutation of Idealism', *Mind* 12.48 (1903), pp. 433–53 at p. 443.
18. Ibid. p. 451.
19. Ibid. p. 446.
20. Ibid. p. 450.
21. Ibid. pp. 446, 450.
22. Joseph Conrad, 'Preface' to *The Nigger of the 'Narcissus'* (London: J. M. Dent and Sons, 1923), p. x. Subsequent references are cited in the text as *NN*.
23. Moore, 'Refutation of Idealism', p. 451.

24. Martin Ray, 'Language and Silence in the Novels of Joseph Conrad', in *Critical Essays on Joseph Conrad* (Boston: G. K. Hall, 1987), p. 56.
25. Joseph Conrad, *The Mirror of the Sea: Memories and Impressions* (London: J. M. Dent and Sons, 1923), p. 14. Subsequent references are cited in the text as *MS*.
26. Ray, 'Language and Silence', p. 56.
27. 'The Silence of the Sea', in Joseph Conrad, *Last Essays* (Cambridge: Cambridge University Press, 2010), p. 173. Subsequent references are cited in the text as 'Silence'.
28. Stephen Donovan, 'Prosaic Newspaper Stunts: Conrad, Modernity and the Press', in Gail Fincham and Attie de Lange (eds), *Conrad at the Millennium: Modernism, Postmodernism, Postcolonialism* (Boulder: Social Science Monographs, 2001), pp. 53–72 at p. 64.
29. Ibid. pp. 66–8.
30. Joseph Conrad, *Heart of Darkness and Other Tales* (Oxford: Oxford University Press, 2002), pp. 155, 176. Subsequent references are cited in the text as *HD*.
31. Matthew Rubery, 'Joseph Conrad's "Wild Story of a Journalist"', *ELH* 71.3 (2004), pp. 751–74 at p. 768. For an earlier insightful discussion of technical language, eloquence and journalism in relation to 'Heart of Darkness', see Jeremy Hawthorn, *Joseph Conrad: Language and Fictional Self-Consciousness* (London: Edward Arnold, 1979), pp. 7–36.
32. J. Hillis Miller, *Poets of Reality: Six Twentieth-Century Writers* (Cambridge, MA: Harvard University Press, 1965), pp. 27–8, 36.
33. As, for instance, in Ian Watt's classic discussion of these streams of influence in 'Heart of Darkness'. Ian Watt, *Conrad in the Nineteenth Century* (Berkeley: University of California Press, 1979), pp. 196, 176, 186.
34. Michael Levenson, *A Genealogy of Modernism: A Study of English Literary Doctrine 1908–1922* (Cambridge: Cambridge University Press, 1984), pp. 1, 35.
35. Joseph Conrad, *The Shadow-Line: A Confession and Within the Tides: Tales* (London: J. M. Dent and Sons, 1950), p. vi.
36. Mark A. Wollaeger, *Joseph Conrad and the Fictions of Skepticism* (Stanford: Stanford University Press, 1990), p. 185.
37. Joseph Conrad, *Under Western Eyes* (London: J. M. Dent and Sons, 1947), p. 122. Subsequent references are cited in the text as *UWE*.
38. Conrad, *Shadow-Line*, p. vi.
39. Richard Niland, 'The Political Novels', in J. H. Stape (ed.), *The New Cambridge Companion to Joseph Conrad* (Cambridge: Cambridge University Press, 2015), pp. 29–43 at p. 30.
40. Joseph Conrad, *Nostromo: A Tale of the Seaboard* (London: J. M. Dent and Sons, 1947), 84. Subsequent references are cited in the text as *N*.
41. Niland, 'Political Novels', p. 32.
42. Joseph Conrad, *Chance: A Tale in Two Parts* (London: J. M. Dent and Sons, 1949), p. 69.
43. Wollaeger, *Joseph Conrad and the Fictions of Skepticism*, p. 129.
44. Joseph Conrad, *Tales of Hearsay and Last Essays* (London: J. M. Dent and Sons, 1955), p. 40. Subsequent references are cited in the text as *LE*.

## Chapter 4

# Conrad's Language of Passivity: Unmoving towards Late Modernism

*Yael Levin*

> Words and language are not wrappings in which things are packed for the commerce of those who write and speak. It is in words and language that things first come into being and are.[1]

This chapter will engage some commonplaces of Conrad scholarship in order to initiate a new line of inquiry into the writer's exploration of language and subjectivity. The analysis will trace the emergence of a new subject and the manner in which its ontological permutations determine the rethinking of plot and event in Conrad's fiction. Such a rereading of Conrad is informed by a quandary that infects literary endeavour well into late modernism. As Samuel Beckett commented: 'The material of experience is not the material of expression and I think the distress you feel, as a writer, comes from a tendency on your part to assimilate the two.'[2] Drawing from a number of canonical texts including *The Nigger of the 'Narcissus'*, 'Heart of Darkness', *Lord Jim* and *Victory*, the chapter will show that the categorical separation between experience and expression – and the problem it poses for an early modernist writer such as Conrad – is everywhere evident in the thematic and stylistic makeup of his fiction. Much has been said about the epistemological uncertainty arising from this divide and the literary techniques to which it gives rise, impressionism and delayed decoding being two familiar examples.[3] This study focuses rather on its distinct ontological articulations in the refashioning of plot, narrative voice and character.

Reframing the above-mentioned works in accord with Beckett's insight will demand we read against three of the mainstays of Conrad criticism. First, *Lord Jim* will be read not as evolving around a series of revisitations of Jim's seminal jump off the *Patna* but as a serial restaging of an altogether different moment of inception in the novel. Marlow describes his initial meeting with Jim as an unsolicited encounter with the language of the other. The novel's many returns to this model of unwarranted interruption contribute to an exploration of a particularly passive and fragmented subjectivity that relinquishes the agency and cohesion afforded the Cartesian *cogito*. To view the novel as evolving from this spring of action is to redefine its thematic focus. Though commonly read as Marlow's attempt to trace the psychological makeup and development of the younger man, the novel will be presented here as the implied author's philosophical grappling with the refashioning of subjectivity consequent upon the historical and ideational shifts at the turn of the century. Second, the insistence on the oral tradition evident in the Marlovian narratives and other works will not be regarded as an attempt to resurrect speech in an essentially silent medium. Instead of viewing these conjured voices as an antidote to the sense of alienation Walter Benjamin famously associates with the novel, I will suggest the quotations within quotations in Conrad's texts be read as a dramatisation of the role of language in the evolution of the modernist subject and the narrative that houses him.[4] Finally, the experimental narrative techniques often associated with Conrad's commitment to an inherently epistemological philosophical inquiry will be attributed rather to the author's effort to chart the ontological coordinates of character and narration. These three rereadings may appear to be only tenuously connected in their stylistic and thematic import. I will suggest that the three meet in the redrawing in Conrad's fiction of language as event. Such a language will be viewed as neither oral nor written, but as a writerly spring of action from which plot and subject are brought into being.

The eponymous narrator in Beckett's *The Unnamable* muses on the ontological confusion generated by an inability to distinguish object from subject, expression from experience: 'I seem to speak, it is not I, about me, it is not about me.'[5] His difficulty is cast in linguistic terms. As the choice of pronouns depends on a clear-cut demarcation of subject and object positions, the tentativeness of the same leads to a grammatical chaos. Admitting as much, the Unnamable finally maintains that 'Any old pronoun will do, provided one sees through it' (*Three Novels* 343). The incongruence underlying the writer's task as noted by Beckett is thus signalled in his work in this pronominal tension. Lene Pedersen suggests that 'If it is the status and function of pronouns which establish subjectivity in language, experiments with pronouns in a literary text may lead to new conceptions of the subject which overcome the "linguistic scepticism" of these novels.'[6]

A similar grammatical oddity is evident in one of Conrad's earlier novels. *The Nigger of the 'Narcissus'* begins with a heterodiegetic third-person narrator which is abruptly forfeited when a homodiegetic first-person plural narration takes its place. The narration then shuttles between the two until it concludes in the voice of a single first-person homodiegetic narrator. Bruce Henricksen argues that

> *The Nigger of the 'Narcissus'* deconstructs the identity of the subject by juxtaposing a third-person narrative voice that refers to the crew as 'they' with a first-person voice that says 'we.' These two pronouns alternate in an apparently random way that has suggested to many readers simple authorial carelessness.[7]

Drawing a clear parallel with the examples seen in Beckett, such a 'violation of the rules concerning point of view exposes the dialogic nature of discourse and consciousness.' Henricksen concludes that

> *The Nigger of the 'Narcissus'* reveals the paradoxes of the storytelling self, who must on the one hand maintain the fiction of a disengagement that offers a perspective from which to 'see' or 'hear' society's speech diversity while on the other hand being always already inhabited and constituted by that diversity.[8]

If we choose to view these transgressive pronoun shifts as an indication of the writer's attempt to work through the refigurations of subject and object and their respective articulations within the grammar available to a writer, we may view this novel as the first of many technical efforts to address this difficulty. That the writer need choose between the first- and third-person voice in order to tell the story is no longer simply a matter of narrative convention, between the sympathy afforded the first-person narrator and the distance and reliability associated with the third-person. In making such a choice the writer must make an ontological commitment; he must conceive what a speaking subject might be and how to cast his relation to the world.

Whether this is the outcome of a deeply cogitated philosophical impasse or the mistakes of an inexperienced writer, the shifting pronouns in *The Nigger of the 'Narcissus'* are an exception in the Conrad canon. In the novels that follow Conrad does not revisit these unmotivated pronoun shifts but relies instead (for comparable effect) on multiple narrators. In choosing the latter technique, Conrad appears to commit to the epistemological doubt raised by competing narratives where Beckett commits to the ontological confusion signalled by linguistic anarchy. The distinction between the two authors that emerges might thus be delineated in accord with these disparate philosophical questions. Beckett's works not only return to the linguistic confusion demonstrated above but also dramatise it further by undermining the narrative convention of cohesive and separate characters. Such is not the case in Conrad's universe. Here, the split between self and other is repeatedly underlined. Compare the following passages from *Lord Jim* and *The Unnamable* respectively:

And that's the end. He passes away under a cloud, inscrutable at heart, forgotten, unforgiven, and excessively romantic.⁹

Malone is there. Of his mortal liveliness little trace remains. He passes before me at doubtless regular intervals, unless it is I who pass before him. (*Three Novels* 292)

Though these two excerpts are hauntingly similar, the impressions recorded by Marlow and the Unnamable diverge significantly. When Marlow brings his narrative to a close and parts with the young man, he does not signal any of the ontological confusion suggested by the Unnamable's addendum. The difference between the two passages might be relegated to the thematic divide Brian McHale addresses in distinguishing between modernism and postmodernism. Delineating the two epochs' diverging foci, McHale suggests that 'postmodernist fiction differs from modernist fiction just as a poetics dominated by ontological issues differs from one dominated by epistemological issues'.¹⁰ Such a position is supported by Marlow's emphasis on Jim's inscrutability, a comment no doubt issuing from his stated project in *Lord Jim*. From the outset, Marlow explains that his is a quest for knowledge:

Was it for my own sake that I wished to find some shadow of an excuse for that young fellow whom I had never seen before, but whose appearance alone added a touch of personal concern to the thoughts suggested by the knowledge of his weakness – made it a thing of mystery and terror – like a hint of a destructive fate ready for us all whose youth – in its day – had resembled his youth? I fear that such was the secret motive of my prying. (*LJ* 51)

Indeed, whether it is the 'fundamental why' or the 'superficial how' (*LJ* 56), it is knowledge and its various coordinates to which the novel and its narrator repeatedly return. That the question of self-knowledge is not without ontological implications is noted in Marlow's comments above; one comes to know oneself by looking to the other.

McHale's categorical separation nevertheless serves us here if we understand it in quantitative rather than qualitative terms; rather than a mutually exclusive thematic divide, modernism and postmodernism provide diverging emphases in subject matter, a distinction to which traditional treatments of the two authors adhere.¹¹ If Conrad's treatment of the relation between self and other is seen primarily as part of an epistemological inquiry, such an inquiry is still held within a world of solid ontological foundations. It is the absence of the same that initiates the alternative focus in the work of the later writer.

Prevalent in the work of both writers, the motif of doubling offers a useful illustration of these diverging emphases. Though the motif serves to highlight similarity between characters, in Conrad, such similarity never approaches that sameness explored in Beckett where characters often entertain the suspicion that they might be easily confused with the doubles that populate their narratives. The Unnamable wonders: 'And is it still they who say that when I surprise them all and am Worm at last, then at last I'll be Mahood, Worm proving to be Mahood the moment one is he?' (*Three Novels* 348). In contrast, such evidence of doubling in 'Heart of Darkness' repeatedly underscores the divisions and boundaries between characters. Summing up his last days in the Congo, Marlow remarks:

> And it is not my own extremity I remember best – a vision of grayness without form filled with physical pain, and a careless contempt for the evanescence of all things – even of this pain itself. No! It is his extremity that I seem to have lived through. True, he had made that last stride, he had stepped over the edge, while I had been permitted to draw back my hesitating foot. And perhaps in this is the whole difference; perhaps all the wisdom, and all truth, and all sincerity, are just compressed into that inappreciable moment of time in which we step over the threshold of the invisible.[12]

The passage here illustrates a telling contradiction. At the same time that it testifies to Marlow's ability to 'live through' Kurtz vicariously, it repeatedly calls on the existence of a limit between the two. That 'invisible' threshold is not only the difference between experience and expression, between moving forward and drawing back. It is also the difference between self and other, between the subject and object of contemplation. Expression is the sum product of *not* having stepped over the edge, not having evacuated one's sense of self by stepping over the threshold into the unknown.

I would argue that in tracing such differences between the two authors' poetic preoccupations we neglect a significant correspondence between their respective explorations of ontology. Both the separation and the collapsing of subject and object repeatedly call attention to the difficulty underlying the writer's task when grappling with that very limit between experience and expression. If such a divide is not explored in the Conradian universe through the thematisation of character confusion, it is nevertheless dramatised through the juxtaposition of two characters who are defined precisely by their respective roles within the dichotomy: one acts; the other remembers and narrates. Such a dynamic is evident in 'Heart of Darkness' and *Lord Jim* where Marlow is repeatedly used as a storyteller bound to tell the story of another man's experience. He witnesses the downfall of Kurtz and Jim respectively, but lives to tell the tale.

In order to reconsider the significance of language in the novel we must forfeit McHale's definitions and turn our attention to the similarities underlying Conrad's and Beckett's writing projects, wherein language functions not as a means to knowledge but as a fact of being. Heidegger's conceptualisation of *Dasein* in *Being and Time* provides a key to fleshing out the difference between the two. Magda King helpfully articulates this distinction:

> It is because Da-sein factually exists in a world with others that the articulated understandability of his hereness comes to word and concretely voices itself (utters itself) in language. The existentiell-ontic phenomenon of language is therefore not a man-made tool consisting of words into which mutually agreed meanings have been infused, but is the signifying voicing of the already disclosed and articulated meaning of man's hereness. Where language is a communicating talk, what is communicated, shared, is not the inner experience of an isolated subject with another isolated subject but the mutually understandable hereness in a mutually shared world.[13]

King notes that any act of communication is not merely a passing of information between two or more individuals but the dramatisation of man's 'thrownness'. The following section will apply this insight to a reassessment of the role of language in *Lord Jim*. While it might not hold the key to a reconceptualisation of being, by repeatedly calling attention to our being 'there', language functions in the novel as an ontologically meaningful event.

## The permeable subject

Daphna Erdinast-Vulcan suggests that the removal of Jim to Patusan in the second part of *Lord Jim* is an 'active, if desperate, attempt to defeat [the modern temper] by a regression to a mythical mode of discourse'.[14] The distinction made is between an individualised, fragmented and modern universe and a communal and integrated epic-mythic one. The coordinates drawn in these respective universes may be seen as definitive also of the differences between the pre-modernist and the modernist subject. The mythic hero is the product of an ideational and perhaps philosophical fantasy that lends itself to the figurative geographical borders of an isolated and clearly demarcated space of an island or remote territory. In keeping with this method, Jim's secluded life in Patusan takes on the figurative force of a door shutting behind him. Marlow emphasises the younger man's isolation and remarks:

> I could make him a solemn promise that [the door] would be shut behind him with a vengeance. His fate, whatever it was, would be ignored, because the country, for all its rotten state, was not judged ripe for interference. (*LJ* 232)

In *Victory*, the protagonist Axel Heyst is similarly brought into isolation where he is refashioned as a romantic hero. On the island of Samburan, we are told, Heyst is 'out of everybody's way, as if he were perched on the highest peak of the Himalayas, and in a sense as conspicuous. Everyone in that part of the world knew of him, dwelling on his little island.'[15] Douglas Kerr notes the similarity between the two characters and their respective settings: 'In both cases of retreat from the business of men and the western traffic around the globe, to an enclosed, apparently timeless, unworldly and enchanted space, the orientalism of the figure of the circle is manifest enough.'[16] Where Kerr highlights the postcolonial significances of such characterisation, the distinction to which I wish to draw attention lies in the subject's relation to language. The peculiarity of this relation might be demonstrated by exploring its antithesis.

In opposition to such a vision of insulation, the modernist subject is constantly open to invasion. Marlow's description of his encounter with Jim at the outset of his narration in *Lord Jim* testifies to this remarkable openness and vulnerability:

> I know I have him – the devil, I mean . . . He is there right enough, and, being malicious, he lets me in for that kind of thing . . . the kind of thing that by devious, unexpected, truly diabolical ways causes me to run up against men with soft spots, with hard spots, with hidden plague spots, by Jove! and loosens their tongues at the sight of me for their infernal confidences; as though, forsooth, I had no confidences to make to myself, as though – God help me! – I didn't have enough confidential information about myself to harrow my own soul till the end of my appointed time. And what I have done to be thus favoured I want to know. I declare I am as full of my own concerns as the next man, and I have as much memory as the average pilgrim in this valley, so you see I am not particularly fit to be a receptacle of confessions. (*LJ* 34)

The particular weakness attested to here is that of an irremediable openness to the other – more specifically, the language of the other. Marlow resists such an invasion on the grounds that, though an empty vessel might contain that which another man wishes to share, he is rather 'full'. Marlow's comment dramatises the death throes of the pre-modernist subject who does not wish to devolve, as it were, into a modernist one. The first, as we have seen, is cohesive, full and impregnable – precisely how Marlow sees himself. The encounter with Jim, however, leads to a dramatic change in the manner in which Marlow's subjectivity is presented. King explains that 'everyday being-together moves largely in a mutual talking-together and in repeating and handing on what has been said. In the course of this the talk loses, or has perhaps never gained, a genuinely disclosing relation to being and beings.'[17] Once Marlow's consciousness becomes riddled with the language of the other, once he begins to reiterate another's words rather than his own, his sense of self and the cohesion and fullness that define it are undermined. He is reborn as a modernist subject who is forced to circulate the words of the other. Such a destabilising effect figuratively fleshes out that poststructuralist vision of a language that is likened to a 'mosaic' or a 'tissue of quotations', where words are always 'anonymous, untraceable, and yet *already read*: they are quotations without inverted commas'.[18]

Following this thematic thread, we may view the narrative as issuing forth from Marlow's encounter with Jim's story and not from the initial jump off the *Patna*. Marlow's attempt to understand Jim is thus shadowed by the story of the implied author's attempts to negotiate the radical refashioning of a peculiarly modernist subjectivity. The stakes of such a reading would not be the question of the ego ideal and its encounter with reality (as Jim's story is so often read) but rather the very foundations of an ego understood as that agency that commands an abiding and coherent self.

The novel's core division has been seen as a symbolic rendering of two distinct types of subjectivity: the pre-modernist (whether mythical, epic or romantic) and the modernist subject. The first is autonomous and whole, active, but on the verge of extinction. The second is invaded, fragmentary and passive, but, much like the Beckettian immortal paralytic, very much a survivor. A careful reading of *Lord Jim* and *Victory* might be instructive, however, in undermining such a dichotomy. Though the difference in the formation of the subjectivity of Marlow, Jim and Heyst appears definitive, the significance of an isolating geography only underlines the fact that there is, in fact, no ontological distinction between them. That Jim and Heyst must be removed to a remote island in order to fulfil fleetingly their vision of self suggests that such an endeavour cannot be imagined in the absence of such a state of seclusion. Like Marlow, Jim and Heyst are both modernist subjects and as such are open to the invading other and his poisonous language.[19] This is evident in the first part of *Lord Jim*, where the young man's many escapes are effected by the voices circulating the *Patna* story. Similarly, the first part of *Victory* shows that the event from which Heyst's narrative unfolds is his chance meeting with Morrison. Morrison himself wonders at his effusiveness in response to the other's charitable gesture:

> Upon my word, I don't know why I have been telling you all this. I suppose seeing a thoroughly white man made it impossible to keep my trouble to myself. Words can't do it justice; but since I've told you so much I may as well tell you more. Listen. (*V* 14)

The effect of the encounter with Morrison, then, is much like the effect of Marlow's and Jim's encounters with the language of the other. Morrison divests Heyst of the illusion of cohesion, without which he is as open to the influence of Lena as he is to that of the trio that invade his island.

As modernist subjects, Heyst and Jim share Marlow's paralysing passivity in the encounter with another's language. It is this fact, perhaps, that renders them as much a pawn of language as those to whom they tell their tales. Jim is finally undone by Gentleman Brown's language, as is Heyst by Schomberg's. It thus transpires that, at the same time that Marlow laments Jim's vulnerability and wishes he could shield the younger man from the aversive echoes that haunt his existence, he is himself the very model for such openness. Language happens to the unwitting Marlow; he is a passive receptacle for the words that invade him. Conrad's famous storyteller thus prefigures the late modernist association of being and language as explored in the work of Beckett. Taken to the extreme, this condition of a language that always already comprehends the speaker drives the emerging subject into a state of inauthenticity, where any attempt at agency is rendered hollow, the sham repetition of another's words. The Unnamable explains the difficulty in communicating one's sense of self:

> It's of me now I must speak, even if I have to do it with their language, it will be a start, a step towards silence and the end of madness, the madness of having to speak and not being able to, except of things that don't concern me, that don't count, that I don't believe, that they have crammed me full of to prevent me from saying who I am, where I am, and from doing what I have to do in the only way that can put an end to it. (*Three Novels* 324)

In their capacity as romantically impenetrable heroes who are created in action, Jim and Heyst are the antithesis of such a conceptualisation of the subject. They are safe from the threat of polyphony. Language, in association with Jim, is always his own. In contradistinction to Marlow, who is bound to cite and repeat, in Patusan Jim enjoys the momentary ownership of the words that fashion him and his world. Such power is particularly striking as it tellingly contrasts with Jim's previous life, where he was trapped in the language of others, light literature and courthouse discourse being two cases in point. Marlow testifies that in Patusan, Jim's word was the one truth of every passing day. It shared something of the nature of that silence through which it accompanied you into unexplored depths, heard continuously by your side, penetrating, far-reaching – tinged with wonder and mystery on the lips of whispering men. (*LJ* 272)

Jim's language is not only impregnable, it is penetrating – precisely the kind of language that contaminates others and is fated to be repeated.

The irony underlying *Lord Jim*, however, is that such a model of communication has become obsolete, as much a romantic fantasy as is the ego ideal Jim struggles to realise. The novel's epigraph is touched by the same irony. Though it may be true that 'my conviction gains infinitely the moment another will believe in it' (*LJ* ii), the encounter with the other is often passive rather than active; it results in the unsolicited invasion of the other's language rather than the psychologically affirmative sharing of one's own. The prototypical subject of communication in the novel is thus not the addresser but the addressee. It is Marlow listening to Jim's narrative, Big Brierly listening at court and Jim silently listening to the voices haunting him from the sailors on the *Patna* to Gentleman Brown in Patusan. Language happens to the subject. Without agency, without words of his own, the subject is forced to accept passively the voice of the other.

The communicative model traced here would suggest that the modernist subject experiences being in the world as a passive attendance on language, a dynamic that is fundamental to Beckett's poetics. Unfolding a similar, if radicalised view of such a state of being in the world, the Unnamable notes: 'you have only to wait, without doing anything, it's no good doing anything, and without understanding, there's no help in understanding, and all comes right, nothing comes right, nothing, nothing, this will never end, this voice will never stop' (*Three Novels* 374).

Though stripped of the sense of urgency and despair articulated by the Unnamable, a similar set of ontological coordinates is dramatised at the outset of each of the four Marlovian narratives. 'Heart of Darkness' famously begins with a scene of waiting. The anonymous first-person narrator reports:

> We looked on, waiting patiently – there was nothing else to do till the end of the flood; but it was only after a long silence, when he said, in a hesitating voice, 'I suppose you fellows remember I did once turn fresh-water sailor for a bit', that we knew we were fated, before the ebb began to run, to hear about one of Marlow's inconclusive experiences. (*HD* 51)

The experience of language described here is one of passive acceptance, an almost noxious inevitability. Waiting for the tide – that experience of waiting without agency – may be seen as the symbolic rendering of the condition of being in the world and falling into language. That stories, experiences, alliances are forced onto the listener thus functions as the metonymical expression of the inevitability of language and its place in the making of subjectivity. Like the spinner of yarns in *Lord Jim*, the anonymous narrator here presents himself as a victim of language. He is 'fated' to encounter Marlow's words much as Marlow in *Lord Jim* is fated to hear Jim's story. The emphasis on the heard voice or oral communication in the Marlovian narratives offers a powerful demonstration of this; one is 'fated' to hear another's story. And yet it is not the speaking voice that determines language as event. A similar dynamic is at work towards the end of *Lord Jim*. The anonymous narrator intervenes here to relate the fact that

> there was only one man . . . who was ever to hear the last word of the story. It *came to him* at home, more than two years later, and it *came* contained in a thick packet addressed in Marlow's upright and angular handwriting. (*LJ* 337; my emphasis)

Though it is now written language, the letter is an extremely evocative example of the interruption of language and the way it intrudes on one's life. The addressee is as much a victim of language as are the listeners on board the *Nellie* and the audience reposing on the veranda after a meal. Language comes uninvited to the privileged man and must be taken in.

### The spring of inaction

My reading has so far teased out the benefits of rereading Conrad's exploration of subjectivity in the light of poststructural theories of language. I would argue further that the shifts consequent upon the ideational breaks at the turn of the century are noted not only in Conrad's characters but also in his reconfiguration of events in narrative. The beginnings of the Marlovian narratives in 'Youth', 'Heart of Darkness', *Chance* and the delayed exposition in *Lord Jim* show that the model of communication employed in fashioning the modernist subject becomes the very event that launches Conrad's plots. While Jim's plot is measured in battles, narrow escapes or a test at sea, the modernist subject's plot begins with the passivity of waiting, interrupted only by the unwarranted language of the other. That is to say that, unlike the traditional plot that sets forth from what is referred to as 'the spring of action', such emplotting is initiated not by an event in language (the representation of a battle or an unexpected arrival) but by an event of language (language happens, as, for example, when someone begins to talk). The difference is significant if we regard language as fulfilling a particularly ontological function.

In order to appreciate this shift in focus fully, I would suggest we briefly turn from the conception of language as issuing forth from an utterer or origin to the idea of an untethered and disembodied discourse that appears to circulate freely between the characters. Marlow's disappearance in the darkness of the night on board the *Nellie* gestures towards such a view of language. The frame narrator relates that

> For a long time already [Marlow], sitting apart, had been no more to us than a voice. There was not a word from anybody. The others might have been asleep, but I was awake. I listened, I listened on the watch for the sentence, for the word, that would give me the clue to the faint uneasiness inspired by this narrative that seemed to shape itself without human lips in the heavy night-air of the river. (*HD* 83)

I would not claim that Marlow is here cancelled out as an individual with a unique idiom and an unusual storytelling style. And yet it is still possible to view that discourse floating in the night as the very fact of language, a language that speaks and in speaking comprehends and predetermines the human subjects that are within its purview. Coleridge's 'The Rime of the Ancient Mariner', one of the obvious intertexts for 'Heart of Darkness', offers a similar illustration of this dynamic. As opposed to the details of the mariner's experience, it is the very communication of his story that marks the quintessential event in the narrative. Accosted as he is about to enter the church, the wedding guest becomes a victim of the mariner's language and is consequently changed by his experience of the other's words. That this transformation is a product of the mariner's lesson is clear. And yet I would argue that it is that passivity and indelible openness to the language of the other that render him other, a paralytic aware of his own beingness.[20]

The difference between these two methods of initiating plot is thus not merely a matter of what occurs – whether it is an event in language or an event of language. It is also determined by agency. The traditional spring of action would necessarily be of the order of Roland Barthes's cardinal event, which he defines as follows:

> In order to classify a function as cardinal, all we need verify is that the action to which it refers opens (or maintains or closes) an alternative directly affecting the continuation of the story, in other words, that it either initiates or resolves an uncertainty. If in a fragment of narrative the telephone rings, it is equally possible to answer or not to answer the call, procedures that are bound to carry the story along different paths.[21]

Barthes's definition of a cardinal function relies on agency, an attribute of that pre-modernist subject that the novels discussed above repeatedly undermine. Such a reconfiguration of plot events or plot beginnings as Conrad initiates renders the matter of choice obsolete. Though Barthes's example of answering the phone is merely illustrative, the point is precisely that it is no longer possible to choose whether or not to answer the phone; as Jim's, Heyst's and Marlow's experiences repeatedly show, one is always already made to listen.

Noting the absence of cardinal events in Beckett's Trilogy, Ruben Borg argues that

> Throughout his career (and with increasing frequency) Beckett tests the possibility of thinking about time without assuming subjective agency as a primary value. A passive consciousness comes to replace the functions of voice and character as the ground of narrative action. In lieu of kernel events, in which characters advance the plot by exerting some sort of free will, Beckett imagines a world in which waiting is the paradigmatic activity.[22]

I would claim that Conrad's reconfiguration of subjectivity and the manner in which it affects the very functions of plot are suggestive of the burgeoning of this philosophy well in advance of late modernism.

The transition from the omniscient narrator of the first four chapters in *Lord Jim* to Marlow's narration provides a further case in point.[23] The description here is uncannily similar to the one in the novella:

> Perhaps it would be after dinner, on a verandah draped in *motionless* foliage and crowned with flowers, in the deep dusk speckled by fiery cigar-ends. The elongated bulk of each cane-chair harboured a silent listener. Now and then a small red glow would move abruptly, and expanding light up the fingers of a *languid* hand, part of a face in *profound repose*, or flash a crimson gleam into a pair of pensive eyes overshadowed by a fragment of an *unruffled* forehead; and with the very first word uttered Marlow's body, extended *at rest* in the seat, would become *very still*, as though his spirit had winged its way back into the lapse of time and were speaking through his lips from the past. (*LJ* 33; my emphasis)

The abiding sentiment, then, is 'Hang exertion. Let that Marlow talk.' This passage further confirms the paradigm traced above. Language unfolds in Conrad's tales as a performative passivity. It occurs at rest, at anchor, in the stillness or in-betweenness of a wary anticipation. It is that which is offered in lieu of action, in lieu of movement. In the staying of action there is an insistence on words, words circulating, unmoored, always belonging to another. A reimagining of plot beginnings in this event of language is the stylistic extension or symbolic representation of the seismic shift at the heart of the modernist subject and his relation to the world. To start a plot in this manner functions as a dramatisation of the tension between experience and expression, between self and other; it is to suggest that the primary event of fiction is the subject's encounter with language, an encounter that harbours the realisation that he is always already within language and as such can never independently author himself.

The event of language is both effected by this loss of agency – occurring, as it does, in that space of involuntary waiting – and further contributes to it by cementing the subject's paralysis. When Marlow's narrative comes to a close in the novella, the frame narrator notes that 'nobody moved for a time' (*LJ* 162). While agency is annulled, made obsolete by the encounter with one's thrownness, *Lord Jim* shows that it nevertheless survives as an illusion. And it is in the survival of this illusion of agency that Conrad's poetics cannot be aligned with Beckett's, where, we recall, one always 'sees through' the tricks of the trade (*Three Novels* 343). As opposed to the disillusioned characters populating Beckett's narratives, Conrad's stories contain a score of 'finished artist[s].' Marlow reflects on Jim's power of imagination:

> Nothing in the world moved before his eyes, and he could depict to himself without hindrance the sudden swing upwards of the dark sky-line, the sudden tilt up of the vast plain of the sea, the swift still rise, the brutal fling, the grasp of the abyss, the struggle without hope, the starlight closing over his head for ever like the vault of a tomb – the revolt of his young life – the black end. He could! By Jove! who couldn't? And you must remember he was a finished artist in that peculiar way, he was a gifted poor devil with the faculty of swift and forestalling vision. (*LJ* 96)

In this association of art and deception Marlow tellingly echoes an earlier comment, where he stated that 'no man ever understands quite his own artful dodges to escape from the grim shadow of self-knowledge' (*LJ* 80). Whether it serves in fleshing out doom or glory, Jim's imagination is continually in the service of his ego ideal. It is through the power of this art that Jim can counter the alienating effects of language as discussed above and effectively author himself.[24] And though Marlow is very aware of the deceptive nature of this enterprise and always ready to diffuse its power with his deliberate asides, he too might be seen to dabble in its seductive power. This is particularly evident at the moment where he gives free rein to his writing:

> At this point I took up a fresh sheet and began to write resolutely. There was nothing but myself between him and the dark ocean. I had a sense of responsibility. If I spoke, would that motionless and suffering youth leap into the obscurity – clutch at the straw? I found out how difficult it may be sometimes

to make a sound. There is a weird power in a spoken word. And why the devil not? I was asking myself persistently while I drove on with my writing. All at once, on the blank page, under the very point of the pen, the two figures of Chester and his antique partner, very distinct and complete, would dodge into view with stride and gestures, as if reproduced in the field of some optical toy. I would watch them for a while. No! They were too phantasmal and extravagant to enter into any one's fate. And a word carries far – very far – deals destruction through time as the bullets go flying through space. (LJ 174)

Marlow is at his desk, a paralytic with nothing but words as the tools of his trade. And yet what emerges in this scene is no less than the power of creation. Much like a demigod staring into the abyss, it is through words that Marlow fashions the world in which the romantic hero will survive or perish, be great or fail. In deliberating Jim's fate Marlow essentially cements his power as creator. His power to author another, however, might be seen as the very extension of that self-deception he had diagnosed in Jim. And indeed, from a narratological perspective, Marlow is as much the pawn of the historical author as is the younger man. To the extent that they are both products of the diegesis, Marlow's power to author Jim is as much an illusion as is Jim's power to author himself. My point, however, is not so much that Marlow and Jim are both fictional characters, and as such do not possess the agency attributed to human subjects, as that in being a subject one is always already predetermined in language. And it is precisely this fact of being that the event of language repeatedly demonstrates.

Though Conrad's poetics are traditionally associated with those of other early modernist writers, a corresponding vision of the subject in language emerges in the work of late modernists such as Beckett. In her discussion of *The Unnamable*, Naomi Greene notes that the protagonist's predicament in this mid-twentieth-century novel is that 'Silence is unattainable', explaining that the Unnamable 'is subject to the onslaught of language which needs to express itself through someone and has chosen him as its unwilling victim'.[25] The juxtaposition of the two writers' thematics demonstrates that Conrad's treatment of the modernist subject heralds the seismic shift associated with a much later aesthetic preoccupation with subjectivity. Greene goes on to note the ramifications of such an unfolding motif and states that the stakes of such a predicament are no less than ontological:

if [the Unnamable] is nothing but the site language has chosen through which to express itself, then without this very same language he would have no existence. His being depends upon the language he abhors for, in effect, he is made of words.[26]

Marlow articulates a comparable ontological anxiety when he comments on the transience of the subject of his story. 'Jim', he tells his listeners, 'existed for me, and after all it is only through me that he exists for you' (*LJ* 224). A subject is not only represented but also created in language; his existence relies on it.

This chapter has addressed a particular and telling relationship between language and subjectivity in the works of Joseph Conrad. Calling attention to the manner in which this network of themes illuminates the author's treatment of the *fin de siècle* crisis of subjectivity, my approach hinges on passivity as one of the abiding symbols attached to the expression of this ontological exploration. Conrad's reimagining of language as an event in narrative in lieu of the action that promotes the traditional fictional or dramatic plot is indicative of the fragmentation underlying the modernist subject and his modernist stories. The modernist subject is defined by openness; it must circulate the language of others while possessing the paralysing self-awareness that the words it issues forth can never be its own. Nevertheless, we have seen that such passivity is not without power. By manipulating the very voices he echoes, by combining and repeating them to others, the modernist subject can turn to artistic creation in striving for the new.

## Notes

1. Martin Heidegger, *An Introduction to Metaphysics*, trans. Ralph Manheim (New York: Doubleday, 1961), p. 13.
2. Samuel Beckett quoted in Dan Gunn, '"Until the Gag is Chewed": Samuel Beckett's Letters: Eloquence and "Near Speechlessness"', *Times Literary Supplement* 5377 (2006), pp. 13–15 at p. 13.
3. See Paul Armstrong, *The Challenge of Bewilderment: Understanding and Representation in James, Conrad, and Ford* (Ithaca: Cornell University Press, 1987); John G. Peters, *Conrad and Impressionism* (Cambridge: Cambridge University Press, 2006); Ian Watt, *Conrad in the Nineteenth Century* (Berkeley: University of California Press, 1979); and Cedric Watts, *The Deceptive Text: An Introduction to Covert Plots* (Brighton: Harvester, 1984).
4. Benjamin writes that 'what differentiates the novel from all other forms of prose literature . . . is that it neither comes from oral tradition nor goes into it. . . . The birthplace of the novel is the solitary individual.' *Illuminations*, trans. Harry Zohn (New York: Schocken Books, 1969), p. 87.
5. Samuel Beckett, *Three Novels: Molloy, Malone Dies, The Unnamable* (New York: Grove Press, 1958), p. 291. Subsequent references are cited in the text as *Three Novels*.
6. Lene Yding Pedersen, 'A Subject After All: Rethinking the "Personalized Narrator" of the Self-Reflexive First-Person Novels of O'Brien, Beckett and Banville', *Orbis Litterarum* 58 (2003), pp. 219–38 at p. 232.

7. Bruce Henricksen, 'The Construction of the Narrator in *The Nigger of the "Narcissus"'*, *PMLA* 103.5 (1988), pp. 783–95 at p. 785.
8. Ibid. p. 792.
9. Joseph Conrad, *Lord Jim* (London: J. M. Dent and Sons, 1967), p. 416. Subsequent references are cited in the text as *LJ*.
10. Brian McHale, *Postmodernist Fiction* (London: Routledge, 1987), p. xii.
11. The understanding that Conrad's contributions to epistemological inquiry mark one of his greatest achievements as a modernist writer is widely held. In 'Conrad and Modernism', Kenneth Graham suggests that the innovation of 'Heart of Darkness' is its 'epistemological ambiguity', which, 'Borne out as it was to be by almost all of Conrad's other major writings, . . . [is] enough in itself to constitute an early manifesto of a Modernism that came to define itself in opposition to the positivistic, mechanical view of the universe that saw meaning as objective and single.' In J. H. Stape, ed. *Conrad and Modernism* (Cambridge: Cambridge University Press, 1996), p. 213.
12. Joseph Conrad, *Youth, Heart of Darkness, The End of the Tether* (London: J. M. Dent and Sons, 1967), p. 151. Subsequent references are cited in the text as *HD*.
13. Magda King, *A Guide to Heidegger's Being and Time* (Albany: State University of New York Press, 2001), p. 253.
14. Daphna Erdinast-Vulcan, *Joseph Conrad and the Modern Temper* (Oxford: Clarendon Press, 1991), p. 35.
15. Joseph Conrad, *Victory* (London: J. M. Dent and Sons, 1967), pp. 3–4. Subsequent references are cited in the text as *V*.
16. Douglas Kerr, 'Conrad's Magic Circles', *Essays in Criticism* 53.4 (2003), pp. 345–65 at p. 356.
17. King, *Heidegger's Being and Time*, p. 84.
18. Respectively, Julia Kristeva, *Desire in Language: A Semiotic Approach to Literature and Art*, trans. Thomas Gora, Alice Jardine and Leon S. Roudiez (New York: Columbia University Press, 1980), p. 66; Roland Barthes, *Image Music Text*, trans. Stephen Heath (New York: Noonday Press, 1977), p. 146; and Barthes again, p. 160.
19. The white other, that is. As Kerr and others have argued, there is a sense that the porousness of the modernist subject is immune to the voice or silence, for that matter, of the native.
20. While the scope of this chapter will not allow for a more sustained engagement with this interext, we could briefly note the symbol of the closed door with which the poem concludes. The wedding goers are all inside, boasting the cohesion of a solid and uniform subjectivity. Having been exposed to the Mariner's language, however, the wedding guest must turn away from the closed door and remain outside; he can no longer entertain such illusions of insulation.
21. Roland Barthes, 'An Introduction to the Structural Analysis of Narrative', trans. Lionel Duisit, *New Literary History* 6.2 (1975), pp. 237–72 at p. 248.
22. Ruben Borg, 'Ethics of the Event: The Apocalyptic Turn in Modernism', *Partial Answers* 9.1 (2011), pp. 188–201 at p. 195.
23. In keeping with the critical tendency to privilege epistemological over ontological concerns, this transition is often associated with the novel's stylistic

and thematic preoccupation with hermeneutics. Indeed, the use of Marlow as a narrator furnishes the text with a subjective prism of interpretation who continuously offers self-reflexive commentary on the partial nature of his narrative enterprise, a technique that results in an inability to see clearly and consequently to know the subject of his investigation. My project here is not to question this interpretation but to illuminate an additional method of reading the novel that has not received due attention.

24. It would be incorrect to suppose that such a view of art is reflective of the author's as it is repeatedly deflated by ironic modifiers that strip it of aesthetic value: Jim is a *finished* artist; his escapes are *artful*. Though Marlow's conflation of art and deception should not be seen as a comprehensive aesthetic treatise, the manipulations brought on by the instinct of self-preservation are nevertheless presented in the novel as a distinctly generative form of art.
25. Naomi Greene, 'Creation and the Self: Artaud, Beckett, Michaux', *Criticism: A Quarterly for Literature and the Arts* 13.3 (1971), article 4, p. 267.
26. Ibid. pp. 267–8.

# Chapter 5

# The Powers of Speech in Conrad's Fiction

*Josiane Paccaud-Huguet*

For the language-minded critic, Conrad's works have always been a privileged field to explore. The 'linguistic turn' in the second half of the twentieth century produced many essays and books, some of which have become Conradian classics.[1] Anne Enderwitz's recent essay on *Chance*, Conrad's most commercially successful novel, argues that whereas in 'Heart of Darkness' Marlow seems engaged in 'melancholy negotiations of the problem of representation', in the later novel Conrad's pragmatic approach to the affective power of language characterises both Marlow as a storyteller and the development of its female protagonist, Flora de Barral.[2] Enderwitz argues that, if critics with an interest in affect tend to turn away from the linguistic, Conrad 'sees no need to introduce a dividing line between affect and language':

> After all, the scene of Flora's abuse is narrated by four different people. In the light of this frame, any thought of unmediated access to affect seems ridiculous. If we take Conrad's approach to language seriously, affects may not be linguistic in themselves but can be effected by words, and they emerge and become intelligible in and through narrative.[3]

There is, indeed, no need to separate affect from language. The argument of this chapter will be that the pragmatic touch is already at work in the early Marlow narratives but in a different mode, which may well account for their different impact on and reception from the reading public. The focus will be on 'Youth', 'Heart of Darkness', *Lord Jim*, *Chance* and *Under Western Eyes* (which Conrad undertook as a respite from *Chance*). My working hypothesis is that Conrad at his best explores the possibilities of narrative *in the act*, both pragmatic and ethical.

## Perlocutionary effects

We owe to Ferdinand de Saussure the distinction between *langue* (language) and *parole* (speech), language being the abstract system of rules of a signifying system, whereas speech concerns the concrete instances of language use, the speech acts performed by a subject.[4] Saussure makes an analogy with chess, *langue* being comparable to the rules of chess whereas *parole* involves the player's moves – there is a choice, therefore an act. Saussure makes no distinction between written and spoken language, as long as there is an individual utterance.

In *How to Do Things With Words*, the language philosopher John Langshaw Austin differentiates several types of speech acts: the locutionary, equivalent to uttering a sentence 'with a certain sense and reference'; the illocutionary, 'done as conforming to a convention' like writing a report or telling a story; and the perlocutionary, which is non-conventional and consists in achieving certain more or less intentional effects '*by* saying something'.[5] Let us take the example of Kurtz's report in 'Heart of Darkness'. On the one hand, Marlow reports to his audience the effects produced by his reading of this text. The peroration is full of Ciceronian perlocutionary effects that make Marlow 'tingle with enthusiasm' at Kurtz's 'burning noble words'.[6] But the handwritten postscript 'Exterminate all the brutes!' produces another kind of unintentional, surprising voice effect. The enigmatic, unsigned, detached expostulation stands in complete contradiction to the philanthropic tonality of the report itself. In addition, its very indeterminacy leaves open the question of who the brutes and who the exterminators may be. The report (the written text) produces an unexpected resonance, an explosive 'noise' – the other meaning of report: it has a *detonating* power which makes us see the tone of the report from a completely different angle. This other kind of perlocutionary effect is surely one of the novella's agents of unrest: it destabilises our epistemological stance, it arouses the desire to know otherwise – or not to know, since, as Marlow also notes in *Lord Jim*, 'the wisdom of life ... consists in putting out of sight all the reminders of our folly, of our weakness, of our mortality'.[7] After all, Marlow tears off the postscript before he delivers the report to the journalist prior to his visit to the Intended.

That Conrad had such effects in mind appears in the formulation of what he famously considers as his task as an artist, namely, 'by the power of the written word, to make you hear, to make you feel – it is, before all, to make you *see*'.[8] The written word comes here as a case of *parole*, that is, an ethical speech act likely to produce bodily effects and affects.[9]

In psychoanalytical terms, the difference between feeling and affect is that whereas the former has a meaning which can be identified and interpreted in social exchange (like love or friendship), affect concerns the body; it involves states of being that leave you speechless, if not petrified: it blocks the process of analytical thought and the possibility of historical continuity – in other words, it makes a hole in knowledge, a tear in the fabric of significance. Even though affect is produced by speech, it is pure speechless intensity, eminently pragmatic: it arises 'in the capacities' of bodies 'to act and be acted upon'.[10] Hence the importance in Conrad's fiction of bodily encounters; hence also the choice of the oral mode of transmission to be conveyed subsequently by a written narrative.

There is in Conrad's texts a permanent tension between the written and the spoken word. This undergoes a shift of emphasis between the early and the late Marlow narratives. In *Lord Jim*, Marlow is wary of the 'weird power of a spoken word' when he wonders if he should speak to Jim of Chester's job offer:

> If I spoke, would that motionless and suffering youth leap into the obscurity – clutch at the straw? I found out how difficult it may be sometimes to make a sound. There is a weird power in a spoken word. And why the devil not? ... And a word carries far – very far – deals destruction through time as the bullets go flying through space. I said nothing; and he, out there with his back to the light, as if bound and gagged by all the invisible foes of man, made no stir and made no sound. (*LJ* 176)

In this case, the speech act would amount to disposing of Jim in a rather brutal way. Another mode will be needed which demands more imaginative sympathy with his case, and an altogether different disposition – for the reader as well.

The perlocutionary effect pertains not to the domain of understanding or judgement, but to the power of speech to touch or to move. In other words it depends less on meaning (the signified) than on the graphic and acoustic substance of the linguistic sign (the signifier). That Conrad was perfectly aware of this appears in the early story 'Karain: A Memory' in the volume appropriately entitled *Tales of Unrest*. The group of Westerners listening to Karain's narrative experience the material presence, the rhythm of speech loaded with sadness and fear, and suggestive of the alarming beat of a war gong: 'His words sounded low, in a sad murmur as of running water; at times they rang loud like the clash of a war-gong – or trailed slowly like weary travellers – or rushed forward with the speed of fear.'[11] Here the perlocutionary power is part of Karain's narrative act, and it also mirrors what Conrad as an artist will consider as his task to perform through the power of the written word.

The signifier, when wrapped within a seductive fiction, can be endowed with a magic of its own, whose pragmatic usage may vary. Karain's Western friends set up a mock-shamanic ceremony to offer him a gilt sixpence bearing the effigy of Queen Victoria, in order to cure his obsession with the ghost of the man he has murdered. The coin (a signifier in a signifying system) stands for the fascinating power of money that itself rests on a certain mode of faith and belief. As Cedric Watts observes,

> It denotes not only fraudulence but also real power, and it amply brings to mind the ways in which, in both the Eastern and Western hemispheres, power may be sustained by story-telling, cheating, myths, faith and superstition. If Hollis's rhetoric makes a damaged coin seem magical, he thereby resembles Joseph Conrad who seeks to invest with magic the defaced currency of language: 'the light of magic suggestiveness may be brought to play for an evanescent instant over the commonplace surface of words: the old, old words, worn thin, defaced by ages of careless usage'.[12]

The power of a fraudulent signifier erases a painful memory, but there is also an important perlocutionary effect in the irony of the scene that raises the issue of the ethical uses of fiction. To invest 'the defaced currency of language' with a 'magic suggestiveness' will certainly be part of Conrad's artistic endeavour, but with a different purpose to that of the Westerners in 'Karain': his aim is to awaken the reader to a memory or a truth not accessible to understanding or judgement.

It is precisely something beyond judgment that binds Marlow to Jim during the tribunal scene in *Lord Jim*. According to J. L. Austin, 'a judge should be able to decide, by hearing what was said, what locutionary and illocutionary acts were performed, but not what perlocutionary acts were achieved'.[13] Marlow here is definitely not in the position of a judge. The narrative focuses on the co-presence of speaking bodies, a notion which is more complex than the linguistic subject and quite close to the Lacanian *parlêtre* – the speaking being.[14] First comes an intense visual contact, an '*act* of intelligent volition' that is at the source of Marlow's willingness to become Jim's mouthpiece (*LJ* 33; my emphasis). Jim's wandering eyes rest upon an unknown white man sitting apart, with 'quiet eyes that glanced straight, interested and clear', unlike the fascinated stare of the others:

> At present [Jim] was answering questions that did not matter though they had a purpose, but he doubted whether he would ever again speak out as long as he lived. The sound of his own truthful statements confirmed his deliberate opinion that speech was of no use to him any longer. That man there seemed to be aware of his hopeless difficulty ... And later on, many times, in distant parts of the world, Marlow showed himself willing to remember Jim, to remember him at length, in detail and audibly. (*LJ* 33)

The desire to tell 'audibly' means on Marlow's part an endeavour to transfer affective intensities rather than to dispose of the case. He has indeed been swayed by something mysterious in this young man struggling with an inconceivable truth – with the spirit of perdition within which is the 'true essence of life'. Jim is himself aware of the effect of his words upon the privileged listener:

> He drew quick breaths at every few words and shot quick glances at my face, as though in his anguish he were watchful of the effect. He was not speaking to me, he was only speaking before me, in a dispute with an invisible personality, an antagonistic and inseparable partner of his existence – another possessor of his soul. These were issues beyond the competency of a court of inquiry: it was a subtle and momentous quarrel as to the true essence of life, and did not want a judge. He wanted an ally, a helper, an accomplice ... the mystery of his attitude got hold of me as though he had been an individual in the forefront of his kind, as if the obscure truth involved were momentous enough to affect mankind's conception of itself. (*LJ* 92–3)

It is in this moment of unrest that the secret sharing establishes itself. Marlow recognises a common bond of humanity that has nothing to do with philanthropic ideals of love. What Conrad aims at here is a truth likely to bring a kind of illumination different from the noble feelings aroused by the powers of eloquence.

In *Lord Jim* the question of the cure is more complex than in 'Karain', if we remember Stein's opinion that 'the question is not how to get cured, but how to live!' (*LJ* 212). It needs something beyond the destructive power of the spoken word: when a passer-by in the street exclaims 'Look at that wretched cur!', the truth borne by the anonymous utterance takes Jim by surprise, leaving him stripped of 'that discretion which is more necessary to the decencies of our inner being than clothing is to the decorum of our bodies' (*LJ* 70). Similarly, a common expostulation like the French lieutenant's 'Mon Dieu! How the time passes!' brings about one of Marlow's rare moments of speechless being (*LJ* 143).[15]

The disruptive effect of the spoken word is indeed very clear in the scene of Flora de Barral's confrontation with 'the hate of an infuriated woman'.[16] Flora is left 'with a deep impression of worthlessness'[17] as the formerly loving governess suddenly turns into a Medusa who savagely attacks the image of her father:

> It seemed that poor Flora had to know all the possible phases of that sort of anguish, beginning with instinctive panic, through the bewildered stage, the frozen stage and the stage of blanched apprehension, down to the instinctive prudence of extreme terror – the stillness of the mouse. But when she heard herself called the child of a cheat and a swindler, the very unexpectedness

this caused in her a revulsion towards letting herself go. She screamed out suddenly 'You mustn't speak like this of Papa!'

The effort of it uprooted her from that spot where her little feet seemed dug into the thick luxurious carpet ... The next few seconds seemed to last for ever so long; a black abyss of time separating what was past and gone from the reappearance of the governess and the reawakening of fear. (*Ch* 121)

This other dark epiphany that leaves Flora rooted to the spot will produce an enduring symptom, a 'mystic wound' (etymologically, 'trauma' means wound) that will show on the 'ghost-like pallor' of her face for years afterwards (*Ch* 122). What Flora has been confronted with is less a question of meaning than one of words loaded with malevolent enjoyment: 'something which more in its tone than in its substance was mere venomous abuse' (*Ch* 119). Marlow is still aware of how 'we live at the mercy of a malevolent word. A sound, a mere disturbance of the air, sinks into our soul sometimes' (*Ch* 264). But in this novel the affective charge finds a resolution in Flora's final 'empowerment', as 'she casts off the passivity and resignation of the eternal victim'.[18] In other words, the symptom finds an outlet in the character's development: it is diegetically resolved, whereas in the early Marlow narratives the affective intensities remain and insist, addressed as they are to an invisible partner which is no other than the reader.

The acoustic substance of the signifier can have unexpected truth effects that appear in another of Conrad's tales of unrest, 'An Outpost of Progress'. Kayerts and Carlier are struck by the uncanny cross-resonances of a conversation between Makola and a slave dealer:

There was something in his intonation, in the sounds of the long sentences he used, that startled the two whites. It was like a reminiscence of something not exactly familiar, and yet resembling the speech of civilised men. It sounded like one of those impossible languages which sometimes we hear in our dreams. (*TU* 97)

The power of sound wrapped in a dreamlike substance obliquely brings forth the unpalatable truth which the two men had rather forget at the time – even though it will return with a vengeance through the irreverent tongue held out silently at them at the end of the story.

## Varieties of voice

There is in Conrad a whole choreography of the voice as a kind of persistent remainder without sense, cleft from a speaking mouth – an independent physical object travelling in space. In *Under Western Eyes*,

Nathalie Haldin's attention is drawn to the sound of a voice holding forth, even though 'she could not make out the language – Russian, French or German. No one seemed to answer it. It was as though the voice had been left behind by the departed inhabitants to talk to the bare walls.'[19] In so far as it does not belong to intersubjective exchange this vocal object may be related to some figure of Otherness and can be endowed with all kinds of uncanny perlocutionary effects – cultural, political, psychological – that make fragile the fabric of what we call 'reality'. The voice to which film theory has given the label 'acousmatic' often comes as the acoustic manifestation of a disturbing modality of the gaze itself detached from a subject, therefore inhuman.[20]

The anonymous voice of hearsay may thus become a powerful medium of fascination and ideological contamination. Flora de Barral's father, the fraudulent financier, was 'a mere sign, a portent' of something that was in the air:

> There was nothing in him. Just about that time the word 'Thrift' was to the fore. You know the power of words. We pass through periods dominated by this or that word – it may be development, or it may be competition, or education, or purity or efficiency or even sanctity. It is the word of the time. Well just then it was the word Thrift which was out in the streets walking arm in arm with righteousness, the inseparable companion and backer up of all such national catch-words, looking everybody *in the eye as it were*. The very drabs of the pavement, poor things, didn't escape the fascination. (*Ch* 74; my emphasis)

Conrad provides here a perfect insight into what Jacques Lacan will later define as one of the four discursive modes that underpin modern intersubjecive relations: the discourse of the capitalist – a variant of the master's discourse which is part of all structures of domination – promotes master signifiers as agents that promise endless enjoyment, like the empty word 'thrift'.[21] The obverse is the discourse of the analyst, where the voice as object enclosed in the fictional process of the cure acts as an agent that resists universalism. As to the artist's discourse – a kind of fifth mode which has no direct function in intersubjective relations – it relies on the same kind of voice as a bearer of a kind of truth likely to produce unexpected affects.

'Youth' presents an interesting case of delayed decoding in which a human voice floating in the air produces a weird effect soon resolved by the decoding process. As Marlow and his companions in ill fortune awaken in the Eastern port, a steamer anchors close to them:

> There was a murmur of voices in her, metallic hollow clangs of the engine-room, footsteps on the deck. Her ports shone, round like dilated eyes. Shapes

moved about, and there was a shadowy man high up on the bridge. He heard my oars.

And then, before I could open my lips, the East spoke to me, but it was in a Western voice. A torrent of words was poured into the enigmatical, the fateful silence; outlandish, angry words, mixed with words and even whole sentences of good English, less strange but even more surprising. The voice swore and cursed violently; it riddled the solemn peace of the bay by a volley of abuse. It began by calling me Pig, and from that went crescendo into unmentionable adjectives – in English. The man up there raged aloud in two languages, and with a sincerity in his fury that almost convinced me I had, in some way, sinned against the harmony of the universe.[22]

The shadowy man's voice loaded with intense anger, preceded by the noises from the engine-room, sounds like the materialisation of some superego's gaze – the 'dilated eyes' of the round shining portholes – as if the East were speaking of the sin committed by modernity 'against the harmony of the universe'.

Hawthorn has argued that *Under Western Eyes* traces the progress of its main character from the prison house of totalitarian discourse, where the written word has a deadly power, to the status of a speaking body. Razumov first makes of himself the voice of 'conservative authority', integrating the inhuman gaze characteristic of the novel's paranoid political universe – represented by General T—'s goggle eyes.[23] In the final interview, Nathalie's presence in the anteroom is perceived as another persecution, 'as unforeseen as the apparition of her brother had been' (*UWE* 341). Then the look of 'dull, absent obstinacy' in his eyes begins to pass away as he awakens to his own status as *speaking being* rooted in time and space:

'I? Going? Where? Oh, yes, but I must tell you first' . . . His voice was muffled and he forced himself to produce it with visible repugnance as if speech was something disgusting or deadly. 'That story, you know – the story I heard this afternoon . . . '

'I know the story already,' she said sadly.

'You know it! Have you correspondents in St Petersburg too?' (*UWE* 346)

An interesting parallel can be drawn here with Marlow's own interview with the Intended, who 'knows' and whose knowledge compels Marlow to lie in order to preserve her from the hidden truth. Here the cards are distributed differently: truth begins to detach itself from knowledge under the effect of the 'exquisite timbre' of Nathalie's voice. The vocal object leads the show: Razumov listens like a man 'listening to a strain of music rather than to articulated speech . . . as if under the spell of suggestive sound'(*UWE* 348). The 'living, acting, speaking lie', which he had so far lived by, loses ground (*UWE* 349). As he also reaches the limits of story-telling, the speaking body comes into play:[24]

> 'There is no more to tell!' He made a movement forward . . . and he kept his ground, though trembling in every limb. 'It ends here – on this very spot.' He pressed a denunciatory finger to his breast with force, and became perfectly still. (*UWE* 354)

As in Flora de Barral's case, the word 'spot' is the signal of the perlocutionary effect which binds the word to the body in yet another kind of 'spot of time'.

'Heart of Darkness' is a different case of the agency of the voice since the question here is more that of trauma, memory and anxiety. In his seminar on anxiety, Jacques Lacan establishes the close link between affect (fear, terror, anxiety) and the lost love object – the Thing[25] – whose fictional representation might be the enfolding body of the silent wilderness, which has 'caressed', 'taken', 'loved' Kurtz and ultimately 'consumed his flesh' (*HD* 26). The soundless life of the wilderness is, as Anika J. Lindskog explains, 'the silence of a sense-making structure', as opposed to the intermittent voice of the surf which is to Marlow 'a positive pleasure, like the speech of a brother' (*HD* 61).[26] How, then, to make us hear, feel and *see* the voice of 'that dumb thing' which is the bearer of anxiety? The 'mysterious stillness' palpable to Marlow seems to hold some hidden, hushed 'inner truth' (*HD* 81), while the sounds of human activity – 'a clink', 'a report' – act upon him like perlocutionary effects that make him turn his head and think:

> A slight clinking behind me made me turn my head. Six black men advanced in a file . . . The clink kept time with their footsteps . . . all were connected together with a chain whose bights swung between them, rhythmically clinking. Another report made me think suddenly of that ship of war I had seen firing into a continent. It had the same kind of *ominous voice*. (*HD* 64; my emphasis)

Such sounds and noises both betray and reveal the central figure of silence which is the voice at its purest, calling for some ethical response.

Kurtz's liminal cry is the other persistent remainder that makes us *see* the silence as long as we are made to hear and feel its material presence as vocal object.[27] It is pure intensity, which has the vibrating force of an object carrying like a bullet from the depths of Africa to the Intended's drawing room in Brussels:

> and the sound of her low voice seemed to have the accompaniment of all the other sounds, full of mystery, desolation, and sorrow, I had ever heard – the ripple of the river, the soughing of the trees swayed by the wind, the murmurs

of the crowds, the faint ring of incomprehensible words cried from afar, the whisper of a voice speaking from beyond the threshold of an eternal darkness. (*HD* 159)

Now the inaudible whisper has contaminated the knowledge of the West. The voice that summed up Kurtz has also migrated into Marlow's own being. It even reaches out to the frame narrator, who listens 'for the sentence, for the word that would give me the clue to the faint uneasiness inspired by this narrative that seemed to shape itself without human lips in the heavy night-air of the river' (*HD* 83). Undoubtedly then, the object voice will be the medium of the hidden truth. Its 'dying vibration' will continue its journey, the remainder of 'one immense jabber, silly, atrocious, sordid, savage or simply mean, without any kind of sense', but not without perlocutionary effect (*HD* 115).

It is this lingering but living memory which 'Heart of Darkness' continues to transfer to the reader: the traumatic secret permeated with a 'strange commingling of desire and hate' has found out Marlow whose inconclusive story is a true work in progress (*HD* 151). In the tension between truth and knowledge, the former will prevail as long as 'the contamination continues'.[28]

## The weird power of the written word

If we admit that ethics concern our acts and their consequences, Conrad's dealing with the power of the written word, however weird the effect, is eminently ethical. What difference is there between the living experience of the word and the lived language of *Chance*? Anne Enderwitz observes 'a new direction' in this novel that seems to put an end to Marlow's 'melancholy negotiations of the problem of representation' in 'Heart of Darkness': whereas the earlier work 'operates on the basis of a potential incompatibility of language and life,' *Chance* traces 'the interaction between language and the full physical body'.[29] I would suggest, however, that this new direction takes place at the cost of the disappearance of the intensely shimmering texture of Conrad's earlier fiction, where the palpitating life of the written word can be felt through every page, and whose correlate is found in the opaque, radiating spots of darkness. The Marlow of *Chance*, by contrast, is presented as a rational being too prone to sagacious general statements. In other words, the voice effect is lost.

If *Chance* is as much language-focused as Conrad's other novels, the focus has shifted from the level of *énonciation* (an act) to that of *énoncé* (a product). The narrative opens on a general confusion in naming – for example between young Powell and his namesake at the Port of London offices – in an atmosphere of distrust as to the ordering power of the word: Mr Powell, young Powell notes, 'made me soon see that an Act of Parliament hasn't any sense of its own. It has only the sense that's put into it; and that's precious little sometimes' (*Ch* 14). The divorce between the sign and the referent is pronounced. As to de Barral, he is another deficient father figure, another hollow man who knows how to concoct pretty fictions out of attractive names:

> The fellow had a pretty fancy in names: the 'Orb' Deposit Bank, the 'Sceptre' Mutual Aid Society, the 'Thrift and Independence' Association. Yes, a very pretty taste in names; and nothing else besides – absolutely nothing – no other merit. Well, yes. He had another name, but that's pure luck – his own name of de Barral which he did not invent. I don't think that a mere Jones or Brown could have fished out from the depths of the Incredible such a colossal manifestation of human folly as that man did. (*Ch* 69)

Unlike Gentleman Brown in *Lord Jim* or Mr Jones in *Victory*, de Barral does not concern himself with the human folly of a fellow human being's intimate soft spot, but rather with the collective credulity of 'poor fools': one day, 'as though a supernatural voice had whispered into his ear', he goes out into the street and begins advertising. Everyone, Marlow recalls, remembers 'his first modest advertisements headed with the magic word Thrift, Thrift, Thrift, thrice repeated; promising ten per cent on all deposits and giving the address of the Thrift and Independence Aid Association in Vauxhall Bridge Road'(*Ch* 79). Conrad's insight here is into the perverse use, the pseudo-magic function of the commodified signifier full of empty promises of enjoyment – whether it be by advertising, the press or politicians:

> The word THRIFT perched right up on the roof in giant gilt letters, and two enormous shield-like brass-plates curved round the corners on each side of the doorway were the only shining spots in de Barral's business outfit. Nobody knew what operations were carried on inside except this – that if you walked in and tendered your money over the counter it would be calmly taken from you by somebody who would give you a printed receipt. (*Ch* 80)

*Chance* indeed 'scrutinizes the power of language to affect and intervene without lamenting the loss of certitudes',[30] but the consequence is that Marlow here, with his 'habit of pursuing general ideas in a peculiar manner, between jest and earnest' (*Ch* 23), has lost his enigmatic aura. If words actually do things, if they acquire a transitory material quality as in the scene of the governess's abuse, they tend to be overinflated with meaning on the level of the novel's narrative discourse, an overinflation that stifles the material *life* of the signifier. One example will suffice from among Marlow's many sagacious ratiocinations on masculine and feminine qualities or on the word 'chance':

> Yes, that very young girl, almost no more than a child – this was what was going to happen to her. And if you ask me how, wherefore, for what reason? I will answer you: Why, by chance! By the merest chance, as things do happen, lucky and unlucky, terrible or tender, important or unimportant; and even things which are neither, things so completely neutral in character that you would wonder why they do happen at all if you didn't know that they, too, carry in their insignificance the seeds of further incalculable chances. (*Ch* 99–100)

We are very far here from the perlocutionary power of speech transferred through the power of the written word, in what Lindskog has called Conrad's 'sense-text'.[31]

The sense-text is experienced rather than comprehended, just as the meaning of Marlow's narrative is brought out by the effects that constitute its living essence, to be searched not in the empty core, which is just a resonant vacuity, but in the 'misty halo' brought out by 'the illumination of moonshine' (*HD* 48). In other words, its perlocutionary effect touches upon the reader as a speaking body. There is a kinship between the frame narrator of 'Heart of Darkness' and the intended reader of the 'Preface' to *The Nigger of the 'Narcissus'*. Paradoxically enough, the sense-text has a voice which speaks silently since it is through the power of the written word, in other words through the letter of the text. Claude Maisonnat has most appropriately named it the 'textual voice': a written avatar of the voice which cannot be represented and can yet be felt through rhythm, sound, intonation – often ironic – which necessitates a hollow to reverberate.[32] We have seen previously how Marlow is made to feel the silence of the wilderness through the inarticulate sounds, noises and resonances that circulate in the diegetic space of 'Heart of Darkness'. The very beat of the wilderness has infiltrated his being so that the rhythm, inaudible but felt, returns during the interview with the Intended. Similarly the perlocutionary power of the silent textual voice is felt in the fragments of affective intensities sprinkled in the particles of the acousmatic halo, diffracted by liminal states of language, for the object voice is present as long as the sound remains unarticulated. And just like the soundscapes and aural elements of the Belgian Congo, the object voice has a 'contaminating' power of its own. In other words the textual voice's effect is potentially disruptive and traumatic in that it produces blank spots in understanding.

Let us take the example of the exchange where Marlow tries to depict to the frame narrator the relation between Kurtz and the wilderness: 'He was its spoiled and pampered favourite. Ivory? I should think so ...' (*HD* 115). The typography – an important aspect of the written word, in particular in its power to create rhythm – is crucial here: the question mark signals a leap from the story to the frame narrative, where someone has misunderstood 'favourite' as 'ivory'. The echo between 'favourite' and 'ivory' produces a kind of narrative syncope which is also a voice effect inscribed in the letter. This brief, accidental lapse provides a glimpse into the nature of the relationship between Kurtz and the silent, loving body of the wilderness, ivory being the metonymic object endowed with desire, torn from 'that thing that couldn't talk and perhaps was deaf as well' (*HD* 81). Claude Maisonnat gives many examples of such 'metaleptic leaps' whose hermeneutic consequences are considerable in *Under Western Eyes*. The holes produced both in meaning and in structure are places for the 'emergent, yet silent and fragmented' voice recuperated by the text, immaterial and yet contained in the most material dimension: their effect is to localise the act of enunciation – deprived of vocality, but not of perlocutionary effect.[33] It may be useful to remember here that etymologically, the word *aesthesis* refers not to judgement or appreciation but to the senses. The gaps in the narrative fabric leave a vacuity which makes it possible for the written word to produce unheard cross-resonances, traumatic in the sense that they have a disruptive effect on our understanding, including our understanding of ourselves. Is it not after all such an inaudible voice effect that Conrad sought when he composed 'Heart of Darkness', whose 'sombre theme had to be given a sinister resonance, a tonality of its own, a continued vibration that, I hoped, would hang in the air and dwell on the ear after the last note had been struck'.[34]

But how can a silent voice be an active agent? The answer is simple: it can be so whenever the power of sound in the written word prevails over meaning, like those 'broken phrases' (*HD* 156) that make the acoustic memory of Kurtz's scream, a kind of subdued roar which is the remainder of the 'horror' and threatens the fragile edifice of meaning, overheard in 'favourite' and 'ivory'. The inarticulate voice emerges in paranomastic effects, as in the portrait of Kurtz as 'an animated image of death carved out of old iv*ory*' with 'a weirdly v*or*acious aspect' (*HD* 134; my emphasis), subtly infiltrating innocent words like 'memory', 'glorious' or 'decorous' in the interview with the Intended. Such fragments in the letter of the text are part of its active memory.

On the level of the narrative economy, the presence of a dark core of silence which does not make sense is indeed the precondition for such resonances to come through, visible in the narrative blind spots where meaning dissolves not as a result of accident, but as a result of Conrad's artistry, for example in the traumatic *Patna* scene which breaks the time-space sequence of *Lord Jim* – a perfect case of cinematic montage which produces a hole from which the text literally looks back at the reader. The recurrence of the eminently ambiguous word 'spot' is itself not an accident since it designates a physical or moral stain, a point in space where time and thought come to a rest. In other words, the affective dimension is located not in the story but in the narrative speech act which conveys the mystery beyond understanding.

Such perlocutionary effects are nowhere to be found in *Chance* because of the primacy given to meaning and general statements; to the Imaginary, rather than the material dimension of the written word. Conrad still uses devices like metalepses, but there is a surfeit of them that simply marks the dialectic exchange with the frame narrator, who is no longer a reader figure built into the text, but simply an interlocutor in the general debate. Here, for example, Marlow elaborates on the governess's behaviour:

> the secret of her envenomed rage, not against this miserable and attractive wretch, but against fate, accident and the whole course of human life, concentrating its venom on de Barral and including the innocent girl herself, was in the thought, in the fear crying within her, 'Now I have nothing to hold him with . . .'
> I couldn't refuse Marlow the tribute of a prolonged whistle.
> 'Phew! So you suppose that . . .'
> He waved his hand impatiently.
> 'I don't suppose. It was so. And anyhow why shouldn't you accept the supposition.' (*Ch* 103)

The Marlow of *Chance* is less a poet of reality than the light holiday philosopher who elaborates on his key 'concept', chance, as the driving force that explains the whole universe.[35] The power of the written word to make you hear, feel and *see* has been sacrificed, the textual voice has vanished, and this may be one more argument in favour of the theory of the decline of Conrad's artistry.

If, for a reader like F. R. Leavis, Conrad 'is intent on making a virtue out of not knowing what he means',[36] the modernist reader certainly appreciates the importance of not knowing. The weird power of the written word can be 'positively' traumatic in the sense that it brings a disruption in the perceptions and representations of our time, and such a disruptive power will be enduring, thought-provoking as long as it cannot be resolved in meaning. Such is, it seems, what makes the living power and the extraordinary literary posterity of a text like 'Heart of Darkness'. A novel like *Chance*, despite its critical interest, has indeed little chance of producing the same kind of prolonged perlocutionary effect in the landscape of our modernity.

## Notes

1. Jeremy Hawthorn's *Joseph Conrad: Language and Fictional Self-Consciousness* (London: Edward Arnold, 1979) is an obvious example.
2. Anne Enderwitz, 'Speech, Affect, and Intervention in *Chance*', *The Conradian*, 39.1 (2014), pp. 36–53 at p. 39.
3. Ibid. p. 51.
4. Ferdinand de Saussure, *Course in General Linguistics*, 3rd edn, trans. R. Harris (Chicago: Open Court, 1986), pp. 9–10.
5. 'We first distinguished a group of things we do in saying something, which together we summed up by saying we perform a *locutionary* act, which is roughly equivalent to uttering a certain sentence with a certain sense and reference, which again is roughly equivalent to "meaning" in the traditional sense. Second, we said that we also perform *illocutionary* acts such as informing, ordering, warning, undertaking, etc., i.e. utterances which have a certain (conventional) force. Thirdly, we may also perform *perlocutionary* acts: what we bring about or achieve by saying something, such as convincing, persuading, deterring, and even, say, surprising or misleading.' J. L. Austin, *How to Do Things With Words* (Oxford: Oxford University Press, 1975), p. 108.
6. See in this respect Tina Skouen, 'Ciceronian Oratory and the Idea of Civilization in "Heart of Darkness"', *Conradian* 40.1 (Spring 2015), pp. 1–6: 'According to Quintilian, the peroration or epilogue is where we are allowed "to release the whole flood of our eloquence" and use "grand and ornate words and thoughts for the sake of moving the audience's emotions"' (p. 3).
7. Joseph Conrad, *Lord Jim* (London: J. M. Dent and Sons, 1946), p. 174. Subsequent references are cited in the text as *LJ*.
8. Joseph Conrad, 'Preface' to *The Nigger of the 'Narcissus'* (London: J. M. Dent and Sons, 1945), p. 5.
9. The affect always concerns the body: 'The Latin root *afficere* has different meanings, all relevant in the key scene of Flora's traumatization by her governess: "(1) to bring somebody into a bodily or organic state, condition or disposition," (2) "to bring somebody into a mental or psychological mood, to excite or stimulate or to move or touch," (3) "to attack, weaken or exhaust someone"'. Enderwitz, 'Speech, Affect and Intervention', p. 41.
10. Ibid. p. 42.
11. Joseph Conrad, 'Karain: A Memory', in *Tales of Unrest* (London: J. M. Dent and Sons, 1923), p. 27. Subsequent references to the volume are cited in the text as *TU*.
12. Cedric Watts, 'Fraudulous Signifiers: Saussure and the Sixpence in "Karain"', in Daphna Erdinast-Vulcan, Allan H. Simmons and J. H. Stape (eds), *Joseph Conrad: The Short Fiction* (Amsterdam: Rodopi, 2004), pp. 12–28 at p. 26.

13. Austin, *How to Do Things*, p. 121.
14. Jeremy Hawthorn notes a similar emphasis in *Under Western Eyes*, which 'includes much comment on language – and the reader ostensibly receives Razumov's story after two stages of transmission: put into words in his diary by Razumov, and then presented to us in the words of the teacher of languages – it is also a novel that is packed with descriptions of what we can term the speaking body'. 'Introduction', in Joseph Conrad, *Under Western Eyes* (Oxford: Oxford Worlds Classics, 2003), p. xxv.
15. See Josiane Paccaud-Huguet, 'The Conradian Flash of Insight: Motion that Stands Still', in Jakob Lothe, Jeremy Hawthorn and James Phelan (eds), *Joseph Conrad: Voice, Sequence, History, Genre* (Columbus: Ohio State University Press, 2008), pp. 118–37.
16. Joseph Conrad, *Chance* (London: J. M. Dent and Sons, 1969), p. 138. Subsequent references are cited in the text as *Ch*.
17. Enderwitz, 'Speech, Affect and Intervention', p. 43.
18. Ibid. p. 48.
19. Joseph Conrad, *Under Western Eyes* (London: J. M. Dent and Sons, 1947), p. 144. Subsequent references are cited in the text as *UWE*.
20. The acousmatic voice 'transgresses the boundary outside/inside, since it belongs neither to diegetic reality nor to the external vocal accompaniment, but lurks in-between space, like a mysterious foreign body which disintegrates from within the consistency of "reality".' Slavoj Žižek, *Enjoy your Symptom!*, 2nd edn (London: Routledge, 2001), p. 120. See also Žižek, '"I hear you with my eyes", or the Invisible Master', in Renata Salecl and Slavoj Žižek (eds), *Gaze and Voice as Love Objects* (Durham, NC: Duke University Press, 1996), pp. 90–126.
21. See Slavoj Žižek, 'Jacques Lacan's Four Discourses'. Available at <http://www.lacan.com/zizfour.htm> (last accessed 25 January 2016).
22. Joseph Conrad, *Youth, Heart of Darkness, The End of the Tether* (London: J. M. Dent and Sons, 1967), p. 39. Subsequent references to the volume are cited in the text as *HD*.
23. 'Responding to the immensity of Russian space and numbers, "A voice seemed to cry within him" and it is this collective voice of conservative authority that Razumov hears and attempts to appropriate as his own.' Hawthorn, 'Introduction', in *Under Western Eyes*, p. xiii.
24. 'It is characteristic of perlocutionary acts that the response achieved, or the sequel, can be achieved additionally or entirely by non-locutionary means: thus intimidation may be achieved by waving a stick or pointing a gun.' Austin, *How to Do Things*, p. 119.
25. 'L'angoisse désigne très probablement l'objet, si je puis dire, l'objet dernier, la Chose' ('Anxiety very probably designates the object, if I may say so, the last object, the Thing'; my translation). Jacques Lacan, *Le Séminaire Livre X: L'Angoisse* (Paris: Seuil, 2004), p. 360.
26. Anika J. Lindskog, '"It was very quiet there": The Contaminating Soundscapes of "Heart of Darkness"', *Conradian* 39. 2 (2014), pp. 44–60 at p. 48.
27. As Žižek reminds us, 'the object is here as long as the sound remains unarticulated; the moment it resounds, the moment it is "spilled out", the object is evacuated, and this voidance gives birth to $, the barred subject

lamenting the lost object. This lament, of course, is deeply ambiguous: the ultimate horror would be that of an object voice coming too close to us . . . voice and silence relate as figure and ground: silence is not (as one would be prone to think) the ground against which the figure of a voice emerges; quite the contrary, the reverberating sound itself provides the ground that renders visible the figure of silence.' Žižek, '"I hear you with my eyes"', p. 93.
28. 'As it turns out, this story is indeed inconclusive, not only because it refuses to offer a definitive version of the events narrated, but also from its being still in progress, as the contamination continues through and after its narration.' Lindskog, '"It was very quiet there"', p. 59.
29. Enderwitz, 'Speech, Affect and Intervention', pp. 39, 42.
30. Ibid. p. 36.
31. Lindskog, '"It was very quiet there"', p. 56.
32. See Claude Maisonnat, 'The Agency of the Letter and the Function of the Textual Voice in *Under Western Eyes*', *Conradian* 4.2 (2009), pp. 90–109.
33. Ibid. p. 95. A metalepsis is defined as a transgression in narrative levels, often made textually visible by aposiopeses and dashes.
34. Joseph Conrad 'Author's Note', in *Youth, Heart of Darkness and the End of the Tether* (London: J. M. Dent and Sons, 1917), pp. v–viii at p. vii.
35. See in this respect John G. Peters, '"Let that Marlow talk": *Chance* and the Narrative Problem of Marlow', *Conradian* 39.1 (Spring 2014), pp. 130–46.
36. F. R. Leavis, *The Great Tradition* (Garden City, NY: Anchor Doubleday, 1954), p. 219.

Chapter 6

# 'Soundless as Shadows': Language and Disability in the Political Novels

*Katherine Isobel Baxter*

> Razumov could struggle no longer. He was exhausted; he had to watch passively the heavy open hand of the brute descend again in a degrading blow over the other ear. It seemed to split his head in two, and all at once the men holding him became perfectly silent – soundless as shadows.[1]

This chapter takes as its starting point the deafening of Razumov in *Under Western Eyes*. At the end of the novel's penultimate chapter Nikita exclaims 'He [Razumov] shall never be any use as a spy on any one. He won't talk, because he will never hear anything' (*UWE* 371). The extraordinary synaesthesic logic of Nikita's claim, in which seeing ('spy') and speaking are annulled through deafness, provokes us to consider the complex relationships between speech, hearing, politics and disability in the political novels.

In the first chapter of *Enforcing Normalcy* Lennard J. Davis explains the prevalence of disabled figures in literature 'as a result of the hegemony of normalcy'.[2] For Davis, the disabled character acts as a necessary counterpoint to the 'normal' character(s), against which their normalcy is measured and secured. Moreover, in constructing this dichotomy of disabled versus normal (whether between characters in the text or between disabled figures in the text and a presumed 'normal' reader consuming it), Davis argues that fiction participates in a larger social programme of normalcy, one that developed out of scientific and sociological thinking in the nineteenth century. A similar position is developed by David T. Mitchell and Sharon L. Snyder, who bring a structuralist approach to what they perceive as the 'narrative prosthesis' engendered by the presence of disability in fiction. For Mitchell and Snyder, disability appears as a textually generative problem: 'a narrative issues to resolve or correct – to "prostheticize" in David Wills's sense of the term – a deviance marked as improper to a social context'.[3] Narratives are thus born of a social desire to resolve into normalcy the problem of, or represented by, disability. These arguments, although more nuanced than in my blunt account of them here, tend to presume that literature cannot help but be imbricated in the dominant discourse of its time. More specifically they imply that novelists such as Zola and Conrad (whom Davis uses as examples) are not just imbricated in, but actually reinforce, the dominant discourse of normalcy in their work, whether consciously or unconsciously, through their depictions of disabled characters. To some extent this is of course true, but it can lead to a reductive account that, in the instance of Davis's discussion of *Under Western Eyes* at least, simply gets things wrong in order to fit the paradigms. Thus, Davis claims that Razumov dies at the end of the novel 'as if life were in fact impossible to survive under those conditions' of his disablement.[4] In fact, contrary to this assertion, Razumov survives, and this complicates Davis's pattern of normalcy versus disability, which he imposes to contrast the disabled and supposedly dead Razumov with the young, beautiful Natalia as the surviving embodiment of normalcy.[5]

Despite being overdetermining, even problematically so, these arguments nonetheless provide an interesting challenge to consider what work is being done by the presence of disability in Conrad's fiction, a presence which is pervasive once one begins to look. From the start I want to suggest that disability is doing different things in different places. Some of the time, disability, or the suggestion of disability, is indeed used either by Conrad or by his characters as a structuring and stabilising counterpart to normalcy: we might think of the Doctor's insinuation of Amy's simple-mindedness, in Conrad's short story 'Amy Foster'; or 'the cripple' in *The Rover*, whose presence reminds the sturdy-bodied Peyrol that he might have been born 'like that'. Elsewhere, though, not least, as it happens, in the two political novels to which Davis draws our attention (he also looks briefly at *Lord Jim*), disability is *not* just there as a foil to a hegemonic normalcy. In what follows, therefore, I take a different approach, one much closer to that espoused by Ato Quayson in *Aesthetic Nervousness*. Nuancing Mitchell and Snyder's structuralist paradigm, Quayson suggests that the 'prostheticizing function [of narrative] is bound to fail, not because of the difficulties of erasing the effects of disability in the real world, but because the aesthetic domain itself is short-circuited upon the encounter with disability'.[6] Quayson suggests, by contrast, that we read disability as a 'fulcrum or pivot'; it is a point out of which 'various discursive details emerge, gain salience, and ultimately undergo transformation within the literary-aesthetic field'.[7] It is this attention to the point of excess that disability represents in a text, what Quayson calls in a different context the 'ex-centric', that informs my approach and that allows for the relationship between disability and language to emerge as a crucial feature in each of the three political novels under discussion.[8]

Before turning to the novels themselves, however, it is worth rehearsing briefly one of the central debates around disability that more broadly informs the analysis of Conrad's fiction that follows. This debate centres on where the cause of disability lies. Medical models locate disability in an embodied physical or mental lack that reduces the capacity of the disabled person to operate according to the norms of a non-disabled (that is, non-lacking) body. For example, an amputee without legs is disabled by her lack of the two legs associated with a normalised human body and with the related normalised mobility of walking. Countering this argument, social models of disability locate the cause in environmental or social barriers that fail to accommodate physical or mental difference: one is thus disabled *by* one's environment rather than disabled *in* one's environment. According to these models the amputee is disabled not by her lack of legs; her mobility in a wheelchair is simply a different mobility to walking. Her disability is caused by steps, turnstiles, narrow lifts and so on, which fail to accommodate her particular mode of movement. The lack is identified here not in the individual but in their physical and social environment. Thus, for these latter models, disability is not embodied per se but emerges in and as the disjuncture between the individual and their environment. This disjuncture, more often than not, is exclusionary in the disability it produces: our amputee is unable to enter a building because of the lack of a ramp. Thus the disabled body is also displaced because it is made to seem out of place.[9] Within disability studies, the vast majority of activists and scholars tend to favour one or another of the social models of disability; by contrast, systems of law, care, health and education continue to operate primarily guided by medical models that attribute a superior value to physical and/or psychical normalcy.[10] In what follows I draw on both models but focus particularly on the social, since it tends to be in the disabled character's encounter with a social or environmental impasse that the significance of their disability appears. As a result my readings demonstrate, in contrast to the work of Davis, Mitchell and Snyder, that the significance of disability in these texts is less borne by the characters themselves, as innately and medically disabled; rather it is located in those places where disability emerges as an event or moment of social displacement.[11]

With this in mind we can now turn to Conrad's three major political novels, *Nostromo*, *The Secret Agent* and *Under Western Eyes*. Each contains both major and minor characters who in some way or another can be categorised medically as disabled. *Nostromo* includes the lame Dr Monygham, as well as Decoud's descent into suicidal synaesthesia; *Under Western Eyes* culminates in the deafening of Razumov; and most famously *The Secret Agent* takes for one of its central protagonists

Stevie, who, as Joseph Valente has recently argued, presents 'attributes at once consistent with and corrective of the dominant contemporary social and scientific construction of the autist'.[12] As we shall see, for each of these protagonists it is possible to trace a relationship between language and disability that is mediated by this characteristic of being 'out of place' to which social theories of disability draw our attention.

In *The Secret Agent* Stevie struggles to communicate and is encouraged to redirect his energies into silent expression, through, for example, his quiet drawing of perfect circles.[13] Nonetheless, Stevie's inarticulacy is deeply frustrating to him since he clearly wants to communicate his thoughts and ideas; and this frustration creates a vicious cycle in which his frustrated outbursts serve as occasions for silence to be reinforced upon him, usually by his well-meaning sister. There are thus several layers of displacement that inhere in Stevie's disability. On the surface, Stevie's ways of expressing himself – setting off fireworks, stamping his feet, stammering – fail to coincide with common expectations for communication in a workplace or domestic environment. Even his sympathetic sister, Winnie, works hard to ensure that Stevie minimises these variant forms of self-expression and encourages him instead to take on normative roles as a way of avoiding 'excited' outbursts, as when she appeals to him to 'look well after me at the crossing ... like a good brother' following his troubling conversation with the cab-driver (*SA* 125). A few pages later Winnie medicalises Stevie's condition, albeit to assure herself of its limited visibility, when she sees him 'amiable, attractive, affectionate, and only a little, a very little, peculiar' (*SA* 128). In attaching 'peculiarity' to this list of visible attributes Winnie is shown to believe her brother's disability is both innate and physically detectable.[14] Winnie is not alone in this diagnosis of Stevie. Comrade Ossipon reads Stevie's actions and his features, such as 'the lobes of his ears', as both symptoms and causes of 'degeneracy' (*SA* 35). In categorising Stevie's appearance and activities through the terms of a medicalising system, Ossipon erases the disruptive potential of Stevie's physical and mental differences.[15] Rather than leave Stevie troublingly displaced by the disjunction of his behaviour and contemporary convention, even the convention of self-proclaimed revolutionaries and anarchists, Ossipon deploys a system of diagnosis to reassign Stevie in ways that conventionalise his difference: 'Very good. Very characteristic, *perfectly typical*. ... Typical of this form of degeneracy' (*SA* 34; italics added).

Beneath this surface layer of medicalised disability, though, we find that the disjunction Stevie experiences between his own understanding of the world and the conventions of the society in which he lives occurs primarily in language. Although critics have often interpreted

Stevie's distress at Yundt's violent rhetoric, and his conversation with the cabman who drives Stevie, Winnie and their mother to the charitable home, as signifying his role as moral compass in the novel, few have pursued the linguistic disjunction which causes that distress in the first place. When Yundt depicts the 'pretty branding instrument' applied 'red-hot' to the 'vile skins' of criminals, he asks rhetorically 'Can't you smell and hear from here the thick hide of the people burn and sizzle', following it up with a gesture of '[sniffing] the tainted air of social cruelty, [and straining] his ear for its atrocious sounds' (SA 35–6). Stevie, who has heard and seen this performance, 'knew very well that hot iron applied to one's skin hurt very much' and consequently his 'scared eyes blazed with indignation: it would hurt terribly' (SA 39).[16] In short, there is nothing wrong with Stevie's knowledge. The disjunction occurs between Yundt's metaphor-inflected use of language to represent experience and Stevie's literal use of language. It is important to recognise that the fault here lies not in Stevie failing to understand Yundt, but rather in his understanding Yundt too well. Both Yundt and Stevie recognise the suffering of the poor and both perceive that suffering in physical terms. But Yundt, in fact, distances himself from the realities of the physical suffering of the poor through the dramatised violence of his performed metaphor of branding. In contrast, Stevie adds the violent reality of branding to his already sympathetic apprehension of the plight of the poor, informed as it is by his daily encounters with Mrs Neale, the Verlocs' alcoholic housekeeper, who entreats Stevie with her 'harrowing tales about her little children' (SA 136).

As Yundt continues, Conrad uses a metaphor of his own to emphasise the literalness with which Stevie takes in Yundt's rhetoric:

> 'Do you know how I would call the nature of the present economic conditions? I would call it cannibalistic . . . They are nourishing their greed on the quivering flesh and the warm blood of the people.'
>
> Stevie swallowed the terrifying statement with an audible gulp, and at once, as though it had been swift poison, sank limply in a sitting posture on the steps of the kitchen door. (SA 38)

Stevie's gulp provides one of several instances of synaesthesia in the political novels that encourage us to associate disablement with political discourse. Whereas in the example of Nikita's judgement on Razumov, with which we opened, Nikita imagines that deafness stops Razamov from both spying and communicating information, Stevie is unable to prevent the information penetrating him bodily and is disabled by it. The uncomfortable nexus of culinary associations – from the nourishing 'flesh', through Stevie's 'gulp', to his place at the 'kitchen door' – seems to trap Stevie and make him both an unwilling participant in and victim of Yundt's intentionally metaphoric rhetoric. In these examples the disabling disjunction for Stevie arises between Yundt's deployment of a melodramatic and metaphoric discourse and the literalness with which Stevie comprehends that discourse. Stevie is thus displaced from the political paradigm which that discourse represents, and this displacement invites the reader to reassess the moral weight of both Stevie's and Yundt's perceptions of the poor in the light of the other's.

If we were to stop here, it would be possible to argue that Stevie's failure to process the metaphors of Yundt's rhetoric signals an arrested development in conceptual thinking. His conversation with the cabby, however, puts pressure on this assumption and once again invites us to reread his disability from a social perspective through the lens of language. In this extended scene, whilst physical disorder and disability are repeatedly alluded to from the outset (in the emaciation of the horse, the cabby's hook and the instability of the cab itself), Stevie's behaviour only becomes visibly disruptive when he leaps down from the cab to lighten the horse's load. Whilst his excited compassion for the horse halts his speech ('he stammered himself into utter incoherence' [*SA* 116]), his solution to the problem is in fact sensible – as Conrad interjects here, 'Stevie could have managed easily to keep pace with the infirm, dancing horse without getting out of breath' (*SA* 116). Winnie, however, is concerned that this solution will only bring the family into disrepute: 'Who ever heard of such a thing' she cries, and she consequently uses threats to Stevie's reputation with Verloc as a way of encouraging him to climb back on the cab: 'Mr Verloc will be sorry to hear of this nonsense' (*SA* 116).[17] The cabby, too, dismisses Stevie's actions as senseless, a 'silly game' (*SA* 117). Thus it is primarily social convention, rather than physical or logical impracticality, that stigmatises Stevie's behaviour at this point.

When Stevie hears the cabby's story, his sympathetic stammering is once again relativised by the fact that the story seems also to strike 'the world dumb' and is itself delivered, moreover, in a 'strained, extinct voice' (*SA* 122; the cabby's strained voice is itself a common disability of the period, brought on by prolonged driving in London's smog). The cabby's whispering and the silence that reigns over the city in response to his story make Stevie's 'concise' response, 'Bad! Bad!', seem eloquent by comparison (*SA* 123). Stevie recognises that 'he could say nothing' for, unlike Yundt who expounds his opinions with metaphorical flourish, he sees no reason to communicate his own metaphorical yearning – in this case to resolve the hardship that the cabby recounts by giving both man and horse a cuddle in a cosy bed:

And that, he knew, was impossible. For Stevie was not mad. It was, as it were, a symbolic longing . . . To be taken into a bed of compassion was the supreme remedy, with the only one disadvantage of being difficult of application on a large scale. And looking at the cabman, Stevie perceived this clearly, because he was reasonable. (SA 123)

It is clear here that Stevie is capable of the kind of abstraction that makes metaphor possible *and* that he is aware of this faculty. Thus, we must be wary of reading this scene, or the earlier scene of Yundt's polemic, too easily as signifying innate naivety in Stevie. If language fails Stevie in the light of the cabby's revelations, it is because he is powerless to articulate a workable remedy. As Conrad notes, if 'Stevie was not wise enough to restrain his passions', he was 'supremely wise in knowing his own powerlessness' (SA 124). Indeed, in the extended dramatisation of Stevie's response to the cabby's plight, Conrad continues to draw our attention to the way in which language, articulation and understanding are related. Thus in Stevie's attempt 'to fit all the words he could remember to his sentiments in order to get some sort of corresponding idea', we see the process by which he maps language onto experience in order to produce communicable ideation (SA 126). This process is hardly unusual but, by atomising it for us, Conrad draws attention to our shared expectation that language will mediate experience and ideation effectively, and to our shared frustration when language fails in this function.

Of course, Stevie does finally manage to articulate his understanding of the situation in his famous dictum: 'Bad world for poor people' (SA 126); and in both his dictum and his solution to the state of affairs it describes – the benevolent interference of the police – he presents an essentially moral and practical (if overly idealistic) response. We need to grasp this if we are also to understand Stevie's later grooming by Verloc and Michaelis. Stevie follows these men not simply because he is naively faithful to Verloc, as Winnie suggests, but also because (we can presume) they offer alternative solutions to the problems of the poor in their conversations with him. Thus Stevie's political enlightenment, begun in his conversation with the cabby, disillusioned by Winnie's dismissal of the police as possible saviours of the poor, comes to fruition in his time with Michaelis and Verloc.[18]

Stevie's anarchic political education is completed in his final displacement, when the bomb he is carrying through Greenwich Park explodes. In the explosion, Stevie's body becomes radically disruptive of and disrupted by its surroundings through the intermingling of 'limbs, gravel, clothing, bones, splinters' that results (SA154). This disruptive effect is exacerbated when his remains are returned to the hospital, where, in a macabre echo of Yundt a few pages earlier, these are presented as 'an accumulation of material for a cannibal feast' laid out upon a 'waterproof sheet ... spread ... in the manner of a table-cloth' (*SA* 64). The apparent incongruity of a hospital and a cannibal feast is only resolved through what they share, and thus what that incongruity makes visible: their unsentimental gaze upon the human body. In a final twist, Stevie's body, once more pathologised through its physical dismemberment and hospital context, disrupts the social fabric of his environment, as Inspector Heat 'required considerable firmness of mind not to recoil' (*SA* 64). Moreover, the scrap of fabric on which his address is inked, which Heat finds amongst the remains in the morgue, on the one hand solves the crime Heat is investigating and, on the other, explodes the narrative into a series of deadly yet inconclusive endings. As a result, this address, handwritten by Winnie, provides the example par excellence of the way in which language, throughout the novel, emerges as the disruptive sign of the body and of the narrative displaced. For if the prior instances of Stevie's disablement drew attention to his bodily disorder in response to injustice, not least the language of injustice, here in the morgue the disordered remains of Stevie's body can only be read through the words inscribed on his destroyed coat lining. The obliteration of Stevie's body by the bomb is a hyperbolic disablement, whose excess (in Quayson's terms) is marked by this inscribed scrap of fabric and whose implications ripple out through not only the plot but the narrative and aesthetic structure of the novel.

While Conrad focuses our attention on a single figure of disability in *The Secret Agent*, in *Nostromo* the relationship between language and disability is revealed in not one but three bodies: Decoud, Hirsch and Monygham. Neither Decoud nor Hirsch is introduced in the narrative as disabled, although both are seen as outsiders to Sulaco society from the start. Instead they are disabled by the mental and physical tortures related to language and truth-telling that they undergo in the machinations of the novel's plot. Furthermore, in both instances that disabling torture is followed swiftly by death: Decoud's suicide, Sotillo's impetuous murder of Hirsch. Monygham too is presented as an outsider, but in contrast to Hirsch and Decoud his disability is made visible from the start: he has a limp that is repeatedly commented upon in the narration, although its cause, also torture, takes place in a time before the novel's main action, and, significantly, he survives it. Monygham makes sense for us of the relationship between politics, language and disability towards which Decoud and Hirsch's own torturous experiences gesture.

As I have noted, Monygham's disability is presented medically from the start and as a physical symptom of a broader misanthropy. He has a 'limping gait and bowed head' when he walks, and is 'old ugly, learned – and a little "loco" – mad'.[19] His deployment of language reinforces his physical features: he is 'a bitter eccentric character . . . bitterly taciturn when at his best. At his worst people feared the open scornfulness of his tongue' (*N* 44). At this early stage of the narrative we might presume Monygham's taciturnity is simply a correlative of his misanthropy; only later do we recognise the significance of why taciturnity might demonstrate Monygham 'at his best', not least in his own eyes. Monygham, we discover in the last section of the novel, had been tortured under Guzman Bento by the 'pitiless' Father Beron (*N* 371). 'The doctor had been a very stubborn prisoner', we are told, 'and, as a natural consequence . . . his subjugation had been very crushing and very complete . . . His confessions, when they came at last, were very complete, too' (*N* 373). Hoping for death as a consequence of the crimes to which he confesses, in fact Monygham was left 'to decay slowly in the darkness of his grave-like prison' until Bento died of a stroke and his prisoners were liberated (*N* 374). Monygham thus staggered forth 'to take possession of his liberty', scarred mentally and physically by the experience of torture *and* by the experience of giving way under torture yet surviving (*N* 375). The effect of these experiences is apparent in the radical doubt expressed in his observation to the chief engineer that if Charles Gould is 'sure of himself' then 'he is sure of nothing' (*N* 310).

In order to live with his scars Monygham makes for 'himself an ideal conception of his disgrace', refusing to rehabilitate himself within society and instead, through his dress and speech, reiterating the social exclusion that his 'maimed' feet signify medically. Indeed, even his limp is made to perform his displacement from a social perspective in so far as Monygham rarely accommodates it by riding or taking a horse and trap. Instead, he determinedly walks everywhere and in doing so makes visible his difference through the very movements of his body. His disruptive appearance, which he maintains with studied care, discomforts both the European and local communities. He both exists 'outside the pale' of the communities in which he operates and at the same time is integral to them by dint of his profession and Emilia Gould's unlikely friendship with him. Thus Monygham maintains, if only in his own conscience, the social rupture that his torture and confession first effect. And we need, once again, to understand that rupture in terms of language. For in so far as Monygham's confessions are betrayals they represent not a failure to speak the truth but rather speaking truth out of place. In the context of torture, taciturnity is 'best'. Monygham's breakdown under torture makes evident that even the value of truth-telling is relative, reliant as it is on its context. Thus, his scrupulous maintenance of his limp as disability in both social and medical terms redirects our attentions to the ways in which political violence can also be understood in social terms to disable language by disrupting its capacity to operate effectively. In Monygham's case, honesty is disabled by being *out of place* in the political context in which he is forced to speak.

The history of Monygham's experience at the hands of Father Beron is hinted at in the narrative at several points before it is finally revealed in the third section. This creates an element of delayed decoding (not least in relation to the value of that 'taciturnity' with which Monygham is first introduced) whereby the reader slowly comes to understand that the initial rumours reported in the narrative about Monygham are in fact true. Nonetheless, the revelation of Monygham's torture and confession comes before the descriptions of Hirsch's torture and finally Decoud's breakdown, and in this sense it acts typologically as an interpretative key to these later episodes. In the light of Monygham's story, whose relationship to the plot is essentially tangential, we are able to read these later scenes as more than elements of dramatic tension and plotting. They certainly serve the narrative in this way, but they also reiterate the rupturing of language's power by political violence through their embodiment of that rupture in physical and mental disablement.

Although Decoud is not marked by disability like Monygham at the start of the novel, he is nonetheless characterised by his social incompatibility with the communities in which he resides. As I have discussed elsewhere, his adoption of 'Frenchified ... cosmopolitanism', belied by his Spanish Creole features, sets him apart as much from his adopted home in Paris as his place of birth, Costaguana (N 152).[20] Whilst this social estrangement is more cultivated than imposed, it nonetheless disables his capacity for self-understanding. We are told early on that 'He had pushed the habit of universal raillery to a point where it blinded him to the genuine impulses of his own nature.' (N 153) As a result, whereas Stevie is dislocated from society by his literal and ethical relationship to language and the world, Decoud is dislocated by another language practice ('raillery') based on his amorality and his refusal to take the world seriously.

As for Stevie, this dislocation has disintegrative and fatal consequences. Whereas Stevie has struggled to communicate and Monygham has opted for bitter taciturnity, however, Decoud has honed a nihilistic persona for himself primarily through constant communication and dialogue. For much of the novel Decoud is presented as engaged in some kind of linguistic activity: reporting for the St Marta's newspaper, *Seminario*, from Paris; writing about Costaguana for 'an important Parisian review' (N 153); corresponding with his sister and with the Avellanos family;

establishing the *Porvenir* in Sulaco; sending news cables; conversing sotto voce with Emilia Gould, Nostromo and Antonia; declaiming to the 'Junta of Notables' (N 234–6); and composing the separatist proclamation of Sulaco, which he had 'written ... furiously' before carrying it away with him on the lighter of silver (N 278). Thus, when he is left stranded on the deserted Great Isabel, he experiences the '[first] day of absolute silence ... he had known in his life' (N 496). This silence is both maddening and depressing to the man for whom words have been lifeblood, and Decoud falls into an irreversible melancholy. At night he perceives the silence as a vibration of 'senseless phrases', 'an ironical and senseless buzzing' (N 499), suggesting his alienation from his facile loquacity. By day, on the other hand, he looks at the silence 'like a still cord stretched to breaking point' (N 499). Eventually this synthesthesia becomes completely intolerable and on the tenth day of his silent isolation he commits suicide. What is intriguing here is that, whether by day or by night, the maddening silence that Decoud experiences is characterised as something that is *not* silence – it becomes sound, it becomes vision. Decoud's synaesthesic apprehension of the island's silence is used by Conrad to characterise the disordering of his senses and his mind in his melancholic state. On the one hand we can therefore read Decoud's synaesthesia as a medical symptom of mental disintegration and disability; on the other we recognise that the cause of that disintegration is his immediate context of displacement from language and communication.

If silence, or the lack of language, is mentally disabling and ultimately fatal to Decoud, it is equally fatal to Hirsch. Hirsch, the hide merchant from Esmeralda, occupies a strange place in the novel. Initially introduced as a figure of ridicule, he is used as an element of plot to heighten dramatic tension in the final chapters of the central section of the book, 'The Isabels', since he has the potential to give away the secret of Decoud, Nostromo and the lighter of silver. In the final section, 'The Lighthouse', he reappears as the captive of Sotillo, to whom he indeed confesses all he knows of Decoud and Nostromo's escape with the lighter of silver. But while Hirsch believes in all sincerity that Decoud, Nostromo and the lighter were sunk by the collision with Sotillo's troop ship, Sotillo refuses to believe the silver can be lost, and in his quest for 'the real truth' he tortures Hirsch with the estrapade (N 446). Hirsch is hoisted on a rope tied to his wrists, which are bound behind his back (thus dislocating his shoulders), and this form of torture creates a parallel between Hirsch and Decoud, who, marooned on the Great Isabel, perceives 'the silence of the gulf like a tense, thin cord to which he hung suspended by both hands' (N 498). This parallel draws our attention to the fact that although both men put their faith in language, in their ability to provide a compelling account of events, such faith is misplaced, something that Monygham's experience of torture has already primed the reader to recognise. Indeed, neither Monygham, Hirsch nor Decoud in the end can say anything that will save them, and this results in their mental and physical disfigurement, fatally so for Decoud and Hirsch.

The pattern of relationships between politics and political violence, language and disability that we have explored in *The Secret Agent* and *Nostromo* is repeated once more in the last of Conrad's political novels, *Under Western Eyes*. At its centre is Razumov, who brings together various of the characteristics we have observed in the prior novels' protagonists. Like Decoud, Razumov pursues his ambitions through writing; specifically, he hopes to attain recognition and thereby secure a career through winning the essay medal at his university. But unlike Decoud he is solitary in his ambition: he has no family with whom to correspond, he avoids social interaction, and (at least initially) has no love interest to spur on his ambition. Similarly, Razumov's familial context – the illegitimate child of a woman with whom he apparently has no contact as an adult and of a senior official who acts as his semi-secret patron – is clearly not the same as Stevie's, but it shares the same characteristics of precariousness in the displacement and dissolution of both maternal and paternal roles. Razumov, like Stevie, is also forced to hear more radical politics than he can bear, but whereas for Stevie it is unbearable because it communicates a terrifying moral danger, for Razumov it represents a danger to his ethos of pragmatic self-preservation. More importantly, whilst silence is enforced upon Stevie by his family in the hopes of minimising the medical and social visibility of his perceived disability, Razumov chooses silence for himself, at least initially. Finally, in this choice of silence there is an echo of Monygham, since for both men their taciturnity is a mark of both personal ethos and political necessity. Indeed, this taciturnity, prized by Monygham, returns not only in the character of Razumov but more broadly as a governing device in the plotting and aesthetic features of *Under Western Eyes*. As we shall see, silences of all kinds are key to the narrative.

'Silences have their character', we are told, when Razumov meets the secret service officer Mikulin for the first time (*UWE* 86). And Razumov finds this out to his chagrin at the start of the novel, when his own silence and aloofness amongst his academic peers are characterised by his fellow student Haldin as a silence sympathetic to the cause of revolution:

> You say nothing, Kirylo Sidorovitch! *I understand your silence.* To be sure, I cannot expect you with your frigid English manner to embrace me. But

never mind your manners. You have enough heart to have heard the sound of *weeping and gnashing of teeth* this man [whom Haldin has just assassinated] raised in the land. (*UWE* 16; italics added)

When Razumov asks Haldin what prompted him to single him out as a likely assistant in his perilous flight from the law, following the assassination, Haldin responds 'Confidence'. This word, we are told, 'sealed Razumov's lips as if a hand had been clapped on his mouth' (*UWE* 19). The simile of the striking hand that silences Razumov reads all the more grimly when we are aware of the circumstances of his deafening at the novel's end. Similarly, Haldin's 'confidence' in Razumov sounds differently when we know that as a result of this encounter Razumov will find he is expected to make a career of inducing confidences, when he is quietly coerced into the service of the secret police. The repeated *mis*-understandings of Razumov's silence thus become a trope of the novel, from this first scene of Haldin's confession to Razumov onwards.

However, Razumov is not the only one to use silence as a way of inducing confidence. Mikulin, in their initial interview, repeatedly leaves his sentences hanging unfinished like bait on a line for Razumov. And despite Razumov's determination 'not to be drawn into saying too much', he falls for this trick almost every time (*UWE* 87). Thus when Mikulin explains that 'I admit that the request for your presence here had an official form. But I put it to you whether it was a form which would have been used to secure the attendance of a . . .', Razumov fills the blank with 'Suspect', helplessly betraying his sense of anxiety and guilt. Mikulin's response demonstrates both his recognition of Razumov's plight and his astute understanding of its usefulness to surveillance: 'I was about to say a "misunderstood person"' (*UWE* 88–9).

With Razumov's arrival in Geneva in the second section of the book, the silences multiply, whether in conversations or in environments. The ability to speak or to hear is constantly under threat of displacement in the croaking, squeaking, rasping, hoarse, whispering, murmuring, muttering voices of the various characters we encounter.[21] The perpetual danger of inaudibility and silence is further reinforced by incidents woven throughout the narrative. Peter Ivanovitch, we learn, lost the faculty of speech in his outlaw wanderings as a runaway convict (*UWE* 124). Returned to civilisation, Ivanovitch drinks his tea impassively 'as if he were deaf' during Razumov's interview with his ghastly patron, Mme de S——. Tekla, we discover, had previously nursed a revolutionary lithographer to his grave, following torture so atrocious that, like Monygham, he 'let some information out'. Crippled mentally and physically by this experience, he wastes away, and Tekla regrets that 'Nothing

I found to say could make him whole' (*UWE* 153). After this experience, we are hardly surprised, then, when sometime later she asks Razumov rhetorically 'What's the good of speech to me?' (*UWE* 237).

Examined retrospectively, the pressure on speech and audibility that Conrad builds up through the details of plot, narrative and atmosphere foreshadow and even determine Razumov's fate at the hands of Nikita: the silences of the novel (such as Peter Ivanovitch's above) anticipate the real deafness that must come to him in the end. Moreover, like Mongygham's limp, Razumov's deafness, resulting as it does from his confession, stands as a physical corollary to the problem of speech, and in particular truth-telling, out of place. It is Razumov's words, in the written confessional of his journal and his oral confession to the revolutionaries, which displace him socially at the very moment when silence would have maintained his inclusion in the émigré society of Geneva. His deafness is thus as much a belated symbol of that prior exclusion brought about by his speech-out-of-place as it is a cause of his physical exclusion from the world of sound.

Following Davis's larger thesis in *Enforcing Normalcy*, it might be tempting to read Razumov's deafening allegorically as a disabling that returns Razumov to his mother country – Russia – geographically, politically and bodily. Such a reading would note that until this point Razumov's physique is notably sturdy, as is remarked by various characters. As such it stands in striking contrast to almost all the other Russians in the novel, whose appearance Conrad is at pains to present, in frequently grotesque detail, as medically disabled. Whether through the dubious corpulence of Nikita or the skeletal horror of Mme de S—, we are made aware of the physical imperfections of all the various Russian characters in the novel, revolutionary or otherwise. This reading, in which Russia is characterised as producing or enforcing a deformation of the soul that is reflected metaphorically in physical deformity, reinstates Davis's argument that disability is used in fiction to counterpoint normalcy either within or beyond the text. One might therefore argue that the multiply disabled Russians that populate *Under Western Eyes* are used symbolically to represent the degeneracy of Russian autocracy in contrast to the implicit normalcy of British and 'Western' democracy. This reading is certainly seductive when we consider Conrad's general attitude towards Russia: his parents had, after all, been political activists against Russian imperial control of Poland, and had both fatally contracted tuberculosis as a result of being sent into exile for their revolutionary activities by the Russian authorities.

Such a reading, however, relies primarily on the medical conception of disability as an embodied state rather than as a socially constructed state, in so far as it implies a symbolic relationship between the inherent physical disability of the Russian characters and the dissolute nature of its political system. What emerges, by contrast, if we read Razumov's disability through a social model? Rosemarie Garland Thomson's description of encounters between non-disabled and disabled people in the opening of *Extraordinary Bodies* is helpful in this regard:

> In a first encounter with another person, a tremendous amount of information must be organized and interpreted simultaneously: each participant probes the explicit for the implicit, determines what is significant for particular purposes, and prepares a response that is guided by many cues, both subtle and obvious. When one person has a visible disability, however, it almost always nominates and skews the normate's process of sorting out perceptions and forming a reaction. The interaction is usually strained because the nondisabled person may feel fear, pity, fascination, repulsion, or merely surprise, none of which is expressible according to social protocol.[22]

Thomson makes clear that although all encounters rely on the interpretation of a multitude of details, 'visible disability' produces a disruptive excess of information that cannot be processed by the non-disabled or 'normate' interlocutor. The discomfort and confusion that Monygham creates amongst both Europeans and locals can be understood in these terms and explains why, despite Conrad's narrative emphasis on Monygham's limp, it goes largely unmentioned by the characters themselves. In contrast, Razumov's deafness is invisible, detectable only through a lack of evidence rather than the surfeit that Thomson describes, and communicated to the reader not through an emphasis on the intense pain he feels in his ears, but rather through another passage of delayed decoding in which the repeatedly 'silent' imagery of lightning, rain and wind is retrospectively interpreted as a result of Razumov's deafening, when on the following page he exclaims '*Je suis sourd*' (UWE 369–70).

Razumov's deafness, then, is as much disruptive of the social systems in which he has operated as it is hindered by a lack of social accommodations to his deafness.[23] Moreover, his disability, whether understood socially or medically, is a rupturing and displacing of language by silence. Razumov is placed beyond the use of the Russian secret service and also beyond the use of the teacher of languages once he becomes deaf, as Nikita surmises, because he can no longer operate in the auditory sphere of language. Thus, as much as he is displaced from the world of sound (and the dangers of that displacement are made evident immediately through his collision with the tram), so he disrupts our social presumption of language itself as a given, for his deafness draws our attention to the limits of the spoken word, limits which the prior silences and failure of voice in the novel have hinted at from the very start.

By way of conclusion, therefore, I want to suggest an alternative interpretation, one which is more in line with arguments that Davis makes elsewhere, in *Bending over Backwards*. For Razumov's deafening, in returning him to the world more generally, returns him to a world in which the excess of difference that Quayson and Thomson draw our attention to in our perception of disability (whether understood medically or socially) is in fact a 'norm'; and in which ideological discourses, including the discourse of normalcy, function as prosthetics (to repurpose Mitchell and Snyder's paradigm) that mask the underlying normality of our inherent disabilities, our silences and our displacements. Disability, then, need not be a symbol of national degeneracy but may be one of the universal human condition, as both Davis and Michael Davidson suggest elsewhere.[24] Moreover, we can extend this argument back through the prior novels to recognise how disability, language, and in particular the disabled languages of silences and speech out of place, draw our attention to the prosthetic function of ideological discourse, whether the radical politics of Yundt and Peter Ivanovitch, the reformist politics of Avellenos and Holroyd, or the reactionary politics of Vladimir, Guzman Bento and General T—. Just as Ossipon, in his harping on Lombroso, seeks to categorise and thereby integrate Stevie's difference into a system by which he can be understood (and ultimately controlled), so these others use their chosen discourse to interpret, contain and control the excess of difference that characterises society and that the moment of disablement reveals. Yet in each novel that control is never achieved, not because of some heroic action on the part of those protagonists whom we have analysed here, but rather because of something that their inevitably compromised and damaged relationships with language make clear: that the excess of difference in society, reflected through disability, language and silence, is irrepressible and irresolvable.

### Notes

1. Joseph Conrad, *Under Western Eyes* (London: J. M. Dent and Sons, 1923), p. 369. Subsequent references are cited in the text as *UWE*.
2. Lennard J. Davis, *Enforcing Normalcy: Disability, Deafness, and the Body* (London: Verso, 1995), p. 44.
3. David T. Mitchell and Sharon L. Snyder, *Narrative Prosthesis: Disability and Dependencies of Discourse* (Ann Arbor: University of Michigan Press, 2000), p. 53. See David Wills, *Prosthesis* (Stanford: Stanford University Press, 1995).
4. Davis, *Enforcing Normalcy*, p. 48.

5. Haldin's sister is called variously 'Natalia' and 'Nathalie' throughout the novel.
6. Ato Quayson, *Aesthetic Nervousness: Disability and the Crisis of Representation* (New York: Columbia University Press, 2007), p. 26.
7. Ibid. p. 34.
8. See Ato Quayson, 'Symbolisation Compulsions: Freud, African Literature and South Africa's Process of Truth and Reconciliation', *Cambridge Quarterly* 30.3 (2001), pp. 191–214.
9. For a helpful introduction to these debates see Carol Thomas, 'Disability Theory: Key Ideas, Issues and Thinkers', in Colin Barnes, Mike Oliver and Len Barton (eds), *Disability Studies Today* (Cambridge: Polity, 2002), pp. 38–57.
10. For a compelling example of how the social model is applied both culturally and politically in disability studies see Michael Davidson, 'Universal Design: The Work of Disability in an Age of Globalization', in *Concerto for the Left Hand: Disability and the Defamiliar Body* (Ann Arbor: University of Michigan Press, 2008), pp. 168–96.
11. Mitchell and Snyder's *The Cultural Locations of Disability* does engage with the significance of environment for disability, but primarily focuses on spaces created purposefully for those defined as disabled and 'in which disabled people find themselves deposited', rather than those spaces that are socially 'open' and yet whose features exclude through displacement and the consequent excess of visibility. See David T. Mitchell and Sharon L. Snyder, *The Cultural Locations of Disability* (Chicago: University of Chicago Press, 2006), p. 3ff.
12. Joseph Valente, 'The Accidental Autist: Neurosensory Disorder in *The Secret Agent*', *Journal of Modern Literature* 38.1 (Fall 2014), pp. 20–37 at p. 21.
13. See, for example, Winnie's anxiety when she notes that 'the sheet of paper and the pencil given him for drawing circles' lie 'blank and idle on the kitchen table'. Joseph Conrad, *The Secret Agent* (Oxford: Oxford University Press, 2008), p. 138. Subsequent references are cited in the text as *SA*.
14. It is worth noting that elsewhere Winnie takes something closer to a social approach to understanding Stevie, when we are told that she affirms there is 'none more affectionate and ready to please, and even useful, as long as people did not upset his poor head' (*SA* 43).
15. Ossipon uses the theories of the nineteenth-century criminologist and physician Cesare Lombroso as his primary guide in interpreting the physiognomy of Stevie, among others (see, for example, *SA* 35). These produced the influential idea of the 'criminal type' and are the ancestor of modern 'profiling'. See Robert G. Jacobs, 'Comrade Ossipon's Favorite Saint: Lombroso and Conrad', *Nineteenth-Century Fiction* 23 (1968–9), pp. 74–84; Robert G. Hampson, '"If you read Lombroso": Conrad and Criminal Anthropology', in Mario Curelli (ed.), *The Ugo Mursia Memorial Lectures* (Milan: Mursia International, 1988), pp. 317–35.
16. We may presume Stevie knows this from the domestic abuse of his father, including 'a poker flung', which Winnie recalls immediately prior to her murder of Verloc (*SA* 178).

17. Winnie chastises her mother similarly over the respectability of her move to the charitable home: 'Whatever people'll think of us – you throwing yourself like this on a Charity?' (*SA* 117).
18. A century later, Emma Sky's *The Unravelling* records 'mentally disabled children' used as suicide bombers in Iraq. See Christopher Dickey, 'No Ends in Sight', *New York Times Sunday Book Review* (12 July 2015), BR1.
19. Joseph Conrad, *Nostromo* (Oxford: Oxford World's Classics, 1995), p. 45. Subsequent references are cited in the text as *N*.
20. Katherine Isobel Baxter, 'Speaking Foreign: Conrad and Modernist Multilingualism', *Studia Neophilologica* 85.1 (2013), pp. 17–28.
21. Almost all the characters are introduced speaking in undertones in Geneva: Natalia speaks in a 'low murmur' (*UWE* 112); the narrator 'mumbles' (*UWE* 113); Mrs Haldin's voice is 'startlingly weak and colourless' (*UWE* 114); Peter Ivanovich's speech is 'like the deep muttering of the wind in the pipes of an organ' (*UWE* 129); Razumov first speaks to Natalia with a 'faint, rasping voice' (*UWE* 180), and then to the narrator in a voice 'practically extinct', and with a 'painful' 'rustling effort' that is 'barely audible' (*UWE* 184–5); Mme de S— also speaks with a 'rasping voice' (215). As the novel continues, conversations are presented almost invariably in murmurs, mumbles and mutters. Inaudible conversations abound, as when Natalia visits Mme de S—'s house and hears an almost silent voice that sounds as if it 'had been left behind by the departed inhabitants to talk to the bare walls' (*UWE* 144).
22. Rosemarie Garland Thomson, *Extraordinary Bodies: Figuring Disability in American Culture and Literature* (New York: Columbia University Press, 1997), pp. 12–13.
23. The tram's aural warning system (a 'clanging' bell [*UWE* 370]) is a precise example of this socially produced disability, whose disastrous consequence means yet further disablement for Razumov.
24. See Lennard J. Davis, *Bending over Backwards: Disability, Dismodernism and other Difficult Positions* (New York: New York University Press, 2002), pp. 4–5; Davidson, *Concerto*, p. xiii.

Chapter 7

# Conrad and Romanised Print Form: From Tuan Almayer to 'Prince Roman'

*Christopher GoGwilt*

'Kaspar! Makan!' These are the first words of Conrad's first novel, *Almayer's Folly,* and this chapter seeks to explore what the Romanised print form of these words reveals about the timing and spacing of Conrad's English. Famously, of course, these opening words are not in English. Almayer's wife is here calling Almayer, by his Christian name Kaspar, to come to dinner – *makan* – meaning 'to eat' in Malay. Conrad's first published words might be considered the first example of what Ian Watt has called 'delayed decoding' in Conrad.[1] It takes at least eight pages before the gist of Mrs Almayer's address is translated into English: 'He had a hazy recollection of having been called some time during the evening by his wife. To his dinner probably.'[2] This delayed translation of Malay into English sets a pattern for things to come: for the plot of *Almayer's Folly*; for the long-delayed completion of the Malay trilogy that frames Conrad's entire writing career; and, too, for successive critical attempts to understand and explain the significance of Conrad's decision to write in English. To the extent that the future of Conrad's English turns on this delayed translation-effect, it is worth noting that Mrs Almayer's words will never – perhaps *can* never – fully be translated into English. Like the later, more famous problem of translation between Malay and English that gives the title to *Lord Jim*, which I will discuss later, the opening words of *Almayer's Folly* set up a dialogic exchange between Malay and English that is at least as lopsided, uneven and difficult as the relationship between Mrs Almayer and her husband. Conrad's English is, from the start, translinguistic, but not all languages are equal. The timing and spacing of Conrad's English turn on a hierarchy of hegemonic relations between languages. One of the key things controlling this hierarchy is romanisation: the transcription, transliteration and translation of linguistic exchange into the Romanised print form of English.[3]

Conrad's English has always posed a great many theoretical and practical problems of translation. Biographically, these problems have typically been traced back to the fact that Conrad came to English late. Critics have long found many instances of French expressions underwriting his English prose – and there may be an example of this in the opening to *Almayer's Folly*: Almayer's 'dream of splendid future' drops the indefinite article one might rather expect in standard English – 'dream of a splendid future'. Critics have also found many instances of Polish – for example, according to Tanya Gokulsing's analysis, in the 'temporal marker' *'now'* in *Almayer's Folly*.[4] Such translinguistic effects organise the temporal and spatial unfolding of narrative in Conrad in ways that might be seen as foundational for English modernism. Those translinguistic effects in Conrad that cross over between European languages – Polish, French and English, above all – might indeed offer a particularly rich kind of *chronotope*, in Mikhail Bakhtin's sense of the word, for modernist narrative form. Bakhtin gives the name *'chronotope* (literally, "time space") to the intrinsic connectedness of temporal and spatial relationships that are artistically expressed in literature'.[5] Later in the same essay he defines 'chronotopes' as 'the organising centers for the fundamental narrative events of the novel . . . the place where the knots of narrative are tied and untied'.[6] Postcolonial criticism has privileged a particular kind of translinguistic knot, following Homi Bhabha's discussion of Marlow's discovery of the English book on seamanship in 'Heart of Darkness', where both the 'Englishness' of the book and its authoritatively bound and printed form produce a privileged space of 'hybridity' and 'ambivalence' towards colonial authority. I want to follow that line of argument, paying attention, though, too, to the point Asako Nakai has made in recalling readers to the 'ciphered marginalia' in the margins of the English book. Nakai claims that 'Bhabha's way of quoting the scene, leaving out Marlow's reference to the cipher, gives readers who are not familiar with Conrad's novella the impression that Marlow's comment, "he must be English", concerns the author of the book.'[7] In fact, 'he must be English' refers to the owner of the book, who turns out to be the Russian 'harlequin', whose notes, in Cyrillic script, look like ciphered code to Marlow. Bhabha describes the discovery of the book as installing 'the signs of appropriate representation'.[8] However, the authority of the 'Englishness' of the book, and the trope of the book itself, are qualified by the interrelation between the English text of the manual on seamanship and the Russian script in the margin. What I call the 'chronotope' of Romanised print is an attempt to specify the translinguistic legacy of this postcolonial displacement of English that Nakai has explored in terms of what she calls the 'discourse of the English book'.[9]

To explore this Conradian chronotope of Romanisation here, I consider three examples. Each highlights a somewhat different kind of Romanisation: the Romanisation of Malay words in *Almayer's Folly*; the Romanisation of Cyrillic script in *Under Western Eyes*; and the Romanisation of Polish in 'Prince Roman'. The first presents an example of the Romanised transcription of a language (Malay) not traditionally written in Roman letters. The second offers an example of the transliteration into Roman letters of a language (Russian) foregrounded as coming from another script (Cyrillic). The third offers an example of the translation between two languages (English and Polish) both presented as sharing the use of Roman letters. Defining the different effects of Romanisation foregrounded in these examples as, respectively, *transcription* (from spoken language into Roman letters), *transliteration* (into Roman letters from another script) and *translation* (from one Roman script to another) may help simplify the range of linguistic questions raised by the Romanised print form of Conrad's English. But it will be important to recognise how the spacing and timing of Romanised print form make it difficult to maintain the distinction between these effects. The first instance of the Romanised transcription of speech will turn out also to hinge on a rivalry between different (Arabic and Roman) scripts. The second instance of transliteration into Roman from Cyrillic script is in many respects an exaggeration of and distraction from the equally significant questions raised by the novel's transcription of and translation from Russian terms. The third instance of a translation between Polish and English (less Romanisation than Anglicisation, it would seem) presents the deceptive illusion of a print space unaffected by the problems of transcription into Roman letters or the transliteration between scripts foregrounded in the other examples. It is this illusion of a neutral space of Anglicised Roman print that Conrad's writing has, from the start, explored, exploited and exposed as an ongoing process of transcription, transliteration and translation that turns English into the site of multiple, discrepant and conflicting histories of language, script and culture.

## Romanised Malay

As noted at the start of this chapter, the opening words of *Almayer's Folly* – 'Kaspar! Makan!' – introduce the novel (and Conrad's career) by rendering Mrs Almayer's spoken Malay in the same form of Romanised print that is the timing and spacing of Conrad's written English. The delayed translation-effect of these opening words is clearly significant for the narrative framing (and also for what Cedric Watts calls the 'covert plotting') of the novel.[10] Anticipating the problem of translation between Malay and English that is addressed explicitly at the start of *Lord Jim* – 'They called him Tuan Jim: as one might say – Lord Jim' – the deferred translation of the first words of *Almayer's Folly* involves a related linguistic question: how does an English reader decode the everyday Malay form of address (Mrs Almayer's calling Almayer to dinner, 'Kaspar! Makan!'; and the way Jim is addressed as 'Tuan' at Patusan)?[11] Both involve questions of translation, transcription and the transliteration of Malay into Romanised print form that have consequential effects on the linguistic space of Romanised English print form. As with the problem of entitlement in *Lord Jim*, the story of Almayer's 'folly' unfolds according to the various ironic shades of familiarity and contempt, intimacy and hostility registered in the transliteration, transcription and translation of Malay. Indeed, the later problem of entitlement in *Lord Jim* (along with the standard English dictionary definition given to the word 'Tuan' as a term of respect) might be read as part of the same delayed decoding effect of Conrad's first printed words.[12] The fact that Mrs Almayer *doesn't* address Almayer as 'Tuan' may not immediately signal the disrespect she harbours towards her husband; but when Almayer *is* called 'Tuan' – when Dain Maroola corrects Almayer, who has mistaken him for his arch-rival Abdulla ('Tuan Almayer is speaking to a friend. There is no Arab here' [*AF* 13]) – the use of everyday Malay forms of address helps establish an unfolding 'covert plot' of intrigue, romance and politics to which Almayer's limited narrative perspective (itself a transcription, transliteration and translation into English from Dutch) remains, crucially, oblivious.

Increasingly more critical attention has been given to the Malay linguistic and historical coordinates of Conrad's work.[13] Of special interest are the parallels between Conrad's literary career and the emergence of the Indonesian language as a vehicle for realising anti-colonial nationalism.[14] What remains under-examined in discussions of this parallel, however, is the role of Romanised print Malay, which plays an important part in the story of the emergence of Indonesian that Benedict Anderson retells in *Imagined Communities*, where it serves as an exemplary story about the role of 'print-capitalism' in the origin and spread of nationalism:

> When print-capitalism arrived on the scene [of the East Indies] in a sizeable way after mid-century, the language [lingua franca Malay] moved out into the marketplace and the media. Used at first mainly by Chinese and Eurasian newspapermen and printers, it was picked up by [native] *inlanders* at the century's close ... By 1928, shaped by two generations of urban writers and readers, it was ready to be adopted by Young Indonesia as the national(-ist) language.[15]

A central part of this story is the way Romanised print Malay displaced the form of Arabic script traditionally used to write Malay since at least the sixteenth century.[16] These different forms of writing Malay – *Jawi* and *Rumi*, Arabic and Roman – coexisted throughout the nineteenth century (their relative linguistic prestige carrying a different weight in British-controlled Malaysia and the Dutch-controlled East Indies). To what extent might these rival forms of writing Malay inflect the rivalry in *Almayer's Folly* between the English Lingard and the Arab Abdulla? To what extent might this historically complex but significant script conversion of Malay writing from Arabic manuscript to Romanised print belong to the narrative structure of all Conrad's Malay work? These are questions to which I will return.

## Romanised Russian

My second example is the contrast in *Under Western Eyes* between the Cyrillic Russian of Razumov's journal and the Romanised print form within which the English narrator reframes that document. The organising narrative function of this contrast is established at the very beginning of the narrative with the narrator's comment that 'the readers of these pages will be able to detect in the story the marks of documentary evidence'.[17] There are many more 'marks' of 'documentary evidence' than the narrator admits to here: besides Razumov's journal, the narrative accumulates a bewildering set of references to texts, records and other documents (including Razumov's spy report).[18] All these 'marks of documentary evidence' are structured in advance by the organising conceit of a Russian document transcribed, transliterated and translated into Romanised English print form. Already encoded in the title-metaphor 'under Western eyes', this conceit is reinforced by the narrator's exaggerated emphasis on the 'cabalistic, incomprehensible' look of Cyrillic writing (*UWE* 99), and structures both overtly and covertly the unfolding of the novel (as the narrator puts it, in the final pages, describing Sophia Antonovna's account of Mikulin's meeting with Peter Ivanovich, 'And this story, too, I received without comment in my character of a mute witness of things Russian, unrolling their Eastern logic under my Western eyes' [*UWE* 279]).

The opposition between Cyrillic and Roman letters that organises this conceit of a Russian document submitted to 'Western' eyes is established in the opening paragraph by the narrator's explanation of the name of 'the man who called himself, after the Russian custom, Cyril son of Isidor – Kirylo Sidorovitch – Razumov' (*UWE* 3). The English rendition of Razumov's Christian name 'Kirylo' as 'Cyril' draws redoubled attention to the contrast between Roman and Cyrillic forms of writing. Unlike the difference, say, between the names Nathalie and Natalia (as Haldin's sister is variously called throughout), this seems to offer something more substantial than two variant forms of the Romanised Russian name; rather, its etymological speculation on the first two names invites a reading of Razumov's unfolding story in relation to the symbolic significance of each successive part of the name: the parts ('Cyril son of Isidor – Kirylo Sidorovitch') whose double transliteration and translation evokes the formation of Cyrillic as Russia's identifiable writing system, and the part (Razumov) that hints at a 'reason' or 'reasoning' (Razumov means 'son of reason') either in accord or at war with that identity. What is proleptically encoded in this overdetermined Romanisation of Razumov's full name is the novel's ideological divisions – between Russia and Europe, and perhaps more significantly between the Westernising and Slavophile strains of its depiction of Russian intellectual debates.[19]

Perhaps the most condensed example of how the novel's ideological divisions are guided by the conceit of a Russian document in Cyrillic script transliterated into Romanised print form is the title-phrase 'under Western eyes'. What might appear to be a simplified, even simplistic distinction between Russia and the West, however, turns on the transcription, transliteration, translation of a Russian term that unsettles the very opposition between Russia and the West it seems designed to frame. This emerges most clearly in the conversation between the narrator and Nathalie Haldin at the beginning of Part Second, where Nathalie's use of the terms 'occidental' and 'western' is taken up by the narrator and transformed from the specifically Russian terms of debate between 'Westernisers' and 'Slavophiles' and used to apply to an English self-characterisation (he calls himself 'the dense westerner' [*UWE* 78]) designed to distance himself from Russian politics ('To us Europeans of the West, all ideas of political plots and conspiracies seem childish, crude inventions for the theatre or a novel' [*UWE* 81–2]), while constructing his imagined readers as 'Western' ('The Western readers for whom this story is written will understand what I mean' [*UWE* 83–4]). Critics have long recognised – and remain themselves divided over – the significance of the title-phrase in framing the novel's representation of Russian politics, but few have paid close attention to the narrator's Romanised transliteration and translation of the keyword 'Western' from Russian intellectual debates.[20] Reading the title as itself divided between a Russian and an English scripting of the keyword 'Western' points towards a reciprocal effect of Romanisation on English. The

Romanised English form of the Russian term adopts and adapts a Russian idea of the West that shapes and transforms in turn the English formulation. The 'documentary evidence' of that Russian term marks the novel's title-phrase in ways analogous to the way the Romanised Malay 'Tuan' inflects (and ironises) the English title 'Lord' in *Lord Jim*.

Arguably the juxtaposition of Cyrillic and Roman print has at least as much claim as the Romanised Malay of *Almayer's Folly*, if not more, for priority in framing Conrad's relation to the space of Romanised English print. Although the Romanised Malay words inaugurate Conrad's entire career as an English writer, the juxtaposition of Roman and Cyrillic writing systems is more intimately bound up with Conrad's personal sense of his own Eastern European profile, 'that peculiar experience of race and family', as he famously puts it in the 'Author's Note' to *Under Western Eyes* (*UWE* 281). The intensity of Conrad's own divided identification both with and against 'things Russian' has often been attributed to his divided loyalties to his Polish inheritance; and notably, as David Smith argues, in the 'duality' Conrad 'felt in himself' between the revolutionary impulses of his father, Apollo Korzeniowski, and the more conservative politics of his uncle, Tadeusz Bobrowski:

> In what one might call a Bobrowskian mode, Conrad clearly identified with Razumov, the meliorist who could get along in a society but who was being prevented from doing so by Haldin, a revolutionary theorist, who symbolized what his father represented in politics and character.[21]

As Smith's argument further illuminates, the intensity of these divided loyalties shows up in the margins of Conrad's manuscript for *Under Western Eyes* in the compulsive repetition of the letter 'K', the mark (Smith argues) of Conrad's preoccupation with the semiotics of his own authorial identity, evident in the multiple signatures used throughout his life:

> These signatures (and their initials) are varied and chosen to suit the occasion, but schematically put, they were *Konrad Korzeniowski* or *K.K.*, *Joseph Conrad Korzeniowski*, or *J.C.K.*, and *Joseph Conrad* or *J.C*. There is an obvious layering in these identities, though *Konrad Korzeniowski* or *K.K.*, or more simply *Konrad*, or still more simply, *K*, was the deepest.[22]

The effect of this letter 'K' and the 'semiotics' of identity it encodes in Conrad's authorial signature is perhaps the most abbreviated form of the chronotope of Romanisation in Conrad's writing. Conrad himself underscores its significance when, in the last year of his life, he regretted not having been able to preserve the 'secret of my origins' beneath 'the neutral pseudonym Joseph Conrad'.[23]

## Romanised Polish

The pseudonym Joseph Conrad is neither Romanised Russian, nor the kind of Romanised Malay Conrad at one point thought of using as his pseudonym (Kamudi). It is, as it were, Romanised Polish. This brings me to the third example, the story 'Prince Roman'. The happy coincidence of the way the Polish 'Roman' translates into English 'Roman' provides a model for the kind of 'neutral' space of print Conrad seems to imagine for the 'neutral pseudonym' Joseph Conrad. Meant to be part of the reminiscences that became *A Personal Record*, the story has been described by Andrzej Busza as an exercise in translation, 'an attempt to give English expression to Polish structures'.[24] In this sense, the unique features of this story might provide a key to unlocking the hidden Polish perspective informing the timing and spacing of Romanised print form in Conrad's English.

To some extent this is precisely the kind of hidden narrative we have been trained to look for by a long and distinguished line of Conrad scholars. Hidden Polish linguistic and literary patterns are surely significant for revealing many aspects of *Under Western Eyes* (as Busza, Najder and Carabine, among many others, have shown) and for revealing many aspects of *Almayer's Folly* (as these same critics and also Jean Szczypien have shown).[25] As I want to argue here, however, it is the surface Romanised print form of 'Prince Roman' that provides a solution of sorts to the linguistic riddle presented by the earlier two examples.

The story merely transcribes the name 'Roman' into the Roman letters of English print – there is no conversion necessary, as happens with the re-transcription of the historical Charles William Olmeijer into the 'Kaspar Almayer' – 'Tuan Almayer' – of Conrad's novel; or in the English narrator's translation of Kyrilo Sidorovich into Cyril, son of Isidore; or in the transliteration of K to C in the adoption of Conrad's own authorial name. Yet this simple transcription is after all only as simple as the other forms of transcription, translation and the writing out of Roman letters that feature in the retelling of Prince Roman's story. To pick only two examples – the 'saying' '*Vae Victis*' in the opening paragraph; and the written confession 'I joined the national rising from conviction'[26] – both involve a complex relation to Roman print form. The first is put in the mouth of the speaker who tells Prince Roman's story – itself a revealing framing of narrative person, since this speaker is surely Conrad himself; a persona, however, distanced by the first-person narrator's opening comment of explanation in the second paragraph: 'The speaker was of Polish nationality' (*TH* 29). This distances, then, the more intense, first-person plural identification with the cause of Polish nationalism (in the key phrase 'for us'). The extent of that plural identification, indeed, is what is marked by the saying '*Vae Victis*' (Latin for 'woe to the conquered'): 'the year 1831 is *for us* an historical date, one of these fatal years when in the presence of the world's passive indignation and eloquent sympathies we had once more to murmur "*Vae Victis*" and count the cost in sorrow' (*TH* 29; my emphasis). The Latin saying aligns Polish historical experience with Roman letters in some ways like the 'old-time habit of larding . . . speech with Latin words' (*TH* 42) ascribed to Prince Roman's loyal servant later in the story. '*Vae Victis*', however, already brings with it a riddle of conquest that is more intimately tied to the way this 'Roman' history is written. The saying comes from Livy's *History of Rome*, where the words are attributed to the barbarian (Gaulish) leader Brennus. After the sack of Rome, asked to adjudicate complaints about the Gauls' unfair weighing of the gold the Romans have given to ransom their city, Brennus throws his sword onto the scales to make the cost even higher, and then 'a saying, intolerable to Roman ears, was heard, – Woe to the conquered! [*Vae Victis*]'.²⁷ The conquered have no rights – this is the bitter lesson of Roman conquest that is also, not coincidentally, an ambiguous and riddling parable of civilisation and barbarism, victor and vanquished, that haunts any transparent identification with a Roman lineage. Even the saying itself is ambiguously attributed, in Livy's passive construction, either to the voice of Brennus or to the murmurs of those witnessing the scene of injustice. This saying (voice or sound: 'vox') is Roman (or Romanised), yet 'intolerable' to Roman ears, transcribed into the written record of Roman history. And it is this ambiguously voiced barbarian–Roman experience of conquest that gives voice to the first-person plural voice of a Polish national identity about whom the first-person narrative voice then writes: 'The speaker was of Polish nationality, that nationality not so much alive as surviving, which persists in thinking, breathing, hoping, and suffering in its grave, railed in by a million of bayonets and triple-sealed with the seals of three great empires' (*TH* 29).

The effect of this framing motto as the immediate experience of a collective Polish national identity is echoed in the scene in which Prince Roman, refusing to accept the leniency extended by the Russian authorities, 'reached for a pen and wrote on a sheet of paper he found under his hand: "I joined the national rising from conviction"' (*TH* 52). Reportedly taken up later as the heraldic device for 'the Princes of the S— family, in all its branches', the last two words, 'from conviction', suggestively echo the effect of the motto '*Vae Victis*' in conveying a defiant adherence to that sense of Polish national communal identity earlier voiced in the first person plural ('for us'). The Latinate English word 'conviction' – echoing the Latin '*Victis*' – might suggest a hidden argument over Roman models of justice, the law and standards of civil rights. What makes Prince Roman's 'written testimony' all the more powerful, indeed, is the Russian emperor's comment, written 'with his own hand in the margin', converting the Latinate echo of Prince Roman's 'conviction' into another Latinate English word, 'convict': 'The authorities are severely warned to take care that this convict walks in chains like any other criminal every step of the way' (*TH* 53).

There is a gravity lent to the words 'from conviction' that both repeats and reformulates the opening motto '*Vae Victis*'. Whereas the Roman words are foregrounded as Latin script, Prince Roman's written testimony is translated into an English word that effaces whatever written form might originally have been used. Simply put, we aren't told what language – Polish, Russian, French or Latin – Prince Roman used for his 'written testimony'. Nor, for that matter, do we know for sure what language Emperor Nicholas used to write 'convict' in the margin of that 'written testimony'. No doubt these are things we might piece together – much in the way the 'extravagant mystery' of the 'cipher' Marlow discovers written in the margin of the English book in 'Heart of Darkness' is ultimately explained by the contrast between Cyrillic Russian and English Romanised print. It is clear that a variety of languages circulate, both in spoken and in written form, but all of these languages come together in the same time and space. One might emphasise the way the story's Romanised print form successfully turns Prince Roman's 'conviction' into an exemplary model of nationalism (along the lines of Anderson's argument about the role of 'print-capitalism' in the rise and spread of nationalism). Or one might emphasise the way it bitterly counts the cost of that 'conviction' (recalling Derrida's critique of the neo-colonial hegemony of 'globalatinisation' [*mondialatinisation*]).[28] Either way (victor or vanquished), these are the things that Conrad makes us *see* in a particular English timing and spacing of Romanised print.

The most transparent example of Roman print in Conrad, 'Prince Roman' might then enable us to reread all those other examples where the timing and spacing of Romanisation don't so perfectly align – as, for instance, in the vexed and obsessive form of transliteration marked by the alternation between the letters C and K in Conrad's authorial signature. In its very singularity, 'Prince Roman' reveals the irreducible plurality of *Romanisation* that makes Romanised print form the site of multiple, overlapping, and contested languages, cultures and histories.

'Prince Roman' effects, then, an idealised mirroring of Roman print and any other language. Everywhere else in Conrad's works, however, including Marlow's discovery of the English book in 'Heart of Darkness', Romanised print effects a doubling and splitting of letters, names and whole narrative segments. So, in *Under Western Eyes*, the doubling and splitting of narrative levels creates a bewildering narrative complexity. This may seem to be based on the opposing logic of two different languages (English and Russian), scripts (Roman and Cyrillic), perhaps even two different spatio-temporal topoi (Geneva and St Petersburg).[29] In fact, the narrative's ghostly effects are generated, rather, by the way Conrad makes Russian and English converge on the shared timing and spacing (*chronotope*) of Romanised print. Despite what the narrator claims about the 'blackened pages' of Haldin's letter – that they appear 'cabalistic, incomprehensible to the experience of Western Europe' (*UWE* 99) – the narrator succeeds in conveying not only Haldin's messianic convictions, but also Razumov's conflicted and divided responses to those convictions (and 'conviction' is the shared keyword here, as Debra Romanick Baldwin points out in her discussion of 'Prince Roman').[30] Directly refuting the narrator, Razumov himself draws attention to the contradictory logic in the narrator's ascribing a Russian ethos to Cyrillic script and a Western European ethos to Roman script: 'In Russia, and in general everywhere – in a newspaper, for instance. The colour of the ink and the shapes of the letters are the same' (*UWE* 139). Contradicting the novel's governing contrast between Cyrillic and Roman scripts, Razumov's statement sounds at first counterfactual: despite the overlap between Cyrillic and Roman alphabets, it is difficult to sustain the argument that 'the shapes of the letters are the same' for both. If by 'shapes' Razumov means the general form, or principle, or idea of the letter, however, one might recognise his point as underscoring the merely instrumental function of writing in providing any reader, potentially, with access to what is written; and, perhaps still more to the point, as insisting that writing is not determining of a national, linguistic or racial character. Razumov's disregard for the narrator's exaggerated contrast between Cyrillic and Roman alphabets might be seen to reciprocate the universalising assumption of Romanisation (the assumption that all languages and scripts can be transcribed, transliterated and translated into Roman letters) with a corresponding universalising assumption about Cyrillisation.

Put another way, the exaggerated English Romanisation of Russian (as in 'Cyril son of Isidor') is matched by a reciprocal Russian Romanisation of English. The most striking example of this is, as we have seen, the keyword 'Western'. The narrator's account of his conversation with Nathalie reveals how this word (and its various cognates) get adapted and adopted – Romanised – from the specifically Russian terms of intellectual debate, used by the narrator (with increasing emphasis and staged incomprehension) to apply to an English self-characterisation shaped by the Romanised Russian word and idea.

## Romanised English

The reciprocal effects of Romanisation are, in some respects, still more striking in the case of *Almayer's Folly*. Opening with the delayed translation-effect of 'Kaspar! Makan!', the novel closes with Abdulla 'piously' reciting the 'bismillah' – 'in a solemn whisper he breathed out piously the name of Allah! The Merciful! The Compassionate!' (*AF* 208). With deliberative irony, the English print of the novel is reframed within the timing and spacing of formulaic Arabic scripture and script. What might certainly be read as Conrad's ironic reversal of the Orientalist opposition between European and Arab interests may also be read, however, in terms of the rival forms of Arabic (or *Jawi*) script and Romanised (*Rumi*) print Malay. The final evocation of Arabic script and scripture, of course, is itself rendered in *Romanised* English print; but this only underscores the reciprocal effects of Romanised Malay on the novel's English. Abdulla is Arab, but also a British subject, whose accommodation with the Dutch is entirely compatible with the logic of both free trade and Islam: he embodies the triumphant ethos of multinational capitalism. Abdulla's final words have something like the same effect as the motto '*Vae Victis*', marking, in the space of Romanised print, the final victory of his trading interests over 'Lingard and Co.'. On the office door of the house that will be renamed in Chinese characters 'House of Heavenly Delight' (*AF* 205), those 'half obliterated words' ('Office: Lingard and Co.') signal early on in the novel the multiplying ironies of Romanised English print forms. Whereas the *telling* of the story invests a great deal (Conrad's literary career, for example) in a future English-language readership, the future of the story itself lies in the Malay-language intrigues to which Almayer, in his 'folly', is deaf. The import of Mrs Almayer's opening Malay words has yet to be decoded fully.[31] Within the story itself, English doesn't seem to have such a splendid future at all. Almayer's knowledge of English, though good for business – playing a role in securing his partnership with Lingard – stands, from the very beginning of the novel, as a misplaced dream of splendid future possibilities that will never transpire. With Lingard gone, he lives in a house of unfulfilled English promises. This returns us, however, to the Romanised Malay form of the novel's opening words: the space of

Romanised print Malay, juxtaposed with the concluding evocation of an Arabic script, opens the Romanised *English* print form of the novel itself – and Conrad's novelistic career to come – to a much wider range of scripts, including by the way Dutch, Arabic, Buginese, Javanese, Thai and Chinese; and, most notably, the form of revolutionary Malay that will forge the language of anti-colonial Indonesian nationalism.

In conclusion, the reciprocal effects of 'Romanisation' on the way Conrad uses English make his work a particularly relevant point of reference for a genealogy of contemporary Romanised print form. Demanding, I think, a reassessment of Benedict Anderson's model of 'print-capitalism' and Jacques Derrida's rather different formulation of '*mondialatinisation*', such a genealogy might make more precise the 'hybridity' and 'ambivalence' Homi Bhabha claims for the privileged trope of the 'English book'.[32] Conrad's work might thus make visible the process of *Romanisation* that continues to turn English into a site of multiple, conflicting histories of language, literature and culture.

## Notes

1. Ian Watt, *Conrad in the Nineteenth Century* (Berkeley: University of California Press, 1980), p. 168ff.
2. Joseph Conrad, *Almayer's Folly* (Oxford: Oxford University Press, 1992), p. 11. Subsequent references are cited in the text as *AF*.
3. For an initial exploration of this argument, see my 'Romanization and the Digital Future of Philology', *Postmedieval: A Journal of Medieval Cultural Studies* 5.4 (Winter 2014), pp. 428–41.
4. Tanya Gokulsing, 'Polishness, Modernism and the Manipulation of Time: Conrad's Use of "Now" in *Almayer's Folly*', in Andrzej Ciuk and Marcin Piechota (eds), *Conrad's Europe* (Opole: Joseph Conrad Society, Poland, 2005), pp. 153–61.
5. Mikhail Bakhtin, *The Dialogic Imagination: Four Essays*, trans. Caryl Emerson and Michael Holquist (Austin: University of Texas Press, 1981), p. 84.
6. Ibid. p. 250.
7. Asako Nakai, *The English Book and Its Marginalia* (Amsterdam: Rodopi, 2000), p. 27.
8. Homi Bhabha, *The Location of Culture* (New York: Routledge, 1994), p. 105.
9. Nakai, *English Book*, p. 20.
10. Cedric Watts, *The Deceptive Text: An Introduction to Covert Plots* (Brighton: Harvester, 1984).
11. Joseph Conrad, *Lord Jim* (London: J. M. Dent and Sons, 1923), p. 5.
12. The significance of the Malay 'Tuan' for the problem of entitlement in *Lord Jim* is discussed in my *The Invention of the West: Joseph Conrad and the*

*Double-Mapping of Europe and Empire* (Stanford: Stanford University Press, 1995), pp. 88–105. More recently, I have explored in what sense the Malay term 'Tuan' (in both *Lord Jim* and *Almayer's Folly*) encodes an effaced reference to the term 'nyai' (the colonial Malay term for mistress, maid and/or concubine) (see *The Passage of Literature: Genealogies of Modernism in Conrad, Rhys, and Pramoedya* [New York: Oxford University Press, 2011], pp. 153–75). Since the term 'nyai' is a transcription and translation from the Javanese into Malay, the volatile racial and sexual problems of entitlement it encodes in the corresponding term 'tuan' emerge from a crossing over between at least three different scriptings of Malay: *Kawi* (Old Javanese), *Jawi* (Arabic) and *Rumi* (Roman).

13. See, for example, Robert Hampson, *Cross-Cultural Encounters in Joseph Conrad's Malay Fiction* (New York: Palgrave, 2000); Sanjay Krishnan, *Reading the Global: Troubling Perspectives on Britain's Empire in Asia* (New York: Columbia University Press, 2007); Agnes S. K. Yeow, *Conrad's Eastern Vision: A Vain and Floating Appearance* (New York: Palgrave, 2009); Andrew Francis, *Culture and Commerce in Conrad's Asian Fiction* (Cambridge: Cambridge University Press, 2015).
14. See my *Passage of Literature*.
15. Benedict Anderson, *Imagined Communities: Reflections on the Origin and Spread of Nationalism*, rev. edn (London: Verso, 1991), p. 133.
16. For an excellent discussion of this within the context of Malay literary traditions see Henk Maier, *We Are Playing Relatives: A Survey of Malay Writing* (Leiden: KITVL Press, 2004).
17. Joseph Conrad, *Under Western Eyes* (Oxford: Oxford University Press, 2003), p. 3. Subsequent references are cited in the text as *UWE*.
18. For an excellent and succinct account of this multiple layering of texts see Shafquat Towheed, 'Geneva v. St. Petersburg: Two Concepts of Literary Property and the Material Lives of Books in Under Western Eyes', *Book History* 10 (2007), pp. 169–91, esp. pp. 177–8.
19. See, for example, Andrzej Busza's 'Rhetoric and Ideology in Conrad's *Under Western Eyes*', in Norman Sherry (ed.), *Joseph Conrad: A Commemoration* (London: Macmillan, 1976), pp. 105–18; Keith Carabine, *The Life and the Art: A Study of Conrad's Under Western Eyes* (Amsterdam: Rodopi, 1996); Daniel Darvay, 'The Politics of Gothic in Conrad's *Under Western Eyes*', *Modern Fiction Studies* 55.4 (Winter 2009), pp. 693–715; my *Invention of the West*; and David R. Smith, 'The Hidden Narrative: The *K* in Conrad', in *Joseph Conrad's Under Western Eyes: Beginnings, Revisions, Final Forms* (Hamden, CT: Archon Books, 1991), pp. 39–81.
20. See, for example, the contrasting readings of Eloise Knapp Hay, *The Political Novels of Joseph Conrad: A Critical Study* (Chicago: University of Chicago Press, 1963); Avrom Fleishman, *Conrad's Politics: Community and Anarchy in the Fiction of Joseph Conrad* (Baltimore: Johns Hopkins University Press, 1967); my own *Invention of the West*; Carabine, *Life and the Art*; and Darvay, 'Politics of Gothic', p. 707.
21. Smith, 'Hidden Narrative', p. 65.
22. Ibid. p. 42.
23. G. Jean-Aubry, *Joseph Conrad: Life and Letters*, 2 vols (New York: Doubleday, 1927), Vol. 2, p. 336.

24. Cited in Owen Knowles and Gene Moore (eds), *The Oxford Reader's Companion to Conrad* (Oxford: Oxford University Press, 2000), p. 328.
25. See Andrzej Busza, 'Conrad's Polish Literary Background and Some Illustrations of the Influence of Polish Literature on His Work', *Antemurale* 10 (1966), pp. 109–255 (Rome: Institutum Historicum Polonicum, 1966); Zdzisław Najder, *Conrad's Polish Background: Letters to and from Polish Friends* (Oxford: Oxford University Press, 1964), and *Joseph Conrad: A Chronicle* (New Brunswick, NJ: Rutgers University Press, 1983); Carabine, *Life and the Art*; Jean Szczypien, 'Joseph Conrad's *A Personal Record*: Composition, Intention, Design: Polonism', *Journal of Modern Literature* 16.1 (Summer 1989), pp. 3–30, and 'Untyrannical Copy-Texts for the Prefatory Essays to Joseph Conrad's *A Personal Record*', *Conradian* 9.2 (1984), pp. 81–9.
26. Joseph Conrad, *Tales of Hearsay* (London: J. M. Dent and Sons, 1928), p. 52. Subsequent references are cited in the text as *TH*.
27. Livy, *The History of Rome*, Books V, VI and VII with an English translation, ed. Benjamin Oliver Foster (London: William Heinemann, 1924), p. 165.
28. See Jacques Derrida, 'Faith and Knowledge', in *Acts of Religion* (New York: Routledge, 2002), pp. 40–101.
29. See Paul Kirschner, 'Topodialogic Narrative in *Under Western Eyes* and the Rasoumoffs of "La Petite Russie"', in Gene M. Moore (ed.), *Conrad's Cities: Essays for Hans van Marle* (Amsterdam: Rodopi, 1992), pp. 223–54.
30. Debra Romanick Baldwin, 'Simple Ideas and Narrative Solidarity in "Prince Roman"', *Conradian* 35.1 (Spring 2010), pp. 17–27.
31. For more on this (and specifically Mrs Almayer's Sulu background) see Andrew Francis's chapter in this volume. See also Julie Beth Napolin, '"A Sinister Resonance": Joseph Conrad's Malay Ear and Auditory Cultural Studies', *Sounding Out! The Sound Studies Blog*, 9 July 2015. Available at <http://soundstudiesblog.com/2015/07/09/a-sinister-resonance-joseph-conrads-malay-ear-and-auditory-cultural-studies> (last accessed 26 January 2016).
32. See Homi Bhabha, 'Signs Taken for Wonders: Questions of Ambivalence and Authority under a Tree outside Delhi, May 1817', *Critical Inquiry* 12.1 (Autumn 1985), pp. 144–65 at p. 150.

Chapter 8

# Languages in Conrad's Malay Fiction

*Andrew Francis*

In Najeeb M. Saleeby's *The History of Sulu*[1] there is a map of the Sulu Sultanate that included the Sulu Archipelago and north-east Borneo, a small part of the region in which Conrad's Malay fiction is set.[2] The map contains no names in English – albeit the Sulu Sultanate was by then a possession of the USA – apart from one example off the remote (to Europeans) north-east coast of Borneo, between Borneo and the Sulu Archipelago. Here, the words 'Alice Channel' cut visually and linguistically across this part of the map, the two foreign, colonial words intruding upon the area and the Sultanate, the long independent history of which prior to Spanish colonisation it was part of Saleeby's purpose to record.

This linguistic intrusion can serve as an exemplar of the complexities of language that characterised the linguistic environment in the Malay Archipelago in the latter half of the nineteenth and early part of the twentieth centuries, when Conrad's Malay fiction is set. This chapter will explore these complexities, assisted by some recovery of the historical context of the Malay fiction's setting in a turmoil of languages. Of the languages mentioned in the Malay fiction, the main focus, for reasons of space, will be on English as a foreign language, Malay and Sulu, although no words in Sulu appear in this fiction. This focus will largely exclude Arabic, Chinese, Dutch, Portuguese and Spanish, not to mention the hundreds of other languages of the Archipelago that are implied linguistic presences, such as the language of the 'Goram vagabonds' with whom Heyst sails in *Victory*.[3] The aim will be to demonstrate a number of aspects of Conrad's use of languages. First, that responses to language use form part of the way in which the colonial enterprise is represented. Secondly, that language use can be seen as not only part of the colonising process (including, with some recovery of historical context, issues of language enforcement and a certain hegemony of alphabets) but also part of the colonised impacting on the colonisers.

Thirdly, that the frequent reference to non-European languages being spoken is part of how Conrad gives the voiceless a voice. And, fourthly, that 'broken' language and language dispossession, sometimes presented as impairments to language, are powerfully symptomatic in the Malay fiction of a confusion of cultural relations recognisable alongside other modes of Conrad's representation of colonialism and of the human condition more widely.[4]

As if to register such issues from the outset, the opening words of Conrad's first novel, *Almayer's Folly*[5] – 'Kaspar! Makan!' – a summons by Mrs Almayer to her husband to dinner, are (as Christopher GoGwilt mentions in the previous chapter in this volume) not English, but a Dutch name and a Malay verb. Furthermore, these words are spoken by someone who originated from the independent Sultanate of Sulu and who, although sometimes regarded rather generally as Malay, is almost certainly a native speaker not of Malay but of Sulu, someone for whom *makan* is therefore almost certainly a foreign word.[6] This linguistic context poses questions about not only linguistic but wider relations: just as Conrad's characters are frequently physically displaced, so in the Malay fiction they are often also displaced from their or others' language, the two opening words adding complexity with regard to cultural relations and issues of communication while also acting as an example of the complexities, alienation and ambivalences inherent in the colonial enterprise.

Much has been written on Conrad's use of language but much less on the literary role that languages play as languages in his fiction, rather than, for example, as instances of the use of foreign vocabulary. Because both Conrad's knowledge of languages and the linguistic environment in the Malay Archipelago at the time of his visits are relevant, brief accounts of these follow.

## Conrad's linguistic inheritance

There has been continuing critical attention to Conrad's interest in, and use of, the languages that are considered to have contributed to his linguistic sensitivity, a sensitivity reflected in the many references to language in his writing. Polonisms and Gallicisms have been observed in Conrad's English, and Barbara Koc observed, from the fact that Conrad's glosses on his letters from Tadeusz Bobrowski were in French, that at that time 'the French language was for Conrad the most convenient to use and that he had spoken it, for a long time, with the greatest fluency'.[7] Such discussions highlight the presence in his mind of three different cultures and their individual modes of linguistic expression.

In an authoritative essay, 'The Gift of Tongues: The Languages of Joseph Conrad', Martin Ray carried out a study of, primarily, the languages Conrad knew.[8] Though not specifically a study of the roles that different languages might play in Conrad's fiction as part of his representation of, for example, human relations or culture, Ray's study focuses helpfully on Conrad's 'interest in multilingualism'. Ray observes that Conrad demonstrates throughout his work 'the interdependence and fragmentary nature of all tongues'.[9] Conrad's own multilingualism is often discussed in terms of his linguistic competences, but it might equally focus on his shortcomings. Indeed, Conrad described the challenge that English posed for him as having 'to work like a coalminer in his pit quarrying all my English sentences out of a black night' (*CL4* 112).[10] Ray remarks that

> it is a matter of contention whether Conrad accepted the limitations and lack of precision in English and proceeded to write in defiance of them, or whether (as is more probable) he was attracted to the language precisely because of the stylistic freedom which these apparent defects gave him.[11]

Ray rightly feels that it is best to concern ourselves with the effects rather than the causes of Conrad's decision: 'two of the most prominent are an acute detachment, even isolation, from his medium, and a fundamental suspicion about the nature of the language he employs'.[12] As we consider the role of languages in his Malay fiction, Conrad's multilingualism can be seen to parallel that of a number of his characters and of the Malay region more widely in his time. The questions of what, for example, constitutes a foreign language, what it is to speak in a language not one's own, and the cultural significance and history of a language are germane not only to Conrad personally, but also to his fiction.

Conrad's knowledge of Malay was of a different order from his knowledge of Polish, French and English. His short spells in the Malay Archipelago in the 1880s cannot realistically have provided sufficient opportunity, whether on land or sea, to master the language. Ray, however, believes that Conrad 'rapidly learned' Malay, citing two sources: Jerry Allen, *The Sea Years of Joseph Conrad*, and Frederick R. Karl, *Joseph Conrad, The Three Lives: A Biography*.[13]

However, Karl does not state that Conrad knew Malay to any extent, simply that 'the ever-present mix of languages of French, English, Malayan, Polish' was one of Conrad's 'several levels of awareness' at the time he was writing *Almayer's Folly*.[14] Allen writes that 'Conrad's own talent as a linguist, so evident in English, also enabled him to pick up Malay, and quickly',[15] but this doesn't necessarily mean any degree of mastery of the language; perhaps a limited number of words needed for ship and shore life in the Archipelago. However, Allen, in a reference not cited by Ray, also quotes Captain F. C. Hendry's recollection of the master of the *Vidar*, Captain Craig, stating that 'Conrad learned to speak Malay fluently, though with a peculiar guttural accent, in an incredibly short time.'[16] This recollection of Captain Hendry's goes back a number of decades from when his book was published in 1950, which may make it less reliable (unless the text was written earlier). It may also be that the remarkable later life of Conrad encouraged exaggerated recollections, to which the nature of Malay grammar – the absence, for example, of conjugation and declension wrongly suggesting to some that the language could be easily mastered – may also have contributed.[17] Amy Houston mentions Florence Clemens's view that 'Conrad knew only the trade Malay language, which he would need in his commercial travels', although Houston demonstrates that Conrad used other types of Malay words as well.[18]

## Taming the languages of the Malay Archipelago

The languages mentioned in Conrad's Malay fiction might appear to be stable elements, the words for those languages signifying vocabularies and grammars readily definable and capable of unproblematic differentiation from other languages. But languages in this fiction are as much a part of the disturbance that Conrad portrays in other aspects of relations – political, economic and social – on which colonial intrusion is the major influence.

Those who wished to record language in Conrad's time in the Archipelago were faced with a very similar challenge to those working in the fields of cartography and hydrography. Pilot guides were ever-growing in size but recognised their limitations in providing a comprehensive view, and for cartographers much remained to be recorded. The languages of the Archipelago had similarly long been recognised as very numerous and little understood. P. A. M. Boele van Hensbroek recorded in 1875 some twenty-seven categories of language in the Malay possessions of the Dutch, but these included some broad summaries of groups of languages and dialects that were not individually listed. For example, for Borneo merely Dayak and 'overige talen en dialekten' ('other languages and dialects'), a phrase that hardly conveys the linguistic variety of Borneo, were noted.[19] Robert N. Cust listed eighty-eight languages and twenty-nine dialects in his 'Malayan Family' (although this included Formosa and Madagascar). Cust gave 'A Language Map of Further India and the Indian Archipelago' to show where some of these languages were spoken, but acknowledged that 'there is great uncertainty'.[20] Modern estimates put the number of languages and dialects at at least several hundred.

Europeans sought to order this variety by creating a linguistic taxonomy, much as their counterparts in botany were doing. Dictionaries were created, and orthographies applied to languages that did not have one or that did not use the Roman alphabet.[21] A start was made with Malay, the language that the respected linguist William Marsden described as 'having commonly received the appellation of the *lingua franca* of the east', an often-used term.[22] Thomas Bowrey had published a Malay–English dictionary in 1701, and James Howison another a hundred years later; William Marsden's appeared in 1812, and John Crawfurd's *Grammar and Dictionary* in 1852; Hugh Clifford and Frank Athelstane Swettenham published their *Dictionary* some fifty years later, and there were others.[23] There was also a persistent attempt to classify Malay into, in effect, two languages, 'Low' and 'High' Malay. N. B. Dennys distinguished between 'high' or 'pure' Malay and that spoken by foreign residents of Singapore. J. Pijnappel, however, the Dutch Indies scholar and dictionary compiler, albeit finding it necessary sometimes to refer to '*Classical*-Malay', argued that the term 'Low-Malay' was misleading and unhelpful.[24] Other languages of the region received similar but less attention from the British. William Clark Cowie edited his brother's vocabulary of Sulu, a book that had been preceded by essays in British Asian journals, such as Alexander Dalrymple's 'Essay towards an Account of Sulu', which speculated on the roots of the Sulu language but acknowledged that it was not clear what other languages there were in the Sulu islands or how, or whether, they were related to each other.[25] So many apparently were the languages that were not properly, if at all, recorded (not only in south-east Asia), and so worthwhile the recording of them, that John Bellows published an *Outline Dictionary* 'chiefly intended for English and American travellers and Missionaries engaged in collecting the words and grammatical forms of new languages or dialects, of which we possess, as yet, either no dictionary or grammar, or only very incomplete ones'.[26]

Both Malay and Sulu had used the Arabic (*Jawi*) alphabet, following the arrival of Arab immigrants particularly from the thirteenth century. This was an additional barrier to Europeans, who set about using the Roman alphabet, although it, like the Arabic, could only approximate the pronunciation of some Malay sounds. W. Robinson, a missionary at the faltering British colony of Bencoolen on the west coast of Sumatra, published a book aptly titled *An Attempt to Elucidate the Principles of Malayan Orthography*, in which he tries to establish 'a more correct system of Roman orthography, than has hitherto appeared'.[27] As William Edward Maxwell remarked, 'those follow but a vain shadow who seek to prescribe exact modes of spelling words regarding which even native authorities are not agreed, and of which the pronunciation may vary according to locality'.[28]

Knowledge of the Archipelago's languages by Britain's south-east Asia rivals, the Dutch, was acknowledged to be superior to that of the British, something that Maxwell observed:

> The extent and value of Dutch works on Malay subjects is, however, but little known to Englishmen in the East, owing to their general ignorance of the Dutch language. It is not too much to say that anyone aiming at a thorough knowledge of the language, literature, and history of the Malay people should commence his task by learning Dutch.[29]

### Languages in transition, language enforcement, 'broken' language and language loss

Other languages were also present, brought in by trade and colonial intrusion, the linguistic fluidity of their use often revealing language loss as well as acquisition. New arrivals, whether from the Archipelago, the wider region or Europe, brought with them their mother tongue but had to adapt linguistically. The Dutch, unable to cope with the many languages of their growing East Indies possessions despite civil servants' training in one or more of the major languages, therefore imposed – in addition to government, law and economic organisation – a linguistic requirement. This prescribed the use of Malay in those areas where it was not the lingua franca, but as Drewes observed, 'it does not seem that this by-language, no matter how well it is studied, will ever be able to replace the country [that is, local] tongue'. Drewes went on to relate the western Sumatran Minangkabaus' feeling that in Malay 'their thoughts were robbed of their "flavour"'.[30]

Thomson writes revealingly about language use in the region.[31] In Malacca – a town with a colonial heritage that had changed from Portuguese to Dutch to British – he communicates the bewildering exchange of personal and ethnic, including linguistic, characteristics, a fluidity revealing itself further in language loss:

> Here the Hindoo features are most remarkably apparent in that Chinese, with shaven head and long tail; there that coal-black woolly-headed personage calls himself a Portuguese; and yonder fair, flaxen-haired, blue-eyed youth says he is a Malay. Again, that yellow-skinned, oblique-eyed, flat-faced, snub-nosed gentleman says he is a Dutchman. The climate of Malacca is a surprising one

in creating such incongruities. In two generations an Englishman becomes a Negro, a Chinaman a Chitty, a Malay becomes a Brahmin, and a round lusty German changes into a dried-up leather-jawed Arab.

The languages are soon forgotten, and all merge into the universal Malay. Not to say that broken-Dutch-English-and-Portuguese are not used; but these are enunciated in the Malay idiom, so that they are so disguised as not to be understood excepting by true-born Malacca men.[32]

The languages of all three successive colonial rulers are seen to be vulnerable, in particular to 'the Malay idiom'.

Arab immigrants to the Archipelago provide a particularly striking example of language loss. Coming without wives, they married Indies women. Though relatively small in number, their political, diplomatic and religious influence was great, and they might, perhaps, have been expected to ensure that their linguistic inheritance persisted. Instead, however, as L. W. C. van den Berg writes:

> The Arabs of the Indian Archipelago have married either indigenous women or the daughters of their fellow-countrymen, women who have never been outside the Archipelago and who as a result are exactly the same as the indigenous women as far as language, culture and customs are concerned.
>
> A primary result of this is that the language spoken in the Arabs' homes is not Arabic but Malay or Javanese, in other words the language of their wives. It is also the language the Arab men speak to their children. When the boys grow up they learn a little Arabic; the girls only learn a few forms of words from the Koran or used in prayer. And once the Arabs have been resident in the Indian Archipelago for some time they speak and read Malay as if it was a second mother tongue. Only their pronunciation remains peculiar to them. As for Malay, they all speak it, even if their wives and children only understand, for example, Javanese.[33]

The tendency for linguistic assimilation, quite apart from other aspects of cultural assimilation, was therefore marked, something that was also observed of Chinese immigrants, who also married indigenous wives and who needed to speak, if not Malay, at least one regional language. Somerset Maugham observed of the Chinese in a fictionalised Malacca: 'Many have forgotten their native language and hold intercourse with one another in Malay and pidgin English.'[34] The Dutch were concerned about their own children, who spoke 'Low Malay' even 'before they know their own Language'.[35] In *Lord Jim*, Cornelius, himself a Malacca Portuguese and able at least to pronounce 'horrible blasphemies in Portuguese', has been 'clerk in some commercial house in the Dutch colonies' and therefore no doubt speaks Dutch (*LJ* 329, 220). He can also speak English and, presumably, Malay. In the same way as Kurtz in 'Heart of Darkness' is of mixed European heritage, so Cornelius is of mixed colonial heritage, speaking the languages (to an extent at least) of all three colonial powers in the Archipelago. His linguistic character subtly conveys something of the history of the region's extensive colonisation, but also provides a fuller sense of his background and heritage than Marlow's description of him as merely 'the awful little Malacca Portuguese' (*LJ* 276).

## The incidence of 'half-uttered expression' (*LJ* 174)

Cornelius's English seems good, even though we might expect otherwise from his past, and Conrad does not represent his spoken English literally, in the way that he does that of some other characters in *Lord Jim* to signify the non-native speaker.[36] Jacques Berthoud lists various non-English characters in *Lord Jim* whose use of English Conrad portrays, remarking of these that '*Lord Jim* could lay claim to being the first novel to exploit the vagaries of international English'.[37] But the implications of, and reasons for, such language representation need to be considered. In the examples cited by Berthoud, the representations of the characters' language use is part of the means by which they are realised by Conrad as characters, their language use not only indicating their foreignness but extending the ways in which Conrad's writing is concerned with displacement and alienation.

Berthoud refers to 'the malaprop volubility' of the master of Stein's brigantine in *Lord Jim*, as if to suggest that the significance of the extended description and of the direct and reported speech of this ship's captain, who is to take Jim to the estuary of the river downstream from Patusan, is muddle.[38] Marlow responds to the captain's use of English with amusement and colonial superiority, as if this is how an Englishman abroad might be expected to react, akin to the Dutch tendency to look down on Eurasians in the Dutch East Indies for not being able to speak Dutch properly.

The episode provides insight into Marlow's colonial attitudes and, by the same measure, questions any assumption that the Englishness, and the language of English, embodied in Marlow or Jim (or indeed Lingard) comprise a foundational and proprietary British perspective through which a reader should expect the world properly and exclusively to be viewed and expressed. Marlow introduces the ship's captain as 'a dapper little half-caste', the adjectives suggesting a man less than man-sized, his dress not conforming to British notions of correct attire, 'dapper' suggesting someone too neat, too well-finished (*LJ* 238). Again, there is a link with Dutch colonial disdain for Indo-Europeans' sense of dress (as implied by Willems's description of his brother-in-law Leonard's dress in *An Outcast of the Islands*). Similarly, the captain has only a 'thin little black moustache' and a 'smirking' expression (*LJ* 238). Further on, Marlow refers to 'that half-caste croaker' and to 'the insufferably conceited air of his kind' (*LJ* 241, 240). The captain's face is also described in derogatory terms: 'the little wretch's face, the shape and colour of a ripe pumpkin' (*LJ* 241).

Marlow's mocking attitude to the captain's use of English parallels his attitude to the captain's appearance and character:

> His flowing English seemed to be derived from a dictionary compiled by a lunatic. Had Mr. Stein desired him to 'ascend,' he would have 'reverentially' – (I think he wanted to say respectfully – but devil only knows) – 'reverentially made objects for the safety of properties.' If disregarded, he would have presented 'resignation to quit.' ... Keeping one eye on the movements of his crew forward, he let loose his volubility – comparing the place to a 'cage of beasts made ravenous by long impenitence.' I fancy he meant impunity. (*LJ* 238–9)

Marlow's disdainful amusement is made more significant by its being positioned between passages in which he shows imaginative sympathy for Jim, a sympathy Marlow is unable to extend to the captain, who is clearly not 'one of us' (*LJ* 43). In fact, the captain is particularly deserving of sympathy, having suffered the terrifying experience when he last went to Patusan of being tied up by the neck for a day and a night in 'a mud-hole before the Rajah's house' (*LJ* 240). Marlow's mockery is expressed in terms of unpleasant dismissiveness: 'devil only knows' and 'I fancy he meant' attempt to locate the captain further and further away from any claim to linguistic competence, even to suggest stupidity (*LJ* 239). Marlow, in fact, is betraying colonial attitudes in what stands as one of the most telling representations of those attitudes anywhere in *Lord Jim*.

While Marlow focuses on the strangeness of the captain's English, it reveals itself in terms of vocabulary as educated and sophisticated, and in terms of its meaning is clear enough. 'Resignation to quit' may be tautologous, and Marlow may describe the language as 'absurd chatter', but it is effective, as is 'propitiated many offertories' – a form of curiously developed English (*LJ* 239–40). The captain rightly has 'pride [in] his fluency' and his use of English has, as Marlow admits, 'the undeniable effect of his phraseology'; the captain's beginning later 'to speak judicially' is a further indication of his command of the language and of registers that 'absurd chatter' attempts to belittle (*LJ* 239–40). The captain's language thus repays closer examination than Marlow's sweeping judgement and resists Marlow's assumptions about apparently normal English: the captain's hybrid English is reshaped just as other aspects of existence and culture were reshaped by colonialism and trade, and shows the colonisers' culture undergoing modification by the colonised. The captain describes Jim, in a powerfully expressive and ironic phrase, as 'in the similitude of a corpse', to which he adds 'already like the body of one deported' (*LJ* 241, 240). The concreteness of 'corpse' and 'body' arrest the reader amid the hybrid English; and the oddly chosen 'deported' recalls the retreating movement Jim has previously enacted in his efforts to escape his past. Marlow merely describes these observations by the captain as having been made 'with the insufferably conceited air of his kind after what they imagine a display of cleverness', a totalising view centred on an ethnic type (*LJ* 240). Tellingly, this hybrid, expressive English is followed by the clipped and somewhat formulaic and impoverished phraseology of Marlow and Jim, when Marlow says: 'I believe I called him "dear boy," and he tacked on the words "old man" to some half-uttered expression of gratitude', language far removed from the captain's imagery (*LJ* 240–1). In the captain's language we are taken away from our linguistic norms, a type of postcolonial language having apparently planted itself in the colonisers' language to make it new and subtly independent linguistically, while the dialogue between Marlow and Jim instantiates the restricted code of their class.[39]

The example of the ship's captain's use of English is but one of a wide range of language use that suggests a turmoil of communication in the Malay fiction. Other characters also speak languages badly, or surprise someone by unexpectedly speaking in a particular language, show signs of language loss or speak the wrong language. 'A strange Chinaman' and Jim-Eng both speak 'bad Malay' (*AF* 134, 205) in *Almayer's Folly*, as does Massy in 'The End of the Tether'.[40] Jewel 'had learned a good bit of English from Jim' (*LJ* 283), but they can also speak to each other in Malay, in which Jim, however, may not be proficient. Heyst and Wang in *Victory* speak 'in such Malay as we are both equal to' (*V* 348). Jörgenson in *The Rescue* declares: 'I can speak English, I can speak Dutch, I can speak every cursed lingo of these islands … but I have forgotten the language of my own country.'[41] Heemskirk finds fault with Nelson in 'Freya of the Seven Isles' for his not conforming to Dutch colonial superiority by learning Dutch. In *Almayer's Folly* Almayer speaks to his servant Ali mainly in English rather than Malay, so that Ali can understand, Malay presumably being a foreign language to Ali, who is from Sumatra. Nina surprises her father by speaking to him suddenly in English instead of Malay. In 'Karain: A Memory' Karain and Pata Matara cannot always be understood in Java; perhaps some in Java, speaking Javanese, could understand neither Karain's and Pata Matara's native Buginese nor, possibly, Malay. And in linguistic terms, reminiscent of the numerous occasions in which the tables are turned, so to speak, on the Europeans in the Malay fiction – as when Leonard in *An Outcast of the Islands* says to Willems: 'You are a savage. Not at all like we, whites'[42] – the colonisers are made the Other of the Other by speaking an 'unintelligible stream of words' as heard by 'the Chinaman marker' in that novel (*OI* 6). And Willems's wife, who usually speaks to her husband in Dutch but who presumably also knows Malay, is revealed as being from Macassar and therefore knowing Buginese (or its related Makassarese), as if placing her even further from the empty European values of Willems. It is as if, in this fiction set at the colonial and modernist edge, language is on the verge of losing its communicative strength. On a linguistic continuum we might place Abdulla's carefully and decorously written communications in *Almayer's Folly* at one extreme. From there language use and proficiency might extend through languages not fully learned, to languages invented out of necessity (such as the old serang's pidgin English in *The Rescue*), to languages not understood, and on, finally, to sound alone, where, for example, Heyst feels of Lena that 'if she only could talk to him in some unknown tongue, she would enslave him altogether by the sheer beauty of the sound, suggesting infinite depths of wisdom and feeling' (*V* 209).

## The significance of Sulu, and further taming

Malay and English feature most commonly as the languages used in Conrad's Malay fiction, with Malay, though occasionally appearing as words in Malay, being mainly referred to as the language in which various characters are speaking as the narrative nevertheless proceeds in English. We have already noted the implied presence of other languages in this fiction, such as Arabic and Chinese, albeit words in these languages are virtually absent as direct speech. We have also seen how the presence of such languages offers the opportunity to reflect on the cultural context of their native speakers, for example as economic migrants in a colonial culture, and the impact of this on the continuing use of their mother tongue.

A further example that illustrates the value of investigating linguistic context is the Sulu language. We are told in *Almayer's Folly* of Mrs Almayer's capture from 'Sulu pirates', pirates much feared for their slave-raiding voyages (*AF* 7). The colonial powers, British, Dutch and Spanish, made every effort to end this activity and Spain finally broke the Sulu Sultanate's power, bringing it under their control in 1878. Sulu settlers were present in east Borneo, the setting of fictional Sambir, and

Babalatchi, being 'of Sulu origin', suggests the heterogeneous composition of Conrad's portrayal of the region (*AF* 38). But it is the Sulu language, a reference to which occurs in *Almayer's Folly* regarding Mrs Almayer and Babalatchi's having long conversations at night 'in Sulu language' (*AF* 38), that conveys a powerful sense of the presence of different cultures, and of different visions, resistant to colonial agendas, that work alongside other marks of resistance in the book, such as in Mrs Almayer's talk of 'white men driven from the islands' (*AF* 152). This linguistic context, with the secretive night-time conversations, adds to the sense of separation from Western culture that is suggested by Mrs Almayer's resistance to Western education, 'assimilating quickly only the superstitious elements of the religion' in the Semarang convent (*AF* 22).

During the nineteenth century there was considerable interest in the languages and dialects of the Sulu Archipelago. Alexander Dalrymple's 'Essay towards an Account of Sulu', which has already been noted, was an early example (though it is not only about the language). In this essay he wrote of Sulu's languages in an exploratory fashion similar to that adopted by writers considering the inhabitants of a newfound island or nation:

> There is a very great variety of languages in the Sulu dominions. The Tiroon and Idaan, are equally foreign to the Sulu, and to each other; nay, particular districts have different languages, which, however, I rather suppose dialects of some of the others, than entirely distinct from them.[43]

Cowie describes Sulu more precisely as 'formed chiefly from Bisaya and Malay. Its similarity to both, in grammatical construction, is very marked, yet the distinction colloquially is most remarkable.'[44] But Cowie goes on to provide a utilitarian, partly colonial, purpose for the study of the language:

> Spanish rule is hateful to [the Sulu people] and many are leaving the Sūlū archipelago for British North Borneo. In time they should make valuable subjects to the Chartered Company, but, whilst taming, they will require very careful treatment.
> The primary object of this work is to assist the Europeans of North Borneo in acquiring a knowledge of Sūlū to enable them to converse with the Sūlūs in their own dialect rather than through the medium of Malay, which, although understood by many, is still a foreign language to them.[45]

Although Sulus are leaving their home territory, which has been colonised by the Spanish, they are moving to another colonial possession, this time colonised by the British and situated at least partly in former Sulu territory, in which British knowledge of their native tongue will assist in their 'taming'.

For Cameron the central issue, while less overtly hegemonic than Cowie's aim, is in effect another form of taming: Cameron wants to transliterate Sulu into the Roman alphabet so that 'more English-speaking people may be encouraged to take up the study of Sulu and other languages of the Philippine Islands which use an adapted Arabic script'. Sulu, 'like the other languages spoken by Muhammadanized groups living in the Philippine Islands, called Moros, . . . has borrowed its alphabetical system from the Arabic through the Malay'. Cameron notes that this transliteration was as forced phonetically in Roman as in Arabic scripts.[46] That there was an *ur*-Malay alphabet, perhaps originating in India and subsequently superseded, was a possibility considered by nineteenth-century philologists, one that in effect offered an enhanced originary standing to Malay.[47]

Conrad's reference to the Sulu language can therefore be seen, with some recovery of context, to introduce a number of points closely related to other aspects of his representation of relations – especially colonial – in the region. The Spanish defeat of the Sulu Sultanate seems to suggest in *Almayer's Folly* the ultimate defeat too of resistance to the Dutch. Despite Babalatchi's hopeful 'There will be fighting. There is a breath of war on the islands', it appears an empty hope (*AF* 206). Even the Sulu linguistic heritage of Mrs Almayer and Babalatchi is weakened in a foreign environment encompassed by other languages in which the Dutch rather than the Spanish are the colonial power. Mrs Almayer has mainly had to speak Malay and Dutch since her capture, and we can expect that her daughter, Nina, would be likely to speak Malay rather than Sulu, as well as both the Dutch her father would have been anxious for her to know as part of her 'white' inheritance and the English taught in her school in Singapore.

### Language dispossession and a Scottish settler on the east coast of Borneo

A compelling historical example of the decay of language brought about by colonial disturbance is evident from a photograph held in the archives of the KITLV in Leiden.[48] This photograph shows Scottish-born Mr Alexander Gray, his wife and seven children on the rear verandah of their house in Samarinda, east Borneo, in 1905. Alexander Gray was born in 1859 and came to the Dutch East Indies to seek his fortune, dying in 1943.[49] As a result of support he gave to the Sultan of Kutai he was given land in Samarinda, where he came to own a sawmill, a lemonade works and an ice factory. He had two children with a Malay woman and more subsequently with his Eurasian wife. One might assume, therefore – and from Gray's living in a remote part of the Dutch East Indies that also necessitated dependence on local people, as well as having children who presumably would have spoken Malay fluently – that he would have been a capable speaker of Malay. However, an anonymous and undated note written in Dutch on the back of the photograph records that he spoke neither Malay nor Dutch well.

It seems unlikely that Gray's case was unique among Europeans in the Dutch East Indies, although as a native English speaker in a Dutch colony his difficulty with Dutch would have been unusual. But what his linguistic situation tellingly illustrates is the isolation of the coloniser, particularly when we consider how he might have had difficulties communicating with his own children, who, like the Arab children discussed earlier, are likely to have spoken the language of their mother. In the Gray household we can reasonably infer that the languages spoken would have been Malay, with possibly some Dutch. It seems unlikely that he would have spoken English with his family, there being no particular need to do so.

Gray, therefore, like the Arabs, is a linguistic stranger in both his adoptive country and his own family. In being dispossessed of the mastery of language that is a fundamental feature of human identity (his mastery of English having become no longer useful), he is a documented historical example of the way in which colonialism could work its process of dispossession not only on the colonised but on the coloniser, the coloniser ironically become, to a degree, voiceless. In this Gray is related to those other examples in Conrad's Malay fiction of linguistic decay, inadequacy or compromise to which colonialism contributed and which are parallel to other manifestations in his writing of the consequences of colonial intrusion and economic migration. In considering the languages of the Malay Archipelago, J. R. Logan wrote that 'theoretically and absolutely speaking, we may say that language is the complete expression of human nature fully developed'.[50] We may therefore consider impairments to language, or modifications of language such as the brigantine's captain's, among the most telling aspects of the human condition portrayed in the Malay fiction. It is all the more fitting therefore that when Captain Whalley in 'The End of the Tether' reflects on the testimony of his life, an existence he feels in the present age to be archaic, he characterises it as 'a screed traced in obsolete words – in a half-forgotten language' (Y 186).

## Notes

1. Najeeb M. Saleeby, *The History of Sulu*, Bureau of Science Division of Ethnology Publications, Vol. IV, Part II (Manila: Bureau of Printing, 1908), map in inside front cover.
2. Conrad's Malay fiction is that which is set, or largely set, in the Malay Archipelago and predominantly in the Dutch East Indies. It differs from his Asian fiction in so far as the latter includes 'Falk' and *The Shadow-Line*, two works with a significant part of their setting in Siam.
3. Joseph Conrad, *Victory* (London: J. M. Dent and Sons, 1923), p. 8. Subsequent references are cited in the text as *V*.
4. Christopher GoGwilt, in the previous chapter in this volume, addresses important issues concerning the Romanisation of languages, including Malay (particularly print Malay), topics that are included within a larger context in his *The Passage of Literature: Genealogies of Modernism in Conrad, Rhys, and Pramoedya* (New York: Oxford University Press, 2011).
5. Joseph Conrad, *Almayer's Folly* (London: J. M. Dent and Sons, 1923), p. 3. Subsequent references are cited in the text as *AF*.
6. The word for 'eat' in Sulu is given by Andson Cowie as 'ka-aun' or 'ka-maun'. *English-Sulu-Malay Vocabulary, with Useful Sentences, Tables, &c.*, ed. W. Clark Cowie (London: printed for the Editor, 1893), p. 59. T. H. Haynes gives it as 'kumaun', in 'English, Sulu and Malay Vocabulary', *Journal of the Straits Branch of the Royal Asiatic Society* 16 (December 1885), Part I, pp. 321–84 at p. 353, and J. Hunt gives it as 'komaowan', in 'Some Particulars Relative to Sulo, in the Archipelago of Felicia, Collected Partly from a Parcel of Shattered and Torn Memoranda, and Recited Partly from Memory', *Malayan Miscellanies* 1 (Paper 10) (1820) (Bencoolen: Sumatran Mission Press), p. 26.
7. Barbara Koc, 'Conrad: The Problem of Language', *Kwartalnik Neofilologiczny* 27.2 (1980), pp. 155–64 at p. 156.
8. Martin Ray, 'The Gift of Tongues: The Languages of Joseph Conrad', *Conradiana* 15.2 (1983), pp. 83–109. Ray discusses Conrad's 'love of' French but 'devotion to English' (p. 89). While his spoken French, according to Jean-Aubry, was grammatically correct, with a perfect accent, his written French was not of such a standard (ibid. p. 90). His spoken English, as Ray also remarks, had a very strong foreign accent (p. 90); his uncle Tadeusz Bobrowski had a high opinion of his written Polish.
9. Ibid. p. 85.
10. Quoted in ibid. p. 91.
11. Ibid. p. 93. As Conrad wrote to Hugh Walpole in June 1918: 'French, which is crystallised in the form of its sentence and therefore more exacting and less appealing' (*CL2* 206). Quoted in Ray, 'Gift of Tongues', p. 91. Marlow shares this view in *Lord Jim*, when he describes the French lieutenant's French as using 'the passionless and definite phraseology a machine would use, if machines could speak'. Joseph Conrad, *Lord Jim* (London: J. M. Dent and Sons, 1923), p. 159. Subsequent references are cited in the text as *LJ*.
12. Ray, 'Gift of Tongues', p. 97.

13. Ibid. pp. 89, 105 n. 32. Jerry Allen, *The Sea Years of Joseph Conrad* (London: Methuen, 1967), and Frederick R. Karl, *Joseph Conrad, The Three Lives: A Biography* (London: Faber and Faber, 1979).
14. Karl, *Joseph Conrad, The Three Lives*, p. 327.
15. Allen, *Sea Years*, p. 229.
16. Ibid. p. 185. 'Shalimar' (pseudonym of [Captain] F. C. Hendry), *From the Log-Book of Memory* (London: William Blackwood and Sons, 1950), p. xi.
17. The notion that Malay is an easy language to learn was expressed by Charles Frederick Noble: 'The Malayan language is spoken by the natives of this island [Java] in a variety of dialects, and is easily acquired, perhaps easier than any foreign living language in the world.' *A Voyage to the East Indies in 1747 and 1748* (London: for T. Becket and P. A. Dehondt; and T. Durham, 1762), pp. 62–3. J. T. Thomson wrote that he 'could converse tolerably well' after twelve months. *Some Glimpses into Life in the Far East* (London: Richardson, 1864), p. 60.
18. Amy Houston, 'Implicit Translation in Joseph Conrad's Malay Trilogy', in Ton Hoenselaars and Marius Buning (eds), *English Literature and the Other Languages* (Amsterdam: Rodopi, 1999), pp. 109–22 at pp. 116, 117–18. Florence Clemens, 'Conrad's Malaysia', in Robert D. Hamner (comp. and ed.), *Joseph Conrad: Third World Perspectives* (Washington, DC: Three Continents Press, 1990), pp. 21–7 at p. 25.
19. P. A. M. Boele van Hensbroek, *De beoefening der oostersche talen in Nederland en zijne Overzeesche Bezittingen 1800–1874* ['The Study of Eastern Languages in the Netherlands and its Overseas Possessions 1800–1874'] (Leiden: E. J. Brill, 1875), p. 84. Translations are mine unless otherwise stated.
20. Robert N. Cust, *A Sketch of the Modern Languages of the East Indies. Accompanied by Two Language-Maps*, Trübner's Oriental series, 4 (London: Trübner, 1878), pp. 168–71; ibid. 'A Language Map of Further India and the Indian Archipelago', in 'Appendix A: Two Language-Maps'.
21. Cust observed unsympathetically of languages without a script that 'now the adapted Roman and adapted Arabic are contending for possession of the uncultivated Languages, as they pass from mere vocalism into writing', a process that is reminiscent of colonial annexation (ibid. p. 20). G. W. J. Drewes, however, observed that 'the language of a certain group of speakers ... reflects the whole of its cultural assets', something that applies whether it is written or not. 'The Influence of Western Civilisation on the Language of the East Indian Archipelago', in B. Schrieke (ed.), *The Effect of Western Influence on Native Civilisations in the Malay Archipelago*, trans. H. J. Bridge (Batavia, Dutch East Indies: Royal Batavia [sic] Society of Arts and Sciences, 1929), pp. 126–57 at pp. 127–8.
22. William Marsden, *A Grammar of the Malayan Language, with an Introduction and Praxis* (London: for the author, 1812), p. ii.
23. Thomas Bowrey, *A Dictionary: English and Malayo, Malayo and English* (London: for the Author, 1701); James Howison, *A Dictionary of the Malay Tongue, as Spoken in the Peninsula of Malacca, the Islands of Sumatra, Java, Borneo, Pulo Pinang, &c. &c. in Two Parts*, 'English and Malay, and Malay and English' (London: John Sewell, et al., 1801); Marsden, *A Dictionary of the Malayan Language, in two parts, Malayan*

and English and English and Malayan (London: for the author, 1812); John Crawfurd, *A Grammar and Dictionary of the Malay Language: With a Preliminary Dissertation*, 2 vols (London: Smith, Elder, 1852); Hugh Clifford and Frank Athelstane Swettenham, *A Dictionary of the Malay Language: Malay–English*, Parts I–V (Taiping, Perak: Printed for the Authors at the Government Printing House, 1894-1902).

24. N. B. Dennys, *A Handbook of Malay Colloquial, as Spoken in Singapore, being a Series of Introductory Lessons for Domestic and Business Purposes* (London: Trübner, [1878]); J. Pijnappel, 'Laag-Maleisch' ['Low Malay'], *De Gids: nieuwe vaderlandsche letteroefeningen* 29.4 (October–December 1865), pp. 148–59 at p. 155. Bowrey remarked that 'the *Malayo* spoken in the *Islands* is called *Basa dagang*, that is to say, the Merchants or Trading Language, and is not so well esteemed as the true *Malayo*' ('Preface', in *Dictionary: English and Malayo, Malayo and English* [p. 1]).
25. A. Dalrymple, 'Essay towards an Account of Sulu', *Journal of the Indian Archipelago and Eastern Asia* 3.8 (August 1849), pp. 512–31, pp. 545–67.
26. John Bellows, *Outline Dictionary for the Use of Missionaries, Explorers and Students of Language* (London: Trübner, 1867), p. v.
27. W. Robinson, *An Attempt to Elucidate the Principles of Malayan Orthography* (Fort Marlborough, Bencoolen, Sumatra: printed at the Mission Press, 1823), p. lxiii.
28. William Edward Maxwell, *A Manual of the Malay Language. With An Introductory Sketch of the Sanskrit Element in Malay* (London: Trübner, 1882), p. vii.
29. Ibid. p. 2. Nevertheless, given the many languages, the distinguished Dutch scholar P. J. Veth wrote: 'A multitude of languages and dialects of the Indian Archipelago . . . lie totally in darkness'. 'Onze kennis der Talen van Nederlandsch-Indië' ['Our Knowledge of the Languages of the Dutch East Indies'], *Tijdschrift voor Nederlandsch-Indië*, third series, 1.2 (1867), pp. 443–4.
30. Drewes, 'Influence of Western Civilisation', p. 153.
31. Recalling incidents from the 1830s, Thomson describes the captain of the ship on which he sailed from Singapore to Penang as someone who spoke in 'broken English, but appeared better at home in Malay and Hindostanee' (*Some Glimpses*, p. 28).
32. Thomson, *Some Glimpses*, pp. 313–14.
33. L. W. C. van den Berg, *Le Hadhramout et les colonies Arabes dans l'Archipel Indien* ['The Hadhramout and Arab Colonies in the Indian Archipelago'] (Batavia, Dutch East Indies: Imprimerie du Gouvernement, 1886), pp. 184–5; my translation from French.
34. Somerset Maugham, 'Footprints in the Jungle', in *The Complete Short Stories*, 4 vols (Harmondsworth: Penguin, 1961; repr. 1963), Vol. II, pp. 369–95 at p. 369.
35. Cust, *Sketch*, p. 134.
36. Houston provides a close analysis for the Malay fiction of what she terms implicit and explicit translation in 'Conrad's textual presentation of the varying languages these characters speak' ('Implicit Translation', p. 111), drawing 'clear distinctions between different nationalities and between different characters in the explicitness with which he represents their voice',

concluding that 'character function and narrative purpose may directly affect the way in which non-English speech is presented' (p. 122). Examples are the 'phonetic distortion' of the pronunciation of the skipper in *Lord Jim* and the crockery agent in *The Rescue* – whose roles are 'incidental, contemptible' (p. 112) – compared with the 'more dignified' (p. 113) representation of Stein's speech.

37. Jacques Berthoud, 'Explanatory Notes' in Conrad, *Lord Jim*, ed. Jacques Berthoud (New York: Oxford University Press, 2002), pp. 317–29 at pp. 324–5.
38. Ibid. p. 324.
39. As J. R. Logan observed, 'all the ends of language are accomplished by the one tongue as by the other'. 'The Languages of the Indian Archipelago. Part II. Preliminary Remarks on the Generation, Growth, Structure and Analysis of Languages', *Journal of the Indian Archipelago and Eastern Asia* 3.10 (October 1849), pp. 637–77 at p. 656. The colonisers' language being altered by the language of the colonised was also noted by P. J. Veth with regard to some of the former colonists' Portuguese words and their adoption in the Dutch East Indies not only by indigenous languages but by Dutch. 'Portugeesche woorden in de taal der Nederlanders in Indië en in het Moederland' ['Portuguese Words in the Language of the Dutch in the East Indies and the Motherland'], *Tijdschrift voor Nederlandsch-Indië*, third series, 1.1 (1867), pp. 295–6.
40. Joseph Conrad, *Youth, Heart of Darkness, The End of the Tether: Three Stories* (London: J. M. Dent and Sons, 1923), p. 267. Subsequent references are cited in the text as *Y*.
41. Joseph Conrad, *The Rescue* (London: J. M. Dent and Sons, 1924), p. 103.
42. Joseph Conrad, *An Outcast of the Islands* (London: J. M. Dent and Sons, 1923), p. 28. Subsequent references are cited in the text as *OI*.
43. Dalrymple, 'Essay', p. 551.
44. Cowie, 'Introduction', in *English-Sulu-Malay Vocabulary*, pp. ix–xlvii at p. ix. C. R. Cameron, in a book published some twenty-five years later and after 'thirteen years of association with the Sulu people and study of their writings', wrote that 'the Sulu language is spoken by about seventy-five thousand Muhammadans, and is the commercial *lingua franca* and vehicle of written thought for about seventy-thousand others, whose usual spoken dialect is Samal, Bajau, or Yakan. All these live in the Sulu Archipelago, eastern Borneo, Basilan, and the southern extremity of the Zamboanga peninsula.' This reinforces the Sulu links with eastern Borneo, the fictional location of Sambir. *Sulu Writing: An Explanation of the Sulu-Arabic Script as Employed in Writing the Sulu Language of the Southern Philippines* (Zamboanga, Philippines: Sulu Press, 1917), pp. iii, 1.
45. Cowie, *English-Sulu-Malay Vocabulary*, p. x. The North Borneo Chartered Company administered the area of north Borneo, a British protectorate that is now Sabah in Malaysia.
46. Cameron, *Sulu Writing*, pp. iv, 1, 4–5.
47. The possibility was discussed by Max Müller (1823–1900), the eminent philologist, in a review of a Spanish book that cited twelve different Malay alphabets in the Philippines. 'The Alphabets of the Philippine Group', review of T. H. Pardo de Tavera, *Contribucion para el estudio de los antiguos*

*alfabetos Filipinos* ['Contribution to the Study of the Old Philippine Alphabets'] (Lausanne: [n.pub.], 1884), *Journal of the Straits Branch of the Royal Asiatic Society* 17 (January 1886), pp. 157–8. Robinson argues against the 'very generally received' opinion that there was a Malay alphabet before the Arabic was employed (*Attempt to Elucidate*, pp. vi, vi–xii).
48. I am indebted to Mr Walter Oliemans of Alkmaar in the Netherlands, Alexander Gray's great-grandson, for bringing this photograph to my attention. Koninklijk Instituut voor Taal-, Land- en Volkenkunde (KITLV) [Royal Institute for Language, Geography and Ethnology, now known in English as the Royal Netherlands Institute for Southeast Asian and Caribbean Studies], ref. 155239.
49. For further information about his life, see Andrew Francis, 'The Olmeijer Family and a Wedding Photograph', *Conradian* 37.2 (Autumn 2012), pp. 126–35.
50. Logan, 'Languages of the Indian Archipelago', p. 647.

# Chapter 9

## Gallicisms:
## The Secret Agent in Conrad's Prose

*Claude Maisonnat*

The macaronic quality of Conrad's prose is a well-documented dimension of his writings, be they fictional or epistolary, and testimonies that he regularly indulged in the habit of mixing several languages in oral conversation also abound. H. G. Wells recalled that Conrad 'spoke English strangely'. Wells went on to say that, 'He would supplement his vocabulary – especially if he were discussing cultural or political matters – with French words.'[1] French idioms clearly came naturally to Conrad and were always relevant, but what makes their status problematic is when they are, as it were, smuggled into the English language through faulty translations, so that to many readers Conrad's English frequently sounded awkward. George Orwell sums up his impression of Conrad's convoluted language: 'He used I believe to think in Polish and then translate his thoughts into French and finally into English.'[2]

Conrad's compulsion to switch from one language to another in the same sentence may originate from different needs. The first one might be to supplement what he found himself momentarily unable to express in the master language of his medium, namely English, by resorting to an idiom with which he was more familiar. To be sure, most of the time the language that fulfilled this function turned out to be French, but he could sporadically use German, Italian or Spanish phrases if need be. This simply goes to show that Conrad could sometimes find it arduous to channel his thoughts through English words. He not infrequently bemoaned his lack of mastery of the language. However, if this reaction is easily understood in an oral context, things are different in a written one because the writer is always free to correct, amend, erase what he considers to be a betrayal of his intention and ultimately scrap everything and start all over again or even enlist the help of competent friends. Yet Conrad kept complaining that English eluded his literary control. For instance, in a letter to Marguerite Poradowska dated 1 January 1908 he confessed,

> I'd rather dream a novel than write it. For dreaming a work is always much more appealing than the reality of the thing in print. And then, English is still for me a foreign language whose handling requires tremendous efforts.[3]

This can only suggest that he was aware that there remained in his third language, which he nevertheless mastered well enough to write novels, some grey areas in which he suspected that uncontrollable forces were at work.

The second need is more culturally oriented, as it was part of the European tradition in the educated classes of the time to drop sentences and phrases, quotations and proverbs into conversation so as to suggest how widely travelled or learned one was. And we know that Conrad decidedly belonged to that kind of world owing to his *szlachtic* (Polish gentry) origins.

The third assumption is that in his fiction such linguistic excursions can be attributed to the conventional literary practice of bolstering the local-colour dimension of narratives when telling stories taking place in a non-English setting. What must not be overlooked, however, is that such words may be not mere embellishment of the narrative but indispensable references to things that do not exist in the English world of the narrators.

The fourth and perhaps most rewarding hypothesis is to argue that Conrad's use of French in his fiction was not only the result of conscious decisions and assumed volition but also had deeper, hidden implications related to the innermost libidinal forces of his creative power, and is part and parcel of the idiosyncratic nature of his creative practice. The massive collection of gallicisms in his narratives suggests that intensive translinguistic negotiations were implicitly taking place when he put pen to paper. A fictional representation of such a process is to be found in *Nostromo* when Mrs Gould and Decoud discuss the revolution: 'And a French phrase came upon them as if, for this Costaguanero of the Boulevard, that had been the only forcible language.'[4] Conversely, it also happened that when expressing himself in French, anglicisms cropped up, as his letters to Poradowska clearly show. His two main foreign languages are thus shown to be intricately interwoven and to constitute what is easily identified as the Conradian voice.

What never ceases to impress bilingual French readers of Conrad is the extent to which his publishers, editors and proofreaders alike allowed him to get away with the incredible number of gallicisms that put a strain on his prose under a wide variety of forms and guises.[5] This is all the more surprising as Conrad wrote in a 1903 letter to his agent J. B. Pinker: 'I can't let a book of mine go into the world without a careful personal revision ... And I *will not* put up with the American spelling in the English edition' (*CL3* 92). Twenty years later he no longer proved so fastidious about similar matters of linguistic precision, as the proliferation of lexical and grammatical gallicisms testifies.

What must not be lost sight of is the fact that in the course of his life in Great Britain between 1878 and 1924, Conrad used three languages simultaneously in conversation and in his letters: Polish, French and English. Inevitably, there were bound to be more or less conscious interferences between them. We can reasonably assume that there were fluctuations in his fluency in the three languages with the passing of time. If, on the one hand, we can expect his grasp of the English language to have improved with his integration and his daily professional, then domestic, immersion into the English-speaking world, on the other hand his hold on French and Polish may be expected to have declined given his infrequent travels to Poland or France. In point of fact, René Rapin has shown that between 1911 and 1924 the number of anglicisms in Conrad's letters in French had increased considerably.[6]

Yet Conrad's novels tell another story. As far as English is concerned, he was constantly plagued by what he considered to be his lack of control over the medium of his choice. As late as 1911, in a letter to Joseph de Smet, a Belgian who translated *Nostromo*, he confessed: 'I've never opened an English grammar in my life. My pronunciation is rather defective to this day. Having unluckily no ear, my accentuation is uncertain, especially when in the course of a conversation I become self-conscious' (*CL4* 409).

The case of Polish is the opposite: as early as April 1891, writing to Poradowska, he conceded that it was too difficult for him to write in Polish to Gabriela Zagorska, born Poradowska, on the occasion of her husband's death:

> What a sad end! I must indeed write to dear Aunt Gaba, but I do not have the heart. The fact is that the effort of gathering my ideas and seeking the Polish for them is, for the moment, beyond me. (*CL1* 76)

If we bear in mind that much later, in 1909, when he was in the course of completing *Under Western Eyes*, Polish sentences cropped up in his delirious state, we can assume that Polish was for him a kind of repressed language, all the more so as he did not deem it advisable to have his two sons learn the language of their ancestors, but insisted on French instead. This suggests that he was in some way reluctant to live with his Polish past, which after all was not a very happy one. Symbolically – if not literally – this was a way of severing direct links with it, a gesture that his flight to Marseilles no doubt anticipated. As far as the Polish language is concerned, critics like Morf, Najder and Morzinski have provided insights that are unavailable to non-Polish speakers, but Yves Hervouet has summed up the case definitively when he argued: 'No doubt the Polish background in particular is valuable, an indispensable key; but a master-key it is not.'[7]

The situation of French is different because it is constitutive of Conrad's art. He abundantly paraded it both in written and in oral forms of communication, and he apparently never had any difficulty expressing himself in his second language. At least he never complained about it and apparently enjoyed himself using it, to the extent that it could be argued that for him French almost operated as a surrogate first language. Indeed, he had a genuinely in-depth knowledge of it and he could use it idiomatically with a wealth of nuances that is rare in a non-native speaker. Rapin even mentions a letter to Poradowska, dated 26 August 1891, in which Conrad switches from French to English possibly without noticing it, later returning to English as if it were the most natural thing in the world.[8] Altogether his grasp of French is extremely assured and confident, and the numerous slight mistakes that he makes are those of a man who does not speak the language on a daily basis but who nevertheless maintains a high level of proficiency. So much so that he never hesitated to meddle with the work of his translators, giving advice, as his letters to them testify. Rapin reports that although unasked, Conrad even went so far as to help Poradowska, making suggestions as she was writing her own novel *Marylka* in French.[9]

Hervouet paved the way for a host of scholars who have done extensive research in this field and have reached the conclusion that Conrad's debt to French literature – which had been systematically underestimated – is huge and manifold. Not only did he study the technique of such masters as Flaubert and Maupassant, or borrow ideas and scenes from their works, but he also translated sentences and even paragraphs to include them in his own prose. This practice reveals the extent to which French and English are positively linked very closely in his writing practices. Sometimes, Conrad deliberately plays with the two languages, mixing them in such a way as to create comic effects, as we see in the case of the character of the French Lieutenant in *Lord Jim* who betrays his linguistic incompetence by producing literal translations and gallicisms. This preposterous stance casts doubts on the genuineness of his speech on honour and makes him sound somewhat ridiculous. Incidentally, that Conrad should engage in such wordplay bears witness to his extensive knowledge of both languages. More often than not, however, the attentive reader can spot the presence of gallicisms whose status is uncertain. The sheer proliferation of their occurrences raises a few questions concerning their interpretation. This chapter will explore them by focusing mostly, but not exclusively, on the case of *The Rover*, because it happens to be the last novel that Conrad could revise for publication, just a year before his death.

## Gallicisms and *The Rover*

By 1923, when *The Rover* was completed, one might have expected Conrad's control over his language to be maximal, but if there is a constant in his texts, it is the number of gallicisms contained in his novels, from *Almayer's Folly* to *Suspense*. The fact that he dictated the novel to Miss Hallowes may have played a part in the proliferation of gallicisms, as his supervision of the written version must not have been as strict as it could have been, all the more so as his strength and his health were clearly declining. From that angle, *The Rover* is the ideal locus to examine the various modalities of the emergence and the poetical function of such gallicisms. Prior to that, however, what is meant by 'gallicism' must be clarified, keeping in mind that the issue of the relationship between English and French is more complex than it appears at first sight.

In truth, gallicisms are inherent in the English language and the earliest date back to the times of the Norman Conquest, as the famous duplicates like 'sheep/mutton', 'veal/calf' and so on remind us. It is therefore not unduly surprising that such lexical items should regularly fall from Conrad's pen, as there is certainly a Latin/French tropism in his diction on account of his extensive knowledge of French.[10] Of course, since such lexical items are widely shared by native users of the language they would mostly pass unnoticed, but their presence did not escape the scrutiny of Virginia Woolf, who maintained

> So Conrad had been gifted, so he had schooled himself, and such was his obligation to a strange language wooed characteristically for its Latin qualities rather than its Saxon that it seemed impossible for him to make an ugly or insignificant movement of the pen.[11]

Such borrowings are not so idiosyncratic as the less standard ones which constitute a major characteristic feature of Conrad's prose. Consequently they do not reveal as much about his literary intentions. But the notion of gallicism cannot be restricted to misguided linguistic usage, as Conrad's knowledge of the French cultural and literary context was wide.

A gallicism can also arise in relation to a typically French custom that has no equivalent in the Anglo-Saxon world, which accordingly does not possess the adequate terms to provide a similar picture. The words and phrases used to refer to such cultural elements are in fact untranslatable and could be called contextual gallicisms. *The Rover* offers a good many of these when it comes down to evoking the French Revolution. The word 'sans-culotte' describes both literally and metaphorically a clog-wearing revolutionary urban proletariat composed mostly of workers and craftsmen fighting for revolutionary ideals. Yet 'sans-culotte' does not only conjure up a dress code composed of trousers with white and blue stripes, worn instead of the knee-breeches of the aristocrats, to which was later added the red cap of liberty called a Phrygian cap. It is associated with a whole historical background that includes, to mention but a few associations, Marat, who popularised the term; Rousseau's liberal ideas about education; revolutionary wars in which the sans-culottes were active participants, though ill-equipped; and the looming Terror engendered by the radicalisation of their ideals. As can be seen, the term carries with it a great number of connotations that conjure up, in one word, a turning point in French history; so much so that the sans-culotte has become an almost mythical figure that is at the same time heroic and threatening, because of the worst excesses of the French Revolution. This explains Peyrol's caution in dealing with the Toulon revolutionary authorities, avoiding direct confrontation with them, asserting: 'Nobody can say I was ever anti-revolutionary in my life.'[12] The same could be said for the word 'citoyen', which stresses the political dimension of the popular movement, promoting Republican ideals like freedom, equality and fraternity and their outcome: revolutionary patriotism. Indeed, the very word 'patriot', which recurs in the novel, became a synonym for 'sans-culotte' and thus largely exceeds its initial connotations.

Accounting for the revolutionary situation in English can occasionally lead to awkward formulations, as when, for example, Peyrol exhibits a 'certificate of civism' (*Ro* 5). This document, issued by the revolutionary authorities, was meant to guarantee the bearer's submission and loyalty to the republican ideal, protecting him from accusation of anti-revolutionary sympathies and ultimately from being beheaded. The guillotine, named after French doctor Joseph-Ignace Guillotin, who was supposed to have 'humanised' the device, is the major symbol of that troubled period. Though not of French origin – among its ancestors we find the notorious Halifax Gibbet and the Scottish Maiden – it has come to stand for the horrors of the revolutionary period. Thus when the narrator in *The Rover* reports that Scevola 'became busy purveying the guillotine as they were purifying the town from all aristocrats', it is the whole revolutionary context that is summoned with its connotations of violence, murder and iniquity, through one word only (*Ro* 20). Incidentally, the power of attraction of the word is so strong that the narrator uses the phrase 'busy purveying the guillotine' to describe the situation. Now, although this is perfectly understandable in English, it nevertheless echoes the French expression 'pourvoyeur de la guillotine', used to refer to the infamous public prosecutor Fouquier-Tinville, who presided over the 'Tribunal Révolutionnaire' with great zeal and was reputed to have sent 2,600 people to death, before being sentenced himself in 1795. In the same way, when Peyrol pays the carriers of his chest 'with a large handful of assignats', it is the whole financial organisation of the economy of the Revolution that is summoned through the force of a single word (*Ro* 5).

As can be seen from the above considerations, Conrad's choice of locating the action of his last completed novel in France, and of selecting a plainly paradigmatic historical period, fully justifies the presence of contextual gallicisms. They stand for a linguistic peculiarity that is hardly translatable because of the specific connotations and resonances that are unavailable in the target language. On the face of it they are necessary because words like 'sans-culotte' or 'citoyen' are not mere lexical items with a distinctive semantic content; most of all, they are both images that are metonymically evocative of a given period and symbols of France itself at a crucial moment in its history.

The likelihood of finding gallicisms in Conrad's texts is reinforced by the fact that, as Hervouet has convincingly shown, Conrad sometimes borrowed heavily from the novels of his favourite French writers. For instance, in *The Rover*, the name of the hero, Jean Peyrol, comes from Anatole France's *Bildungsroman*, *Le Petit Chose*, in which Jean Peyrol, the husband of Daniel Eyssette's former nurse Annou, proudly gives Daniel a treat before he starts his first job as study supervisor. Here Conrad makes no attempt to conceal the wellspring of his muse, a sure sign that there is no feeling of unease or guilt attached to this writing practice. *The Rover* abounds with French idioms[13] incorporated as such in the textual fabric. They may be quotations from the characters allegedly addressing each other in French, in which case they are immediately followed by the rejoinder in English, so that with the second half of the exchange the reader can roughly guess the import of the French phrase: '"Hé! La mère," hailed Peyrol. "Have you got a man to lend a hand with my chest in the house?" ... "Mais oui citoyen. He will be here in a moment"' (*Ro* 9). This short dialogue shows Conrad's remarkable in-depth knowledge of the vernacular.

A second variety of linguistic gallicisms is not of a lexical order, but of a grammatical one. They are easily caught by the writer and therefore are few and far between, but nevertheless, they remain symptoms of Conrad's French tropism through sheer repetition. His problem with the use of past tenses is well known, and he not infrequently used the present perfect favoured by the French tense system instead of the preterite required in standard English. When Réal and Peyrol, keeping an eye on the manoeuvres of the patrolling English man-of-war, wonder at the beauty and quality of the ship, the older man is moved to say: 'She has been built by French shipwrights' (*Ro* 72). The temporal slip is quite revealing here. Instead of saying that the ship was actually built in France, which amounts to establishing a clear distinction between the bygone past and present moment, thus implying a feeling of nostalgia for the antebellum period when the sloop used to be French – presumably before its capture by the English – Peyrol resorts to the present perfect. This choice of tense creates an ambiguity, seeming to deny the temporal break and to suggest a form of continuity – as if he unconsciously denied the loss of the ship and all the unpleasant memories associated with it.

Though they may not be so prominent as they are in other novels, non-lexical gallicisms, which have been called by Lucas 'stylistic eccentricities', regularly struck English readers.[14] Rudyard Kipling, for example, could not help admitting, 'When I am reading him . . . I always have the impression that I am reading an excellent translation of a foreign author.'[15] These 'stylistic eccentricities' include postposed adjectives, nominal modifications, verbal phrases and the nominalisation of adjectives, difficulties with the conventions of determination in English and particularly the use of deictics like *this* or *that*. Orwell also mentions 'his tendency to put the adjective after the noun',[16] which we can see in chapter XI when Catherine expresses her relief at Peyrol's arrival at the farm: 'But all the same I was glad when you appeared here, a grey headed-man, serious' (*Ro* 168).

Word order and syntax can also become problematic in Conrad. They are mostly the outcome of the literal translation of a French syntagmatic structure. For instance, when Peyrol, discussing the bloodthirsty behaviour of the revolutionaries with Scevola, exclaims 'You showed no mercy, you other sans-culottes, to the enemies of the republic at home', the phrase 'you other sans-culottes' is unmistakably a gallicism, the first two words a faulty translation of the familiar phrase 'vous autres' (*Ro* 27). In French this is mostly emphatic and insists on the responsibility of the interlocutors, called upon to assume the consequences of their actions, as opposed to the speaker, who distances himself from them. Besides, the notion of alterity implicit in 'others' is not present – 'autre' is purely reflexive in this context – whereas the position of 'others' in the English syntagm foregrounds it. A proper English equivalent might be: 'you hopeless sans-culottes'. The adjunction of the word 'other' is redundant in English. As it stands, the phrase could equally refer to other sans-culottes (that is, additional ones). It is easy to see why a translation of Conrad's phrase back into French is challenging. What is the translator supposed to do: correct the message by doing the work proofreaders did not do? Or try to find a faulty equivalent? This is the paradox with which translators of Conrad's fiction into French are constantly faced.

The same applies for a phrase uttered by Catherine: 'I recognised the son Bron' (*Ro* 91). What Conrad obviously meant when he spoke of 'the son Bron' was something like the equivalent of 'the son of the Bron family' or 'the Bron son' in French. However, the only way to consider his rendering of the phase as correct would be to assume that he meant 'the son named Bron' to the exclusion of any other, which does not correspond to French usage or to Conrad's intention. Such discrepancies highlight the fact that even when French and English offer similar lexical possibilities they can provide different semantic contents. In other words, when a literal translation of the source language into the target language is acceptable, connotations may vary all the same, and what remains is the presence of the French language underneath the English phrase. Such phrases as 'the last two islands' or 'as you say yourself', which are distinctly mistaken syntactical 'calques', are indeed indelible markers of this pervasiveness (*Ro* 261, 167).

So are, in this respect, the innumerable loan translations that are equally acceptable in French and in English, like 'While Michel was executing that order', 'The great affair is to keep our life in our bodies' or 'I used to count for something in that house' (*Ro* 124, 155, 250). Although, as some critics have argued, such gallicisms are partially justified because the characters who utter them are of French origin, I do not think that kind of argument really holds because, the master discourse of the narrative being English, the narrative agent who commits such linguistic slippages would have to be a French person expressing his ideas in English. It looks as if – unwittingly perhaps – Conrad insisted upon consistently choosing the English formulation that was closest to the French idiom. Thus, when the bilingual Marlow in *Lord Jim* produces gallicisms they are strictly his own, as he is addressing an English-speaking audience. This implies a sort of double voicing. Daphna Erdinast-Vulcan gives a telling example of this singular feature of Marlow's language in *Lord Jim*:

The conversation, we are to understand, took place in French, but it is rendered in English, as translated by Marlow for his listeners, with occasional phrases in the original French, italicised and put within parenthesis, following the English rendering. 'His broad bosom heaved regularly while he went on telling me that it had been the very devil of a job, as doubtless (*sans doute*) I could figure to myself in my quality of a seaman (*en votre qualité de marin*).' ... Marlow's rendering of this last phrase is clearly yet another case of 'false friends': *En votre qualité de marin* is rendered by *in my quality of a seaman*. The resemblance of sound and spelling is misleading, since the French *qualité* should have been translated as *capacity* rather than quality.[17]

Moreover, it is a signal fact that Conrad's narrators make the same kind of slippages in novels in which the background has no relationship whatsoever with anything French. In this respect, Conrad's own admission of his difficulties with the English language opens up a silent zone of uncertainty that makes it possible for gallicisms to creep into his prose.[18] As a result, it becomes strictly impossible to decide whether a gallicism is intentional or not, except in the (not so rare) cases when the ungrammatical nature of the French phrase renders the English translation unidiomatic too. This happens when Conrad, as Fleishman noticed, falls into the traps awaiting naive learners, with false friends such as *dispose*, *affair*, *pass* and so on (*Ro* 23, 33, 65). More interesting are the instances of a source-language idiom translated literally into the target language, both being standard lexical and grammatical usage, because, in this instance, the gallicisms remain undetected if not totally undetectable.

### Gallicisms, reading and interpretation

The impressive number of gallicisms in Conrad's novels has sometimes led critics to pass severe strictures on his use of English. Avrom Fleishman argues, in 'Conrad's Last Novel', that 'Not only are we appalled by the reversion to learner's English and the clumsy stringing out of clichés, but we may suffer an uneasy sensation that perhaps this is what Conrad had done all through his career.'[19] He is right that gallicisms tend to destabilise those readers who do not have a smattering of French, but he errs when he interprets their inclusion in strictly negative terms: because they cannot be considered as pure mistakes, being actually part and parcel of Conrad's writing strategies, as this section will demonstrate. George Orwell is nearer the mark when he acknowledges, 'In the earlier books, such as *Almayer's Folly*, his English is sometimes definitely incorrect, though not in a way that matters.'[20] The object of this section is to show why Orwell was right when he urged Conrad's readers to look beyond the notion of incorrectness and to examine how gallicisms have in fact become the staple of Conrad's aesthetics of writing.

To start with, the specificity of Conrad's engagement with gallicisms is that they provide a perfect illustration of what Derrida called 'the monolingualism of the other'.[21] The French philosopher argues that because language is the only source of the process of identification, the speaking subject has in fact one language at his disposal, and that it is ultimately not his own for the simple reason that it is exterior to him, it precedes him and does not belong to him, so that the subject can only be decentred, which means that a split is inherent in the very definition of the subject. This applies to Conrad the cosmopolitan because as an artist he has only one language, English, and it is not his own, as it is parasitised primarily by French and secondarily by Polish, his actual native tongue. One of the corollaries of this secondary division is that the subject is fallaciously led to the conclusion that the other is monolingual, in other words that this other speaks only his own language and he is the only one that can guarantee its purity. This genuine obsession is expressed in a letter of 22 August 1903 to Davray in which, referring to a translation of a few Maupassant tales into English by Elsie Martindale, Conrad betrays his vision of English: 'You who know the language thoroughly will see that the English of the translation is perfectly idiomatic; entirely pure' (*CL3* 54).

This idealisation of the other's monolingualism induces the conclusion that the language of the other is self-assured, established and stable, and thus almost inaccessible; hence Conrad's fantasy, shared with Ford Madox Ford, of attempting to find the holy grail that is Flaubert's *mot juste*. As a matter of fact, Conrad's quest for the *mot juste* is foredoomed because it supposes the transparency of language, the possibility of communication without any remainder, as if the aim of writing was to make the word disappear behind the message. Gallicisms have the opposite effect; they foreground the materiality of the word and by so doing introduce an irreducible element of alterity into speech that makes purity impossible. Whenever he takes pen in hand Conrad is faced with a contradiction: on the one hand he would like to be recognised as an idiomatic English writer, and on the other hand he finds that it is almost an impossible task. In a 1909 letter to Davray he claimed, 'Don't forget, dear friend and translator, notwithstanding the special flavour that people here find in my prose, I write idiomatic English' (*CL4* 337). Some time later, in a 1914 interview with Marian Dabrowski, a press magnate who questioned him about his relationship with Poland, he maintained: 'The English critics – and indeed I am an English writer – when speaking of me always add that there is in my work something incomprehensible, unfathomable, elusive. Only you can grasp this elusiveness, understand the incomprehensible. It is Polishness.'²² This last argument, however, ought to be taken *cum grano salis*. Indeed, he probably overstated the importance of his Polish past because he was addressing a Polish interlocutor and the accusations of treason still rankled with him. And besides, beyond his exaggerated politeness may loom the idea that the Polish tycoon who was interrogating him could be instrumental in the promotion of his oeuvre.

Be that as it may, one of the most obvious consequences of the persistence of gallicisms in Conrad's novels is that it undermines the reading process on two accounts. First, it introduces a textual blank for those who have no idea of the French, and secondly, it perturbs the smooth operation of interpretation because the split between signifier and signified is not necessarily the same in both languages. Let us take the example of the word 'navigator' on the second page of *The Rover*. The French version just states that the man is a seafarer of some kind, presumably a skipper or captain – which Peyrol definitely is – whereas the English version refers mostly to someone who steers a course. Something is lost in the process of translation, or at least is displaced, but what is gained is a more productive textuality. In clearly established gallicisms, the source text is as it were betrayed at the same time as the target text is given a measure of opacity. However, most of the time the gallicisms in Conrad are silent, by which I mean that they are not earmarked as gallicisms, being perfectly idiomatic English phrases, but a close observation of the context shows that they are directly borrowed from the French. Such is the case of the opening sentence of chapter VII, in which the narrator reports: 'A single cover having been laid at the end of a long table in the salle for the lieutenant, he had his meal there while the others sat down to theirs in the kitchen' (*Ro* 79). The proximity to the French word 'salle' (for dining room) is a first clue, and it is confirmed by the suspicion that the word 'cover' comes from the French phrase *mettre le couvert*, meaning to set the table or to lay the table. Of course the word 'cover' does exist in English (in relation to restaurants), but apart from being less common in such a context, it loses the homely connotations of the French word. The same could be said of a host of phrases whose origin is therefore blurred, as are indeed the boundaries between the two languages. As Derrida has suggested in the subtitle of his book, the monolingualism of the other can only be a prosthesis of origin because the actual origin of the utterance is always already lost. Conrad's glorification of the English language is clearly the chimerical prosthesis he constructed to fuel his creativity, even if it is ultimately a fool's errand. His own way out of this predicament is highly innovative in the sense that it consists neither in repressing the gallicisms that came naturally to him nor in preserving the illusory purity of the target language, but in arranging a sort of complementarity between the two that is the hallmark of his aesthetics.

As Umberto Eco has pointed out, the word is not solely a linguistic unit, it is most of all a cultural unit; by which he suggests that what he calls the encyclopedias[23] inherent in the two languages differ, so that reading is somewhat perturbed. To be sure, the interpretation of the sign-word is also a social and cultural act, and it depends on semantic categorisations and pragmatic rules that are different in the two languages. For instance, when the narrator in *The Rover*, describing Peyrol's arrival at the inn on his way to Escampobar, reports, 'Citizen Peyrol went heavily upstairs to rejoin his luggage', the sentence is misleading, since 'to rejoin' in English is used intransitively to mean the activity of replying to someone, and, less frequently, transitively to mean going back to one's regiment, whereas the implied French verb that is thus translated is perfectly commonplace and simply states that Peyrol goes back upstairs to keep an eye on his luggage (*Ro* 11).

Correspondingly, when Peyrol complains about the revolutionary phrases that have become fashionable, the narrator comments in free indirect speech that 'They seemed the invention of landsmen' (*Ro* 8). What he is actually driving at is that, seen from the other end of the world, the phraseology sounded like a fabrication, which is the actual meaning of the French word 'invention' in such a context. Thus a shade of meaning is lost in the passage from one language to the other. It appears minimal indeed, but if we relate it to the sheer multiplication of such discrepancies, the effect becomes colossal.

Ultimately, because the *Weltanschauungen* of the readers – and the encyclopedias that support them – are different, depending on whether they express their thoughts, and therefore their vision of the world and of themselves in it, in this or that language, the interpretation of the message will vary since the interpretative task of the reader, according to Grice's principle of cooperation, entails that they rely on two different encyclopedias.[24] This kind of textual pragmatics is fundamental to the extent that it relies on the amount of knowledge shared by each interlocutor and on their assumptions. In *The Rover*, when Peyrol has landed at Toulon and, confronted with the reality of the revolutionary troubles, ironically mentions 'these times of equality and fraternity', it stands to reason that understanding the import of the text is not based on the semantic contents of the two keywords only (*Ro* 4). In this case, the meaning of the statement is more than the sum of the meanings of each constituent, since what looms behind them is the motto of the French

Republic, and the depth and extension of the reader's encyclopedia are crucial here. From this standpoint, as we have seen, Conrad's gallicisms function as obstacles to the cooperative principle in so far as the shared knowledge and assumptions that reading as communication requires may ostensibly differ.

At times Conrad solves the problem by providing a translation both ways. As Peyrol enlightens his prisoner Symons as to the truth of his situation, he refers to the enigmatic behaviour of a passing tartane: 'Every time she goes to sea she makes a pied-de-nez, what you call thumb to the nose, to all your English cruisers ... You will soon learn French now'. It looks as if Peyrol wants to make sure that his prisoner understands the ironical message of superiority contained in the disrespectful gesture, but at the same time Conrad provides a double layering of the text as a reminder of the French subtext that underlies the narrative (*Ro* 137).

More unexpectedly, the narrator offers the French translation of an English phrase, as if to insist on the French linguistic substratum in the novel. In chapter VIII of *The Rover*, as Réal and Peyrol respectfully discuss Nelson's naval competence, Peyrol is moved to say 'What – That Nelson? Ah! but he is a cunning one.' The narrator makes his point, but in French this time by stating that Peyrol 'repeated his opinion deliberately: "Celui-là est un malin"' (*Ro* 112). On the face of it, the reformulation may look gratuitous. The necessity of such a translation is not plain to see. It is semantically superfluous, the message being self-evident, but on second thoughts it is a way of reasserting the fact that the whole novel should be construed, if not as a direct translation from the French, at least as a linguistic game involving the two languages that consequently appear to be inextricably linked.

Most of the time, the effect of this kind of linguistic manipulation is to introduce a dose of alterity into the master language of the novel, which consequently sounds strange or awkward to conventional English readers even if they are not confronted with blatant nonsense. This is what happens with such expressions as 'capable of jumping on his best friend' (*Ro* 104), used to say that the French naval officers of the Toulon authorities were ready to fly at one another's faces to avoid being declared traitors and counter-revolutionaries. This far from exhaustive survey of the status and function of gallicisms, whatever their linguistic form, is, however, enough to allow us to conclude that their overall effect on the textual fabric is eventually to blur the limit between the two languages, and consequently to make it impossible to trace the authentic source of a given phrase.

Gallicisms can also be apprehended in terms of what Bakhtin named polyglossia, or the coexistence of two different tongues or national languages within the same textual space. In Conrad's work a combination of French, Italian, Spanish and German phrases is often found to the exclusion of Polish, whose influence remains mostly subterranean. But gallicisms also pertain to the realm of heteroglossia to the extent that they stand as the basis of a discordant discourse in French that runs imperceptibly all through his narratives, and which sometimes surfaces either directly as statements in French or obliquely as gallicisms, but in any case challenging the authority of the master language: English. I would consequently argue that gallicisms are the perfect instance of a cross between heteroglossia and polyglossia, whose features they combine, being at the same time tongue and voice, language and discourse, and therefore intrinsically dialogic.

In this respect, gallicisms constitute the ideal instrument with which to break out of the hermeneutic circle that readers inevitably confront in their interpretative activity. Because of the circular nature of interpretation, no reader is free from the conditions of possibility of knowledge available to her in a given language and circumscribed by the related encyclopedia. By contrast, gallicisms prevent any form of closure, each language challenging the predominance of the other, and thus postponing the emergence of stable meaning so that comprehension demands a deeper inquiry, because the French-permeated subtext thus generated is bound to be the locus of a larger freedom of interpretation, Conrad's unconscious desire being less submitted to the forces of repression.

Gallicisms, then, tend to give a spectral dimension to the narrative as they conjure up another text that remains silent but is mostly present in the mode of absence. What complicates matters further is the fact that in *The Rover* the narrator expresses himself in English whereas almost all the characters are supposed to speak French. The split implies the co-presence of two texts and gives the narrative a metafictional dimension.

This oscillation between languages testifies to the instability of the subject of the enunciation and implies that, as Galt Harpham has suggested, the mastery of Conrad's art is not strictly a linguistic mastery.[25] Artistically, his mastery came precisely from his acceptance of the loss of linguistic control and his submission to the contingency of *transcription*.[26] His keen suspicion that translation is the hidden secret of his art is betrayed by a remark he made to William Rothenstein, in a letter dated 15 November 1909, apropos of his revision of the translation of *The Nigger of the 'Narcissus'*: 'How could I resist the chance of putting something of my real self in the translator's prose?' (*CL4* 290). To the extent that gallicisms are a form of translation they can but be forms of inscription of himself in his text, a reflection of his divided self.

The parting words of Conrad's nurse in his well-known reminiscence in *A Personal Record*, 'N'oublie pas ton français, mon chéri', are prophetic but have to be reversed, since it is rather his French that never forgot him.²⁷ In other words, he accepted the vagaries of the unreliable textual voice to support his writing practice because he could not repress the intrusion of the French idiom into his fiction. Ultimately, when Conrad, in a letter to Davray dated 22 August 1903, marvelled, 'I myself, who am, without boasting, saturated with Maupassant, have been astonished at the Maupassantesque style one can give to English prose' (*CL3* 54), he was indirectly arguing his own cause, since evidence of the influence of French is everywhere in his prose. The inextricable knot that ties French and English within Conrad's particular brand of English can be seen as the hallmark of his voiceprint. His English is not, as Ford Madox Ford would have it, 'French in drag', but French is an indispensable constituent of his aesthetics of writing.

## Notes

1. H. G. Wells, *An Experiment in Autobiography*, Vol. 2 (London: Victor Gollancz, 1934), p. 616.
2. George Orwell, *The Collected Essays, Journalism, and Letters of George Orwell. Vol. 4: In Front of Your Nose, 1945–1950* (London: Secker and Warburg, 1969), pp. 488–90.
3. René Rapin (ed.), *Lettres de Joseph Conrad à Marguerite Poradowska* (Geneva: Librairie Droz, 1966), p. 186.
4. Joseph Conrad, *Nostromo* (London: J. M. Dent and Sons, 1958), p. 213.
5. French diacritics are preserved in the English text, and that tells us that he did not wish to cover his tracks.
6. Rapin, *Lettres de Joseph Conrad*.
7. Yves Hervouet, *The French Face of Joseph Conrad* (Cambridge: Cambridge University Press, 1990), p. 215. See also Gustav Morf, *The Polish Heritage of Joseph Conrad* (London: Sampson, Low, Marston, 1930); Zdislaw Najder, *Conrad's Polish Background: Letters to and from Polish Friends* (Oxford: Oxford University Press, 1964), and *Conrad Under Familial Eyes* (Cambridge: Cambridge University Press, 1983); as well as Mary Morzinski, *Linguistic Influence of Polish on Joseph Conrad's Style* (Lublin: Maria Curie-Skłodowska University, 1994).
8. Rapin, *Lettres*, p. 91.
9. Ibid. p. 130.
10. For instance, nearly half the words (grammatical ones excluded) appearing in the *incipit* of *The Rover* are of French origin.
11. Virginia Woolf, *The Common Reader. Vol. 1* (London: Hogarth Press, [1925] 2003), p. 224.
12. Joseph Conrad, *The Rover* (London: J. M. Dent and Sons, 1965), p. 4. Subsequent references are cited in the text as *Ro*.
13. On the basis of this conception of gallicisms, a rapid computation con-

cludes that the novel contains nearly two hundred French phrases quoted verbatim and nearly a hundred linguistic gallicisms. Contextual gallicisms are of course innumerable owing to the French background of the action.
14. See Michael A. Lucas, 'Conrad's Adjectival Eccentricity', *Style* 25.1 (Spring 1991), pp. 123–50.
15. Quoted in Najder, *Conrad Under Familial Eyes*, p. 162.
16. Orwell, *In Front of Your Nose*, p. 489.
17. Daphna Erdinast-Vulcan, 'Traduttore/Traditore: Language, Exile and Betrayal in Lord Jim' in J. Paccaud-Huguet (ed.), *L'Écrivain et l'Étrangeté de la Langue* (Caen: Lettres Modernes Minard, 2006), pp. 45–60 at p. 49.
18. 'In writing I wrestle painfully with that language which I feel I do not possess but which possesses me, – alas!' (*CL4* 409).
19. Avrom Fleishman, 'Conrad's Last Novel', *English Literature in Transition, 1880–1920* 12.4 (1969), pp. 189–194. Available at <http://muse.jhu.edu> (last accessed 25 January 2013).
20. Orwell, *In Front of Your Nose*, p. 489.
21. Jacques Derrida, *Monolingualism of the Other, or, the Prosthesis of Origins*, trans. Patrick Mensah (Stanford: Stanford University Press 1999).
22. Quoted in Najder, *Conrad's Polish Background*, pp. 152–61.
23. Umberto Eco defines the encyclopedia of a language as the intersubjective network of relationships that constructs a system of knowledge and context available for the semiotic activity. The question is then: how do the writer's and the reader's encyclopedias intersect? *A Theory of Semiotics* (Bloomington: Indiana University Press, 1976).
24. See Paul Grice, 'Logic and Conversation', in *Studies in the Way of Words* (Cambridge, MA: Harvard University Press, 1989), pp. 22–40.
25. Geoffrey Galt Harpham, *One of Us: The Mastery of Joseph Conrad* (Chicago: University of Chicago Press, 1996).
26. This neological construction is meant to describe the act of writing as such (from the Latin *scriptio*), consisting in penning words that involve the more or less deliberate passage from French to English that occurs when a gallicism is produced. Thus when Conrad writes the words 'the spectre of fatality' (*Ro* 217), he does not necessarily refer to impending death as the English suggests, but merely to the working of fate as the French 'spectre de la fatalité' does.
27. Joseph Conrad, *A Personal Record* (London: J. M. Dent and Sons, 1923), p. 65.

# Chapter 10

## 'The speech of my secret choice': Language and Authorial Identity in *A Personal Record*

*Andrew Purssell*

*A Personal Record* is Conrad's only major work of autobiography. It was serialised under the title *Some Reminiscences* in the *English Review*, a new literary periodical founded by Conrad's friend and occasional collaborator Ford Madox Ford, between December 1908 and June 1909. The subsequent book edition appeared in January 1912, and soon went into a second printing, in early March. A second English edition followed in 1916, and a third edition in 1919, anticipating the collected English and American editions of 1921, and underlining the gathering interest in Conrad, from both publishers and the reading public, either side of his popular breakthrough with *Chance*.[1] Conrad had planned further instalments of his 'Reminiscences' – 'under the general title Some Portraits' – and revisited the topic again in early 1922, two years before his death in 1924 (*CL5* 21).[2] However, these further volumes were never realised. The only additions Conrad would make to this slim autobiographical corpus were his two introductions to *A Personal Record*: 'A Familiar Preface' (1912), for the first English edition published by Eveleigh Nash, and his 'Author's Note' (1919) for the third English edition, published by J. M. Dent.[3] Although *The Mirror of the Sea* (1906), an early collection of autobiographical essays, marks his first attempt at the form, and the late essay 'Poland Revisited' (1915) a continuation, *A Personal Record* would remain the single planned, public account of his life.[4] *A Personal Record* is also significant as a sustained reflection, across its serialised parts, book editions and prefaces, on the circumstances surrounding Conrad's entry into public life in the first place: namely, his decision to become a writer, and in particular, a writer in his third language, English.

## Geographical expressions and the adoption of English

Conrad saw himself as having three lives and identities. Accordingly, *A Personal Record* encompasses his upbringing in Polish Ukraine, his early sea years in the south of France and the Mediterranean, and his subsequent apprenticeship as a writer in Britain. As noted in the Introduction, Conrad was born Józef Teodor Konrad Korzeniowski on 3 December 1857 in Berdychiv, a part of northern Ukraine that had formerly belonged to the Kingdom of Poland. Divided between the occupying powers of Austria, Prussia and Russia in 1795, Poland was now a political idea without territorial existence – 'a mere geographical expression', as Conrad memorably puts it in 'The Crime of Partition' (1919).[5] Another of Conrad's late essays, 'Geography and Some Explorers' (1924), recalls a childhood spent poring over maps, in particular the 'exciting spaces of white paper' generated through European imperialism, and this contemplation of cartographic absence offers a comment on Poland's erasure from the map by its imperial neighbours: Conrad's personal history here doubles as political parable.[6]

In fact, Conrad's personal history and that of Poland were deeply intertwined. Conrad's parents were ardent Polish nationalists – though not Revolutionists, as he makes clear in the 'Author's Note' (1919) to *A Personal Record*:

> Why the description 'revolutionary' should have been applied ... to the Polish risings of 1831 and 1863 I cannot really understand. These risings were purely revolts against foreign domination. The Russians themselves called them 'rebellions', which, from their point of view, was the exact truth.[7]

In making this political distinction between the language of one truth regime and that of another (namely, Poland's oppressor Russia), Conrad underlines that what matters is not the intrinsic truth (or not) of such labels, but rather 'control over their classification as such', as Barbara Herrnstein Smith has shown.[8] This would certainly inform the production of *A Personal Record*, which was written partly as a response to his continued subjection to similar forms of categorisation: 'I have always felt myself looked upon somewhat in the light of a phenomenon, a position which outside the circus world cannot be regarded as desirable' (*PR* v). Such categorisation would also have disastrous implications for Conrad's family. His father's anti-Russian activities led to his arrest and imprisonment, and the family's eventual exile: it was during these years that Conrad's parents died, in quick succession, leaving him orphaned at the age of eleven.[9] Although Conrad does not dwell on these circumstances in *A Personal Record* (perhaps out of consideration for the readership he was trying to court), they lend particular weight to his claim to have been 'adopted' in the years since by the symbolic systems of another country and culture: 'well, yes, there was adoption; but it was I who was adopted by the genius of the [English] language' (*PR* vii).

Correspondingly, the floating home of the ship – 'destined for so many years to be the only roof over my head' (*PR* 138) – provides an appropriate emblem of his rootless early life and exilic status. Conrad's nautical career began in 1874, when he made several voyages out of Marseilles to the French Antilles, and ended in 1894 after an abortive voyage transporting emigrants out of Rouen to French Canada. Conrad's sea years therefore began and ended in France, just as his 'first introduction to the sea in literature' was through his father's translations of Victor Hugo's *Les Travailleurs de la mer* (*PR* 72). Yet he spent most of his years as a sailor in the British Merchant Service, and it was during this period that he acquired the prodigiously wide experience of the further reaches of the colonial world to which he later returned in his fiction. Conrad's nationality had barred him from long-term employment in France, yet there was no such restriction in the British merchant marine in the late nineteenth century, the 'Britishness' of which was to a significant degree nominal, and where foreign sailors were common, and, moreover, essential. The service may have been contracting when Conrad joined, thanks partly to the switch from sail to steam, and partly to rising competition from America, Germany and Japan; however, as 'Heart of Darkness' famously announces, Britain remained at the centre of the world economy, with British shipping still accounting for over forty per cent of the world's tonnage.[10] Conrad's entry into the British Merchant Service was therefore the result of a coming together of circumstances, rather than the premeditated decision he claims in *A Personal Record*: 'Already the determined resolve, that "if a seaman, then an English seaman", was formulated in my head though, of course, in the Polish language' (*PR* 122). It was, of course, through his service in British ships that Conrad learned to speak and write (and as *A Personal Record* suggests, write fiction) in English, cementing the connection with Britain and with British culture celebrated here. Conrad's sea-fiction is notable for depicting the British Merchant Service as a distinctly polyphonic, cosmopolitan space, reflecting the conditions of his own entry into it. Beyond this, as Allan H. Simmons has argued, the late nineteenth-century celebration 'of the sea as a defining national myth' is something to which Conrad had, in no small part, latterly given shape through his own output.[11] In this way, *A Personal Record* is not simply a reflection on the English seaman Conrad became, but rather a continued construction of that becoming, where what it means to be 'an English seaman' has been, and is being, recalibrated and expanded throughout Conrad's works.

Towards the end of *A Personal Record*, Conrad charts his entry into this professional body by revisiting his master mariner examination. As Andrea White observes, Conrad imagines 'his merchant mariner self in ancestral terms, terms he felt he needed to appropriate, having an inappropriate genealogy himself'.[12] Thus Conrad suggestively withholds or downplays details of his Polish biography such as his surname ('it has twelve letters' [*PR* 118]), nationality and place of birth, details which tie him to the sign systems – bureaucratic, juridical, linguistic, 'the machinery of official relations' (*PR* 118) – of another country. Meanwhile, by presenting his date of birth in terms of a nationally significant event ('The Mutiny Year' [*PR* 118]), he writes himself into the sign systems of his adopted country. At the same time, he casts his examiner as 'a professional ancestor, a sort of grandfather in the craft' (*PR* 119), reaffirming *The Mirror of the Sea*'s assertion that 'all sailors belong to one family'.[13] These tropes of continuity and inheritance are further plotted in the examination itself, which sees Conrad tasked with setting 'a homeward passage' (*PR* 115), the coordinates of which are implicitly 'England', and which ends with Conrad exiting the examiner's office on Tower Hill, 'the Hill of many beheadings' (*PR* 120), a facetious reflection on the possible outcome of his examination, but also an evocation of English national history that in the context seems far from incidental. According to White, the way in which Conrad writes himself into the hierarchy of the merchant service 'reveals his own need to compose a self while suggesting the positional and discursively constructed nature of all identity'.[14] In fact, it is tempting to view this scene as emblematic of the narrative strategies of the memoir as a whole, whereby the assertion of this new professional identity also plays to his assertion of an 'English' authorial self.

This 'English' self is more fully laid bare at the end of the memoir, where Conrad recalls his physical encounter, while still a sailor in France, with the British steamer *James Westoll*.[15] Conrad describes reaching out to touch 'the smooth flank of the first English ship I ever touched in my life' (*PR* 137), and offers this as retrospectively signalling a foundational moment of cultural identification:

> it was then that, for the very first time in my life, I heard myself addressed in English – the speech of my secret choice, of my future, of long friendships, of the deepest affections, of hours of toil and hours of ease, and of solitary hours too, of books read, of thoughts pursued, of remembered emotions – of my very dreams! (*PR* 136)

Conrad's presentation of this moment of identification as a process of 'hail and response' is significant beyond the immediate context of maritime communications, recalling Althusser's theorisation of '*interpellation* or hailing', those 'procedures of individuation' which rest upon an external determinant, and which play a central role in the emergence and existence of individuals as subjects.[16] Conrad's reconstruction of his final, abiding memory of the vessel – also the final lines of the memoir – is equally freighted:

> Before she had gone in a quarter of a mile she hoisted her flag as the harbour regulations prescribe for arriving and departing ships. I saw it suddenly flicker and stream out on the flagstaff. The Red Ensign! ... the symbolic, protecting warm bit of bunting flung wide upon the seas. (*PR* 137–8)

It seems appropriate that having asserted his immersion in the symbolic systems of the country in which he would later settle and become a writer, Conrad should reinforce this by focusing on 'the symbolic' apparatus through which this particular ship self-identifies herself as 'English'.

This is the last in a series of represented first encounters, which, taken together, lend an air of inevitability to Conrad's subsequent claim in the 'Author's Note' to *A Personal Record* that 'if I had not written in English I would not have written at all' (*PR* viii).[17] These range from his 'first contact with British mankind' (*PR* 39) while travelling with his tutor as a boy in the Swiss Alps (in the shape of his 'unforgettable Englishman' [*PR* 40]) to his first encounter with English literary culture through his father's translations of Shakespeare (*PR* 71) and his subsequent reading of Dickens, Scott, Thackeray and Trollope, 'one of the English novelists whose works I read for the first time in English', and whose 'political novels' Conrad dimly recalls reading 'the day before my writing life began' (*PR* 71, 73). That writing life is threaded throughout *A Personal Record*, to the point that it unsettles the generic origins and ostensible purpose of the memoir as a piece of life writing – the 'established conventions' of which Conrad deliberately 'throws off' (*PR* 'A Familiar Preface', xxiii), along with the generic models laid down and 'discredited' (*PR* 95), as he irreverently puts it, by literary predecessors such as Jean-Jacques Rousseau, whose *Confessions* (1782–9) arguably marks the first modern work of autobiography. It is a strikingly modernist gesture: from its memorable opening, 'Books may be written in all sorts of places' (*PR* 3), *A Personal Record* often seems to be as much about the origins and growth of Conrad's first novel, *Almayer's Folly* (1895), from the 'blackening over' of its 'first ... page' (*PR* 68–9), as it is about the life of its author.

As all of this suggests, *A Personal Record* is not a 'record' in the conventional sense: as with Conrad's fiction, it eschews a linear chronology for a more discursive, digressive form, and in this sense its serial title 'Some Reminiscences' offers a more suitable description of its contents. In their introduction to the Cambridge edition of *A Personal Record*, Zdzisław Najder and J. H. Stape suggest that the memoir 'remains Conrad's most concerted attempt to discern a pattern in his life, or perhaps to impose one *a posteriori*'.[18] If *A Personal Record* is about this, then it could be argued that the attempt failed, as its contemporary reception in Britain, which stressed its 'formlessness' and 'incoherent' substance, emphasises.[19] Indeed, *A Personal Record* is less about the retrospective imposition of pattern and order than a reassertion at the level of narrative of the facility with which Conrad, to adapt Stephen Greenblatt, shifting restlessly from one role to another, self-consciously constructed the phenomenon known as 'Joseph Conrad'.[20]

Nor is *A Personal Record* a document of fact, as its reception through the years has repeatedly underlined. Edward Said has called it 'a mixture of laconic honesty and evasion', and even a 'mock biography', putting it somewhere between what Conrad refers to as the 'exact rendering of authentic memories' (*PR* 25), on the one hand, and 'the debasing touch of insincerity' (*PR* xix), on the other.[21] Similarly, Najder has observed that 'most of [Conrad's] accounts of events require correction, and there are also surprising omissions'.[22] This might be ascribed to the substance of the memoir itself, as Robert Hampson has suggested: 'Memory is notoriously creative, and Conrad regularly adjusts and fictionalises his past in his retelling of it.'[23] A prime example is precisely Conrad's 'choice' of English as the language of his literary work. In the 'Author's Note' (1919) to *A Personal Record*, Conrad chides his friend and former stablemate at *Blackwood's*, Hugh Clifford, for having erroneously claimed he had 'exercised a choice between . . . French and English' (*PR* vi) when becoming a writer; in so doing, he appears to overlook that in the work being introduced he refers to English as the 'speech of my secret choice' (*PR* 136) – creating the double paradox of a secret which in the moment of its disclosure ceases to be so, but which also never *was*.[24] If Conrad regularly adjusts and fictionalises his past in his retelling of it, in this case that adjustment occurs within the pages of a single volume. As a contemporary reviewer, probably Ford, put it at the time: 'These reminiscences will not be of much use to chroniclers.'[25] At the same time, and putting aside that Ford's relationship with the historical record was also typically more selective than scrupulous, all of this is to overlook that throughout Conrad's works the sovereignty and truth value of 'facts', and the stability of signs and their signifiers more broadly, are frequently questioned and unsettled, as Andrew Michael Roberts and Cedric Watts, among others, have shown.[26] In other words, to measure Conrad's memoir against the historical record rather than view it in the context out of which it emerged is in many ways to miss the point. Its gaps, suppressions and creative adjustments are all integral to its retrospective construction of a mythology of cultural affiliation: what matters is not the 'facts', but that Conrad chooses to present them as such, and this includes his relationship with English.

## Linguistic nationalism and global English

As Terry Eagleton notes, theorists of literary reception have long argued that 'a work's reception is never just an "external" fact about it, a contingent matter of book reviews and bookshop sales'. Rather, it 'is a constitutive dimension of the work itself. Every literary text is built out of a sense of its potential audience', and 'includes an image of whom it is written *for*: every work encodes within itself ... an "implied reader"', and 'intimates in its every gesture the kind of "addressee" it anticipates'.[27] This is certainly true of Conrad generally, who, as Fredric Jameson points out, was able to gratify both the 'limited coteries' of modernism and the popular market by straddling '"high" culture and mass culture' within the same covers.[28] It is particularly true of *A Personal Record*, which was written at a time when Conrad was becoming increasingly involved in the efforts of his publishers to market him to a growing audience in Britain and America, and which was partly conceived with self-promotion in mind. As Conrad explained to his agent J. B. Pinker, 'I believe there is a good deal of curiosity as to my personality in the US and ... in this country as well' (*CL4* 138). This relationship with the reader is foregrounded in the memoir's prefatory notes, which, as Frederick R. Karl suggests, were 'conceived ... as a way of establishing rapport with his ... audience', offering an extension rather than an 'explanation' of the work they introduce.[29] The faint outlines of this textual relationship are also implicit in Conrad's encounter with the Port of London examiner, in which he reflects, while presenting his potted biography to this 'professional ancestor', upon the assumed expectations of his auditor: 'It was the exact truth, but he would not have understood the somewhat exceptional psychology of my sea-going, I fear' (*PR* 119).

*A Personal Record* was written not only with the 'curious' reader in mind, but also as a considered response to Conrad's developing critical reputation. In particular, Najder has suggested that *A Personal Record* was written as a response to the critic Robert Lynd, whose review of *A Set of Six* (1908) for the *Daily News* had labelled Conrad a writer 'without either country or language'.³⁰ Though Conrad may have agreed with Lynd's valuation of the collection, which he himself acknowledged to be 'a fairly varied lot' (*CL3* 509), he may have been surprised by Lynd's cultural stance, the logic of which enabled him to downplay, and even dismiss, Conrad's entire output: 'the works of Joseph Conrad translated from the Polish would ... have been a more precious possession on English shelves than the works of Joseph Conrad in the original English'.³¹ Conrad alludes to Lynd in *A Personal Record* as that 'gentleman ... who, metaphorically speaking, jumps upon me with both feet' (*PR* 106). He goes on to assert that 'the writer's substance is his writing; the rest of him is but a vain shadow, cherished or hated on uncritical grounds' (*PR* 107). Though aimed at Lynd, Conrad's remark about the vagaries of critical opinion also acknowledges the unpredictable set of relations which exist between author and audience more broadly – that is, that 'our understanding of authors derives principally from the books in which their texts circulate'.³² This in turn acknowledges the purpose as well as the unpredictable outcome of his current literary project. As a work of autobiography, *A Personal Record* marks an attempt to try to shape the way that posterity will view his life and works, just as the construction of a collected edition (the idea of which was floated by his US publisher F. N. Doubleday in 1913), or the authorisation of a biography (for which Conrad would later select his French translator G. Jean Aubry), might mark others. At the same time, Conrad was clearly aware, as someone who closely followed the critical fortunes of his works, that 'authors can never have complete control over their reputations'.³³

In this regard, Lynd was not alone: other reviewers had pronounced Conrad's works as 'alien to our national genius', and Conrad himself an 'alien of genius'.³⁴ Unsurprisingly, Conrad complained to Edward Garnett that 'I've been cried up of late as a sort of freak, an amazing bloody foreigner writing in English' (*CL3* 488). Garnett's own sustained (and for Conrad singularly problematic) view of the author's 'Sclavonism' (*PR* viii)³⁵ meant that he was well acquainted with – and even partly responsible for – Conrad's othering by the critical establishment, which is enshrined in Virginia Woolf's obituary of Conrad for the *Times Literary Supplement* following his death in 1924, where she suggestively refers to Conrad as 'our ... guest'.³⁶ The extent to which this view of Conrad prevailed can also be felt in F. R. Leavis's *The Great Tradition* (1948), a widely influential and, for the thirty years or so after its publication, inescapable work in Conrad criticism.³⁷ In it, Leavis offers the first systematic, full-length construction of a Conrad canon, and places Conrad at the leading edge of a radically revised tradition of the English novel, together with Jane Austen, George Eliot and Henry James: 'Conrad is among the very greatest novelists in the language – or any language.'[38] In this way, Conrad's entry into the English literary canon almost a quarter of a century after his death seems, paradoxically, to confirm his outsider status: Conrad's English is both beside, and yet partly, the point.

Conrad's years in the British merchant marine situated him in the same imperial networks through which 'English as a language . . . spread around the globe', as Robert J. C. Young has argued, where it underwent 'cultural encounters with the language[s] of others who dwel[t] far beyond the limits of its own originating continental space'.[39] This is not to say so much that English becomes 'globalised, overpowering all other languages, as that it has a constant facility of self-hybridization', being 'already a hybrid compound of the languages of Europe: just as with Conrad's Kurtz, all Europe went into the making of it'.[40] Yet Conrad's years as a writer also coincide with a concerted attempt in Britain 'to remove the later encrustations of French and scholarly Latin and restore English to its purer plain Anglo-Saxon forms, a strategy endorsed by many from Hazlitt to Hopkins to Herbert Spencer, from George Eliot to George Orwell'.[41] Thus the reception of *A Personal Record* has Conrad caught somewhere between domesticating cultural difference, as in the *Outlook*'s pinpointing of a peculiarly 'English humour', or dangerously estranging the language, as in the *Spectator*'s complaint that Conrad's English remained a 'foreign language', irretrievably corrupted by the Polish and French which preceded it.[42] The *Spectator* also remarked that Conrad frequently 'misuses words', making the work 'less easy to understand',[43] typifying a conceptual sleight of hand in Conrad's reception more broadly, whereby the complexity of his prose is proof of his 'foreignness' rather than the mark of a modernism founded on literary experimentation.

Conrad remained acutely attentive to these kinds of views, which reflected less a growing critical consensus than a gathering typology. This is made clear in the 'Author's Note' (1919) to *A Personal Record*, which, he admits, is prompted as much by the need to redress the sustained appearance of 'certain statements about myself . . . bear[ing] upon the question of language' – including a recent review damning *The Arrow of Gold* (1919) with the faint praise that English was not his native tongue – as by the need to introduce the 're-issue of this book' (*PR* v).[44] Conrad also uses the 'Author's Note' to respond to the misreading of his life and works through the prism of 'Sclavonism' by

Garnett and H. L. Mencken (*PR* viii–ix), and to revisit his first meeting with Hugh Clifford, who, drawing on his time as a colonial official in Malaya, had questioned the authenticity of the Malay fiction on which Conrad had begun to build his reputation: 'he ended by telling me with the uncompromising yet kindly firmness of a man accustomed to speak unpalatable truths even to Oriental potentates ... that as a matter of fact I didn't know anything about Malays' (*PR* vi). Revealingly, Conrad groups those who would contest his ability to represent the 'real Malay' together with those who would proclaim him not really 'English', and in so doing he makes a broader point not just about cultural identity but also about the self-arrogation and safeguarding of the privileged cultural position from which such statements are made. Though his popular legacy was by now assured, as the new English edition for which this preface was commissioned attests, Conrad clearly felt that he remained on the outside of the literary establishment. In this light, his assertion of a 'secret choice' in *A Personal Record* marks a claiming of autonomy and authority which speaks directly to the politics of his contemporary reception: that of one denied the cultural privileges that should come with the adoption of English as his chosen medium of literary expression.

## Authorial identity and composite texts

*A Personal Record* is less the product of one individual, as its title suggests, than of several contributors, and this inevitably raises questions about its projection of authorial identity. Debilitated by gout, Conrad dictated most of the text to a secretary, and possibly part of it to his wife Jessie, after Ford had initially offered to take it down from dictation himself – no doubt to help spur the prompt delivery of copy on which the fledgling *English Review* depended, from an author for whom writing was a far from fluent process, as his struggle and eventual failure to finish his 'Reminiscences' underlines. Conrad's reference in the memoir to his 'sacrosanct pen of authorship' (*PR* 91) is, in this case, more figurative than literal, since the text was heavily dependent on his amanuenses for its initial spelling and punctuation.[45] In addition, *A Personal Record* was subject to the same mechanisms of publishing as the rest of his output. These ranged from editorial revision and correction (notably the tidying up of verbs and articles, which Conrad, writing in his third language, typically found challenging) to the imposition of the characteristically heavy house punctuation of the period, where textual idiosyncrasies were regularised, and even led to the introduction of errors through misimpression, such as the ironic substitution of 'spoi' for 'spoil' in the first English edition,[46] or through mishearing at the level of dictation, where the impact of Conrad's heavily inflected pronunciation – 'his strange yet fascinating accent'[47] – can be felt on the printed text, along with his habitual gallicisms and polonisms. As editor of the *English Review*, Ford would have been part of the same machinery through which *A Personal Record* was seen into print. Although the extent of his input is contested, Conrad was certainly indebted to Ford as a prose stylist for refining 'his occasionally unidiomatic phraseology and syntax – those tell-tale marks of foreignness'.[48] As all of this suggests, and as the pre-print materials of *A Personal Record* underline, Conrad's works are always to some degree composite texts, 'his' English the product of numerous – sometimes competing – hands.

As an exploration of the origins of its author, a self-exiled Pole writing in the language of the country in which he had recently settled, *A Personal Record* is also an appropriately polyphonic text. It could be argued that, in *A Personal Record*, 'a certain kind of reader is already included within the very act of writing itself, as an internal structure of the text', because 'the language [it] uses already implies a range of possible audiences rather than another'.[49] This is not quite the case with Conrad's memoir, one of whose aims, after all, was 'to make Polish life enter English literature' (*CL4* 138), as Conrad put it to Pinker. Yet the 'Polish life' presented in *A Personal Record* is not always Conrad's own. Parts of his 'Reminiscences' are not about him at all, but rather about distant relations such as his great-uncle 'Mr. Nicolas B.', a veteran of the Napoleonic Wars, whose culinary encounter with a Lithuanian dog during the Grand Army's retreat from Moscow a century earlier is wryly recast, in a playful interleaving of family myth and Polish history, as epitomising the 'patriotic' hunger of his fellow dispossessed countrymen (*PR* 35). In addition, some of Conrad's 'Reminiscences' are based on and, in places, are direct translations of another Polish memoir, *Pamiętnik mojego życia* (1900), by his uncle and guardian Tadeusz Bobrowski.[50] Although Conrad highlights these borrowings by placing the parts lifted in inverted commas,[51] this act of cultural ventriloquism would surely have been lost on the majority of his British readership, as the contemporary Polish reception of the memoir makes clear.[52] If, as Conrad asserts, 'A writer of imaginative prose ... stands confessed in his works' (*PR* 95), in *A Personal Record* the cultural coordinates of this confession often appear confused.

One reason for this is that *A Personal Record* was motivated not just by Conrad's reception in Britain, but also by his reception in his native Poland. Though particularly stung by Lynd's criticism, Conrad was also aware that several Polish writers and intellectuals had charged him with abandoning his country and cultural heritage.[53] Where Conrad found himself 'jumped upon' in Britain for writing in English, he found himself attacked in his homeland for taking 'a standing jump out of his racial surroundings' (*PR* 121), and not writing in Polish. For instance, in a remarkable attack in the Polish weekly *Kraj* (to which Conrad's father had been a contributor), the Polish novelist and nationalist Eliza Orzeszkowa accused Conrad of draining away 'the life blood of the nation' in order to enrich the 'Anglo-Saxons', as well as himself.[54] As with Lynd's criticism, such a view is not far removed from the 'language nationalism' of the late nineteenth century, 'which produced the idea that nations and races should be sealed homogeneous units comparable to a language, with the corollary that the nation should have a single language with borders as clearly marked as those on the map', as Young explains.[55] In this heavily politicised context, Conrad's use of English entails not only the creation of an authorial, public self, but also the self-erasure of his Polish identity. In this way, Conrad's presentation of some of the obscurer branches of his family tree and his palimpsestic deference to an already published family history, which simultaneously allow him to address his Polish heritage while revealing little about himself, has a certain cultural logic.

So, too, does Conrad's choice of narrative form. In its elliptical, fragmentary and foreshortened narrative, *A Personal Record* draws upon the Polish literary form the *gawęda*, which in turn grew out from the influence of Laurence Sterne's *Tristram Shandy* (1760–7) and *A Sentimental Journey* (1768), popular, and much copied, following their appearance in translation in Poland during the late eighteenth and early nineteenth century.[56] The *gawęda* typically features a narrator who 'relates events from his personal experience', and whose implied audience is 'composed of his own milieu'.[57] For an author 'without country or language', this seems doubly significant. *A Personal Record* sees Conrad reflecting on his 'adoption' by the British merchant marine and by the English language on behalf of his new English audience. At the same time, it also sees him addressing his Polish heritage, and even a covert Polish audience, through the discursive formations of the Poland he had left behind. Fittingly, Conrad's preface to the first book edition is signed 'J.C.K.' – a combination of his English pen name and his Polish surname, unprecedented and unrepeated in his works, which recalls the famous reference to himself in his letters as 'Homo duplex' (*CL3* 89), pointing to an identity split between his native Polish and adopted English cultures.

In this regard, the *English Review* was an appropriate choice for the serialisation of Conrad's reminiscences. *A Personal Record* appeared in the inaugural issue of the *Review* in December 1908, where it ran for a further six instalments. On the one hand, this was a periodical that was founded by Ford, the author of the recent *England and the English* trilogy (1905–7), and whose inaugural issue carried original works by Thomas Hardy, H. G. Wells and John Galsworthy, the last being, along with Ford, a prominent member of Conrad's English literary circle. On the other, it was also 'a periodical that promised to be singularly international' – even 'un-English' – in tone, as Ford later remarked.[58] Thus the inaugural issue of the *Review* also carried stories by Henry James ('The Jolly Corner') and Lev Tolstoy (a translation of 'The Raid'), while subsequent issues carried works by Anatole France and Ezra Pound and, under the editorship of Ford's successor Austin Harrison, by W. B. Yeats, Katherine Mansfield, Herman Hesse and Anton Chekhov. As E. V. Lucas later complained to Conrad, the *English Review* seemed 'generally too foreign for its title' (*CL4* 246) – or as Ford put it elsewhere, 'a contradiction in terms'.[59] According to Ford, '[i]t was Conrad who chose the title' of the new periodical,[60] whose content was intended to reflect more the international currents and cosmopolitan makeup of English literary modernism than a shoring-up of the 'national' literature. These currents are, of course, reflected in Conrad's works: English may be Conrad's chosen vehicle of representation, but it is not always the language represented – as is exemplified by his debut novel *Almayer's Folly*, which features throughout *A Personal Record*, where the represented discourses are Dutch and Malay. If the 'Englishness' of the *Review* was nominal, it is surely apt that Conrad – whose background and works are representative of the transnational currents and polyglossia of modernism and empire – should be behind its naming. Similarly, if *A Personal Record* marks a stage in the continuing process, as well as a reflection on the process, of the construction of Conrad's public identity, it seems equally apt that the hand of its author can be felt on the vehicle of its dissemination.

## Conclusion: linguistic self-fashioning

In *A Personal Record*, Conrad discusses the events in his life which he considers to have shaped his identity, from the January Uprising of 1863 in his native Poland, 'an event which . . . has coloured my earliest impressions' (*PR* 56), to 'the English and Scots seamen . . . who had the last say in the formation of my character' (*PR* 100). At the same time, *A Personal Record* is not just a public revelation of the 'coherent, justifiable personality . . . behind the books', as Conrad puts it in 'A Familiar Preface' (*PR* xxiii), but also a continued construction of that personality – a form of self-fashioning. As Stephen Greenblatt has argued, 'self-fashioning . . . functions without regard for a sharp distinction between literature and social life': 'It invariably crosses the boundaries between the creation of literary characters, the shaping of one's own identity, the experience of being moulded by forces outside one's control, the attempt to fashion other selves.'[61] This seems especially germane to *A Personal Record*, which offers a reconstruction of the 'feelings and sensations connected with the writing of my first book', *Almayer's Folly* (*PR* xxiii), and is itself a response to the critical pressures of the literary career inaugurated by that novel's publication in 1895. Similarly, Greenblatt's thesis is a response to a critical tendency to 'wall off literary symbolism from the symbolic structures elsewhere, as if art alone were a human creation, as if humans themselves were not [also] cultural artifacts'.[62] In other words, the figure of the 'novelist' described in 'A Familiar Preface' (1912) is not just a creator of selves which are mediated and manipulated through the literary text – 'the only reality in an invented world [of] imaginary things, happenings and people' (*PR* xv) – but also an entity which can be 'authored'. This is exemplified in the 'Author's Note' (1919) to *A Personal Record*, in which Conrad claims that rather than consciously choosing between his second and third languages, French and English, in embarking on a career as an author, the language 'chose' him: 'I . . . was adopted by . . . the language, which directly . . . fashioned my still plastic character' (*PR* vi–vii). As a statement on the fundamental centrality of language in the formation of the self, Conrad's remark bears a striking similarity to subsequent theorisations of language during the twentieth century's 'linguistic revolution', whereby language is seen as something which 'always pre-exists the individual subject, as the very realm in which he or she unfolds'[63] – unsurprising, perhaps, for an author given to punctuating his novels with Schopenhauerian philosophising, and whose works have since provided a rich seam for the turn towards theory in the decades after the Second World War.[64] In the immediate context of *A Personal Record*, it is a statement of malleability that is itself supremely manipulative, marking a response to the shaping of his public image by forces outside his control, to adapt Greenblatt, and a countervailing attempt to assert control over that image.

## Notes

1. *Chance* began serialisation in the *New York Herald* in January 1912, and marked a turning point in Conrad's popular reception and personal fortunes.
2. According to Jessie Conrad's memoir of her husband, 'A Personal Record would have had a successor if Conrad had only lived a few more years.' See *Joseph Conrad as I Knew Him* (London: William Heinemann, 1926), p. 138.
3. The Nash edition retained the serial title, *Some Reminiscences*. The first American edition, published by Harpers, appeared under the title *A Personal Record*, also in January 1912. This title was chosen for all subsequent book editions.
4. Conrad's slight autobiographical output stands in sharp contrast with the number of memoirs and biographies on Conrad (or works drawing on biographical matter) published since G. Jean Aubry's two-volume *Joseph Conrad: Life and Letters* (1927) was rushed into print soon after Conrad's death. For a survey, see David Miller, 'Biographies and Memoirs', in Allan H. Simmons (ed.), *Joseph Conrad in Context* (Cambridge: Cambridge University Press, 2009), pp. 42–8.
5. Joseph Conrad, 'The Crime of Partition', in *Notes on Life and Letters* (London: J. M. Dent and Sons, 1924), p. 118. Subsequent references are cited in the text as *NLL*.
6. Joseph Conrad, 'Geography and Some Explorers', in *Last Essays* (London: J. M. Dent and Sons, 1926), p. 13. Subsequent references are cited in the text as *LE*.
7. Joseph Conrad, 'Author's Note', in *A Personal Record* (London: J. M. Dent and Sons, 1919), pp. iii–x at p. ix. Subsequent references are cited in the text as *PR*.
8. Barbara Herrnstein Smith, *Contingencies of Value: Alternative Perspectives for Critical Theory* (Cambridge, MA: Harvard University Press, 1988), p. 132. For a discussion of Conrad's political novels in this context of language and political identity, see Katherine Isobel Baxter, 'Speaking Foreign: Conrad and Modernist Multilingualism', *Studia Neophilologica* 85 (2013), pp. 17–28.
9. For a discussion, see Zdzisław Najder, *Joseph Conrad: A Life*, trans. Halina Najder (Rochester, NY: Camden House, 2007), pp. 3–47.
10. Mark D. Larabee, 'Joseph Conrad and the Maritime Tradition', in John G. Peters (ed.), *A Historical Guide to Joseph Conrad* (Oxford: Oxford University Press, 2010), pp. 55–60 at p. 53. See also Eric Hobsbawm, *The Age of Empire, 1875–1914* (London: Abacus, 2005), p. 51.
11. Allan H. Simmons, 'Identity and Representation in Conrad's Early Career', *Conradiana* 29.1 (2004), pp. 1–26 at p. 5.
12. Andrea White, 'Writing from Within: Autobiography and Immigrant Subjectivity in *The Mirror of the Sea*', in Carola M. Kaplan, Peter Lancelot Mallios and Andrea White (eds), *Conrad in the Twenty-First Century: Contemporary Approaches and Perspectives* (Abingdon: Routledge, 2005), pp. 241–9 at p. 246.

13. Joseph Conrad, *The Mirror of the Sea: Memories and Impressions* (London: J. M. Dent and Sons, 1923), p. 148.
14. White, 'Writing from Within', p. 247.
15. Hans van Marle suggests this vessel was actually the *James Mason*. See 'An Ambassador of Conrad's Future: The *James Mason* in Marseilles, 1874', *L'Époque Conradienne* (1988), pp. 63–7.
16. See Louis Althusser, 'Ideology and Ideological State Apparatuses (Notes Towards an Investigation)', in *Lenin and Philosophy and Other Essays*, trans. Ben Brewster (New York: Monthly Review Press, 2001), pp. 85–126 at p. 118 (emphasis in original); and Robert J. C. Young, *White Mythologies: Writing History and the West*, 2nd edn (London: Routledge, 2004), p. 116.
17. For a discussion of first sightings elsewhere in Conrad, see Robert Hampson, 'First and Last Sights in *Lord Jim*', in Fausto Ciompo (ed.), *'One of Us': Studi inglesi e conradiani offerti a Mario Curelli* (Pisa: Edizioni ETS, 2009), pp. 33–48.
18. Zdzisław Najder and J. H. Stape, 'Introduction', in Joseph Conrad, *A Personal Record*, eds Zdzisław Najder and J. H. Stape (Cambridge: Cambridge University Press, 2008), pp. xxi–xlix at p. xxii.
19. *Manchester Guardian*, 2 February 1912, p. 4. Rpt. CR3 32–3.
20. Stephen Greenblatt, *Renaissance Self-Fashioning: From More to Shakespeare* (Chicago: University of Chicago Press, 2005), p. xiii.
21. Edward Said, *Joseph Conrad and the Fiction of Autobiography* (New York: Columbia University Press, 2008), pp. 23, 79.
22. Najder, *Conrad: A Life*, p. 35.
23. Robert Hampson, *Conrad's Secrets* (Basingstoke: Palgrave Macmillan, 2012), p. 2.
24. Published anonymously, Clifford's essay marks one of the first sustained critical engagements with Conrad's work. See Hugh Clifford, 'Mr. Conrad at Home and Abroad', *Singapore Free Press*, 30 August 1898, p. 142. Rpt. CR1 277–82.
25. *English Review* (April 1912), p. 158. Rpt. CR3 65–6.
26. See Andrew Michael Roberts, 'Conrad, Theory and Value', in Andrew Gibson and Robert Hampson (eds), *Conrad and Theory* (Amsterdam: Rodopi, 1994), pp. 178–202; and Cedric Watts, 'Fraudulent Signifiers: Saussure and the Sixpence in "Karain"', *Conradian* 28.2 (2003), pp. 13–28. There is a similar tendency to view Conrad's private correspondence as 'a repository of Conrad's fixed beliefs', as Gene M. Moore and Owen Knowles have pointed out. See Gene M. Moore and Owen Knowles (eds), *The Oxford Reader's Companion to Conrad* (Oxford: Oxford University Press, 2000), p. 204.
27. Terry Eagleton, *Literary Theory: An Introduction* (Oxford: Blackwell, 1983), pp. 73–4 (emphasis in original).
28. Fredric Jameson, *The Political Unconscious: Narrative as a Socially Symbolic Act* (Abingdon: Routledge, 2002), p. 191. See Joseph Conrad 'Author's Note', in *Chance* (London: J. M. Dent and Sons, 1923), pp. vii–x at p. viii.
29. Frederick R. Karl, *Joseph Conrad, The Three Lives: A Biography* (London: Faber and Faber, 1979), p. 822.

30. Robert Lynd, 'Mr. Conrad', *Daily News*, 10 August 1908, p. 3. Rpt. *CR2* 446. For a discussion, see Najder, *Conrad: A Life*, pp. 390–2. For a wide-ranging discussion of Conrad and Lynd, see Richard Niland, '"Who's that fellow Lynn?": Conrad and Robert Lynd', *Conradian* 33.1 (2008), pp. 130–44.
31. Lynd, 'Mr. Conrad', p. 3.
32. Andrew Nash, 'The Culture of Collected Editions: Authorship, Reputation, and the Canon', in Andrew Nash (ed.), *The Culture of Collected Editions* (Basingstoke: Palgrave Macmillan, 2003), pp. 1–15 at p. 3.
33. Ibid. p. 2.
34. Norman Sherry (ed.), *Conrad: The Critical Heritage* (London: Routledge and Kegan Paul, 1973), pp. 195, 185.
35. As Conrad complained to Garnett: 'You remember always that I am a Slav ... but you seem to forget that I am a Pole' (*CL3* 492).
36. Virginia Woolf, 'Joseph Conrad', *Times Literary Supplement*, 14 August 1924, pp. 493–4 at p. 493.
37. For a discussion, see Andrew Purssell, 'Making the Conrad Canon', in J. H. Stape (ed.), *The New Cambridge Companion to Joseph Conrad* (Cambridge: Cambridge University Press, 2015), pp. 1–14.
38. F. R. Leavis, *The Great Tradition: George Eliot, Henry James, Joseph Conrad* (London: Chatto and Windus, 1948), p. 226.
39. Robert J. C. Young, 'English and the Language of Others', *European Review* 17.1 (2009), pp. 203–12 at p. 203.
40. Ibid. p. 204.
41. Ibid. p. 205.
42. See 'Mr. Conrad's Autobiography', *Outlook*, 17 February 1912, p. 253. Rpt. *CR3* 49–51; and 'Joseph Conrad', *Spectator*, 13 July 1912, p. 60. Rpt. *CR3* 68–70. For a discussion of Conrad's Polish linguistic heritage, see Mary Morzinski, *Linguistic Influence of Polish on Joseph Conrad's Style* (Lublin: Maria Curie-Skłodowska University, 1994). For a corresponding account of Conrad's French heritage, see Yves Hervouet, 'Joseph Conrad and the French Language', *Conradiana* 11 (1979), pp. 229–51, and 'Joseph Conrad and the French Language 2', *Conradiana* 14.1 (1982), pp. 23–49.
43. 'Joseph Conrad', *Spectator*, p. 69.
44. David S. Meldrum, 'The Romance of Mr. Conrad', *Book Monthly* (September 1919), pp. 697–700. Rpt. *CR3* 626–7.
45. For a discussion of Conrad's use of dictation in the memoir, see Conrad, *Personal Record*, eds Najder and Stape, pp. 133–9.
46. Ibid. p. 145.
47. John Galsworthy, *Castles in Spain and Other Screeds* (Leipzig: Tauchnitz, 1928), p. 93.
48. Jeremy Harding, 'The Englishness of *The English Review*', in Dennis Brown and Jenny Plastow (eds), *Ford Madox Ford and Englishness: International Ford Madox Ford Studies 5* (Amsterdam: Rodopi, 2006), pp. 137–45 at p. 141.
49. Eagleton, *Literary Theory*, p. 73.
50. Zdzisław Najder, *Conrad in Perspective: Essays on Art and Fidelity* (Cambridge: Cambridge University Press, 1997), pp. 44–67.
51. Najder and Stape, 'Introduction', p. xxxiv.

52. For a brief survey of the work's Polish reception, see Najder and Stape, 'Introduction', pp. xlii–xliii. Reviews in Britain tended to focus on the work's deviation from the conventions of autobiography rather than on its overlaps with (or, as here, its overwriting of) Polish literature: 'Most writers of autobiography have the decency to tell us where and when they were born. Mr. Conrad deigns to tell us nothing of the kind' ('An Elusive Personality', *Nation*, 24 February 1912, p. 857. Rpt. *CR3* 55).
53. For a discussion, see Najder, *Conrad: A Life*, pp. 292–6.
54. Orzeszkowa's essay was pointedly titled 'The Emigration of Talent'. Cited in Najder, *Conrad: A Life*, p. 294.
55. Young, 'Language of Others', p. 206.
56. Wit Tarnawski, 'Conrad's *A Personal Record*', *Conradiana* 12 (1969), pp. 55–8.
57. Najder and Stape, 'Introduction', p. xxxvii.
58. Ford Madox Ford, *Return to Yesterday: Reminiscences 1894–1914* (London: Victor Gollancz, 1931), p. 379.
59. Ford Madox Ford, *The Critical Attitude* (London: Duckworth, 1911), p. 4.
60. Ford, *Return to Yesterday*, p. 379
61. Greenblatt, *Self-Fashioning*, p. 3.
62. Ibid. p. 3.
63. Eagleton, *Literary Theory*, p. 55.
64. On the emergence of 'Heart of Darkness' as a touchstone of contemporary critical practices, for instance, see Val Cunningham, *In the Reading Gaol: Postmodernity, Texts and History* (Oxford: Blackwell, 1994).

# Chapter 11

## The Russian Redemption of *The Secret Agent* and *Under Western Eyes*

Ludmilla Voitkovska

Readers of world literature rely heavily on translations. In Russia, translation has been used as a form of censorship that was exercised through the careful selection of works for translation. Russian censorship banned foreign works that criticised the existing political regime, as well as those that portrayed Russians as 'non-European barbarians', and, if necessary, allowed publications of world texts only with excisions.[1] This practice lead to the erasure of some authors, like James Joyce, and the misrepresentation of others, like Joseph Conrad. Conrad's political novels have been noticeably absent from the list of his works published in Russia after 1925. Focusing on Conrad's sea-stories, Russian critics branded him as a neo-romantic and aligned him with the likes of Robert Louis Stevenson and Arthur Conan Doyle, defining him as a master of sea adventures, exotic tales and romantic melodramas. They dismissed Conrad's works about any other topic as inferior and insignificant. Kagarlitsky and Katarsky suggest that 'Conrad's weakest works are the ones where he gives up his favorite themes and gets fascinated by the analysis of the broken immoral psyche.'[2] Russian critics have also portrayed Conrad as a European novelist whose work is littered with the expected errors, illustrative of outmoded aesthetics and, despite all of this, still somewhat commendable. Critics praised him for choosing to dramatise the real efforts of real men engaged in struggles with natural forces, rather than indulging in the temptation to chart the vapid lives of the bourgeoisie. With his political novels played down, repudiated or erased, in Russia Conrad remained in the literary backwater, his status marginal when compared with that of Shakespeare, Dickens, Graham Greene, H. G Wells, Galsworthy and Somerset Maugham, all of whom had long been staples in any university course of British literature.

Given that the political novels were de-emphasised in the Russian corpus of Conrad's oeuvre, the 2012 translations of *The Secret Agent* and *Under Western Eyes* in one volume are events of extraordinary significance for Russian Conradian scholarship. The translation of Conrad's 'Russian novels' fills the gaps of the Russian readers' perceptions of the writer; moreover, the status of the publications signals a re-evaluation of Conrad's place in the Russian canon of British literature. The novels were published by the Russian Academy of Sciences as part of the authoritative academic series Literary Monuments, specifically intended for readers seeking in-depth and comprehensive understanding of works that have been established as classics in the Russian canon of world literature. The translations of Conrad's works by A. Antipenko are accompanied by extensive reference tools consisting of an academic article by V. M. Tolmachev, as well as a thorough textual and historic commentary, a chronology of Conrad's life and works, and eighty-nine illustrations.[3]

The 2012 publication is particularly valuable as it follows a century of either negative or mixed critical reception of the novels that were not available to a wider readership, as both *The Secret Agent* and *Under Western Eyes* had a poor publication history in Russia. After *Under Western Eyes* was first published in 1912 (translated by E. K. Pimenova) and 1925 (translated by A. V. Krivtsova), the next publication was A. Malyshev's translation of a small fragment of the novel in the newspaper *Literaturnaya Rossia* ('Literary Russia') in 1991, after liberalisation brought on by *perestroyka*. *The Secret Agent* has been treated more favourably by the Russian state-controlled publishing industry: fragments of the novel in Z. Vengerova's translation were first published in 1908 in the journal *Vestnik Evropy* ('European Messenger'). It was followed by the publication of the full novel in 1915 in Vengerova's translation, and in 1925 in M. Matveeva's translation. However, both novels quickly became a bibliographical rarity that could only be obtained in central research libraries in Russia by scholars employed by state universities and research institutions. Presented as a detective novel, *The Secret Agent* was reprinted in 2003, 2008 and 2010 in response to the current Russian vogue for political thrillers and detective novels. In his notes to the 2012 translation of *Under Western Eyes*, Tolmachev points out the inaccuracy of Conrad's information (as expressed in his 1920 'Author's Note') about the favourable early reception of his novel by the Russian reader, since by that time the novel had been published only once, rather than 'in many editions', as Conrad (no doubt sincerely) indicated.[4] It would seem that one would have to search for hard evidence of the 'universal recognition' Conrad believed it enjoyed (*UWE* viii).

## Things Russian

One recurrent objection regarding Conrad's representation of Russia in *The Secret Agent* and *Under Western Eyes* that is hard to dismiss is the insufficiency of the writer's first-hand adult experiences of the country, which undermines his credibility with the Russian reader. The first critical review of *Under Western Eyes* points out Conrad's lack of familiarity with the subtleties of Russian culture:

> As soon as the author of the novel leaves the learned facts and events – and an author of fiction must resort to his imagination – he begins to tell things that cause the Russian reader to smile against his will. This, however, refers only to everyday details.[5]

In order to avoid Russian readers' negative reaction to Conrad's representation of everyday details, Antipenko changes Conrad's version of Russian names to the correct ones: Kirylo becomes Kirill, Peter Ivanovitch becomes Piotr Ivanovich, and Tekla becomes Fiokla. This practice is in line with earlier translations, which dealt with the problems of Conrad's Russian names in a similar fashion by modifying them to correct Russian versions. Conrad's attempt to address Natalia Haldin in an intimate register as Natalka is corrected to the appropriate Russian diminutive Natasha. Natalka, being short for Natalia in Ukrainian, which Conrad no doubt heard living in Ukraine, would have signalled for the Russian reader the character's Ukrainian descent. There is a similar problem, in *The Secret Agent*, with Mr Vladimir's name, which incorrectly combines the title Mr and the character's first name Vladimir. Mr Vladimir's short spy name is Conrad's attempt to make the character sound undeniably Russian in a way that will be understood by the English speakers who know the common Russian name Vladimir but are not sensitive to the subtleties of the way it is used in formal and familiar registers. Its incorrectness, lost on the English reader who does not know that Russian men are addressed by name and patronymic, cannot be remedied.[6] Since Russian *gospodin*, 'Mr', cannot be used with first names, such as Vladimir, Antipenko leaves the character with the English title 'Mr'. As a result, in Russian translation the name acquires an inexplicable foreign connotation. Its effect on the Russian reader is that of kitsch: they know they are in the presence of a narrative authored by somebody who either does not know their culture or writes for an audience who does not know it. Either way, as a Russian name, 'Mr Vladimir' does not appear culturally authentic.

Ziemianitch's name creates a different set of problems for the translator. Antipenko turns him into Zimyanich (Зимянич), 'man of winter', assuming that the name is a derivative from the Russian word for winter, *zima* (зима). As a result, because of the translator's inability to understand the meaning of the name of Conrad's Ziemianitch, a derivative from Polish *ziemia* ('earth, soil'), its original significance is lost for the Russian reader. The adequate translation of the name into Russian would be Ziemlianich (Землянич), derived from the Russian *zemlia* (земля, 'earth, soil'); however, this translation requires familiarity with both the Russian and Polish languages. Antipenko is not the only Russian reader who failed to comprehend the linguistic origin and symbolic meaning of Ziemianitch's name due to a lack of knowledge of Polish. In his 1991 translation, Malyshev also translates him as Zimianich (Зимянич), 'man of winter'. Dimitry Urnov exasperatedly notes that Conrad 'made up some coachman with the impossible name Zemianych, who of course should have been Demianych'.[7] Demianych, as proposed by Urnov, is, again, not a last name but a shortened patronymic of Demianovich. In essence, however, neither Conrad's Ziemianitch, nor Antipov's Zimianich, nor Urnov's Demianych is a Russian last name.

Other instances of Conrad's erroneous or unclear cultural details are referred to and corrected in the Notes to the text. For example, Tolmachev points out that the Order of St Procopus did not exist in the Russian Empire and that Korabelnaya Street was made up by Conrad. In the nineteenth century, there existed the Korabelnaya Embankment in St Petersburg, which would have been referred to as such by Russian speakers. Mere 'Karabelnaya', as it is in *Under Western Eyes*, would have been a reference to a street. Moreover, Conrad's spelling of the name of this imaginary street, Karabelnaya, betrays his ignorance of the differences between written and spoken Russian.[8] In unstressed syllables, the Russian letter 'o' is pronounced as 'a', and therefore this word should be transliterated into English as Korabelnaya. Although it may seem insignificant, a mistake like that, if uncorrected, would have discouraged the Russian reader, since spelling unstressed syllables the way they are pronounced is considered an egregious mistake addressed in elementary school. Conrad's mention of eighty million compatriots, which is taken to illustrate the Russian population at the time, is rectified in the Notes: by 1914 Russia's population was 166 million, of whom 80.5 million were ethnic Russians. Tolmachev also sets the record straight regarding Conrad's statement in the 'Author's Note' that 'the book had been republished there [in Russia] in several editions' (*UWE* viii): by 1920 there was only one edition of the novel (Pimenova's 1912 translation).

Elsewhere Conrad's Russia seems to be based on stereotypes of Russia familiar to the British reader, and certain cultural details of Russia are modified to fit their expectations. For example, Haldin wears an Astrakhan cap, translated by Antipov as *smushka* (смушка). Astrakhan caps, or *smushkas*, were made of lambskin, which was quite expensive in nineteenth-century Russia. Imported from Bukhara, lambskin was worn as a symbol of wealth and high social status. As a student of St Petersburg University, Haldin would always have been required to wear a uniform that included a military-style cap. A lambskin cap, unaffordable for a student, hardly makes Haldin's attire credible for a Russian reader, particularly given the character's populist political convictions. It can scarcely be justified by Conrad's intention of making Haldin go unnoticed during the assassination of the minister Mr de P—, for a lambskin cap would have stood out in the nineteenth-century Russian crowd. The only explanation is that Haldin wears what the British reader expects a Russian man to wear: a hat made of exotic Oriental fur.

Conrad's recurrent attempts to distance himself from the Russian language and culture have not escaped Russian critics' attention; they point out the inconsistency between the writer's lack of interest and expertise in the culture and his attempt to engage with it in a major way. Tolmachev believes that although Conrad had legitimate grave grievances against Russia, he did not have sufficient life experience to write about its culture. This insufficiency 'could not have been compensated by foggy childhood memories (no matter how intense they were), nor by literary borrowings from *disliked* Dostoyevsky, ... nor vivid imagination'.[9] In contrast, Conrad had intimate personal knowledge of the Congo, which he wrote about in 'Heart of Darkness', not to mention the Borneo and the sea of his other fiction. However, since he did not have lived adult memories of Russia and its people,

> the scenes of St Petersburg, Russian characters ... , conversations between Razumov and Haldin in Part I, possibly believable for the Western reader of Conrad, could be called either 'tall stories' or convention bordering on fantasy or a repertoire of Russophobic clichés and inaccuracies.[10]

Tolmachev goes as far as to compare Conrad's delivery of the Russian theme to that of Hollywood.[11]

Conrad's use of various printed and oral sources for his novels (some of which would have been second-hand accounts), without having a formal education in Russian or first-hand knowledge of Russian society, resulted in a number of cultural blunders. Among written sources Tolmachev refers to literature about the Russian nihilist Narodnaya Volya movement (S. G. Nechaev, V. Zasulich and others), about socialist-revolutionary terrorism, and about Mikhail Bakunin, one of the possible prototypes for Peter Ivanovitch. Among oral sources for Conrad's information about Russia, Tolmachev points to Conrad's long-time friendship with Edward and Constance Garnett, who cultivated notable Russian immigrants, such as Prince Piotr Kropotkin and Felix Volkonsky, in particular. Tolmachev suggests that Constance Garnett, no doubt, knew a great deal about the Russian revolutionary movement from her lover, anarchist and terrorist Stepniak (Sergei Kravchinsky), who had fled to Switzerland after stabbing to death the chief of the Separate Police Corps, N. B. Mezentsov, in St Petersburg and who then lived in London from 1884 until his death in 1895.

Conrad's rejection of Russian culture was undoubtedly passed on to him by his father. According to Tolmachev, Apollo Korzeniowski moved his son to the Austrian part of Galicia, where there were Polish schools, so that his son would not have to study Russian. This resentment is 'felt in his overall delivery of the Russian theme'.[12] Urnov, who echoes this sentiment in blunter language, does not believe Conrad's statements that he did not know Russian. 'He knew relatively little', the critic maintains:

[he] was learning reluctantly and forgetting gladly even what he had previously known – this attitude to Russia is obvious from Conrad's treatment of details, which he confuses, sometimes deliberately, sometimes even offensively for the national sensibility, which . . . could represent a conscious goal to revenge all his abused civil and national feelings, wounded forever by tsarist satraps, police and bureaucratic obtuseness and inhumanity.[13]

Some critics go so far as to attribute Conrad's motives for writing both *The Secret Agent* and *Under Western Eyes* to crass opportunism. Both were written at the time when the 'Russian vogue' took Europe by storm. Kashkin believes that in *The Secret Agent* and particularly in *Under Western Eyes*, Conrad, while professing ignorance about Russia, exploited the trendiness of Russia by 'reflecting', 'as in a false mirror', caricature figures from Dostoyevsky's *Demons*, 'spicing them up, in the Western fashion, with speculations about the mystically transcendental Eastern soul'. *Under Western Eyes*, for Kashkin, is nothing but another 'malicious conjecture'.[14]

Conrad relies on the early twentieth-century British perceptions of Russian culture and Russian people reflected in myths, distorted ideas, clichés and absurd and grotesque stories. The image of Russia, shaped in the Western consciousness during the 1830s and 1840s, remains the same with some small modifications now in the twenty-first century. Traditionally, Western public opinion either demonised or idealised Russia – not so much because of its role in history and politics but as a reflection of people's frustrations, hopes and expectations in Western European society, which was laden with its own problems. In many ways, the image of Russia has over time assumed the status of a culturological category, which explains its irrational aspect. For centuries, for the West, Russia has served as a means of self-cognition, but it has been cognition *ad absurdum*, by contradiction. Tsarist despotism reinforced Western society's commitment to its own social and political institutions. The despotic reality of tsarism planted fear in some, and the revolutionary response to it inspired hope in others.

Conrad's representation of Russian people also follows an established German, French and Anglo-American literary tradition, which depicted the Russian character as that of a barbarian, gradually adapting to Western civilisation. This image, created by German Romantics, was revived at the beginning of the twentieth century. An influential Danish literary critic, Georg Brandes, whose extensive work *Impressions of Russia* was published in English translation in 1888, paints Russians as 'a people of imitation, a people without originality' who 'have invented very little, have contributed nothing ... to the development of civilization'.[15] The whole character of the people is stamped by winter 'where the snow for two hundred days together covers everything, woods and fields, roads and streets and roofs of the houses, with its monotonous sheet'.[16] St Petersburg, according to Brandes, is an unhealthy, half-educated, artificial city built in 'grand style, with half European and half barbarian splendor' that marks the founding tsar's desire to bring his country nearer to the West.[17] Brandes's stereotype of 'the Russian' is based on the idea of the 'incomprehensible, darkly mysterious' Russian soul, the 'womb of new realities and new mysticism' that inhabits 'the broad, unlimited expanse which fills the mind with melancholy and hope'.[18] This 'enormously large', 'very backward' country needs to be elevated by European culture.[19] Russian people are passive, as demonstrated 'in public and private life, in the submission to the powers that be'.[20] Those powers are, first and foremost, the patriarchal and bureaucratic state, 'where official power has destroyed all spontaneous and natural growth in the relations of public life'.[21] This form of government in Russia does not allow an outlet of 'independent thought in political affairs'.[22] The publication of books is subject to strict censorship, as there is 'constant exertion on the part of the rulers to make knowledge impossible and to destroy all individual and independent will'.[23] The profound scepticism of discontented youth has led to the creation of groups that resorted to 'bombs and murderous weapons to inspire terror'.[24]

The Russian characters in Conrad's *Under Western Eyes* could have stepped out of the pages of Brandes's *Impressions of Russia*; Conrad's descriptions of the physical environment in which they exist, and his general statements on Russian culture, echo Brandes's observations. Brandes describes St Petersburg coachmen as uprooted peasants who recall Scythians and look like 'genuine barbarians'; they cross themselves incessantly before every one of the numerous churches, chapels and shrines.[25] Conrad's Ziemianitch, the St Petersburg coachman, whose name, we remember, is derived from Polish *ziemia* ('soil'), recalls one of Brandes's Russian types who 'exactly embodies' the black earth, a broad belt of fertile soil, 'which extends from Podolia to Kazan'. This 'richest and broadest Russian nature' is contrasted with the nihilistic force that springs from the intelligentsia's scepticism regarding existing social institutions, such as the church, marriage and property. This nihilistic force, according to Brandes, extends everywhere in Russia, 'into all circles, and finds support and stronghold at widely spread points'.[26] This force is parallel to Conrad's student and terrorist Haldin, with his conviction that 'true destroyers are they who destroy the spirit and progress and truth, not the avengers who merely kill the bodies of persecutors of human dignity' and his reasoning that people like him are necessary 'to make room for self-contained, thinking men' like Razumov (*UWE* 19). Brandes's account of the activities of young women as propagandists who had 'peculiarly Russian plans for the improvement of the world' focuses on a young girl of sixteen who was arrested in St Petersburg for hosting weekly meetings of students in her mother's house. This young woman, 'homely, with beautiful eyes; difficult to become acquainted with', who had 'the whole severity of youth' and 'youth's naïve faith in the efficacy of every kind of propaganda', seems like a mirror image of Natalia Haldin. Her emotional life 'had been absorbed by the intellectual', and she manages her mother 'as if she had been her own grown-up child', just as Natalia looks after Mrs Haldin.[27]

In *Under Western Eyes* the Russian landscape becomes an essential part of Conrad's metaconcept of Russia.[28] First and foremost, Russia is a cold and infinite space, covered with snow:

> Several times in the night [Razumov] woke up shivering from a dream of walking through drifts of snow in Russia where he was completely alone as any betrayed autocrat could be; an immense, wintry Russia which, somehow, his view could embrace in all its enormous expanse as if it were a map. (*UWE* 66)

In the part of the novel set in Russia, the action takes place in winter despite the fact that the real event at the centre of Conrad's plot, the assassination of the Minister of the Interior, Vyacheslav von Plehve, took place in the middle of summer, on 28 July 1904. This gives the impression that there are no other seasons in Russia. Conrad also uses snow as a means of characterising the existential hopelessness and despair of the people who inhabit the space:

> Razumov stamped his foot – and under the soft carpet of the snow felt the hard ground of Russia, inanimate, cold, inert, like a sullen and tragic mother hiding her face under a winding sheet – his native soil! – his very own – without a fireside, without a heart! (*UWE* 32–3)

Conrad's depiction of Russia presents a significant departure from the way nature is depicted within the Russian literary tradition. For Russian writers, their native land has a profound sustaining significance: it is viewed as a place of renewal, absolution and purification from the corrupting influence of the political system on the human body and soul.

Conrad's Russia is thus based on stereotypes of Russia familiar to the British reader. Conrad had no personal reason to attempt to break the British perception of Russia, a task that would have proven unattainable. As the German-American film director Ernst Lubitsch confessed, 'we can only show Russia in a "style russe"', because 'otherwise it would appear unconvincing and atypical. If we show St. Petersburg as it is, the non-Russian public would not believe us and would say: "That is not Russia but France."'[29] This reality of Western Europe's perception of Russia influenced even Russian émigré artists: early twentieth-century filmmakers who worked in Europe and Hollywood 'were forced to adapt their culture and history to a variety of cultural expectations and clichés, or else they would not be recognized as Russian'.[30] While Conrad does not project the extreme, phantasmagoric 'style russe', he undoubtedly draws on it, which does not help his relationship with the Russian reader. In addition, he incessantly repeats the words 'Russia' and 'Russian' as if to make sure that the intended reader does not forget what country is being represented. However, for the Russian reader this signals that the novel objectifies their culture for the entertainment of a foreign readership.

### Russian language

The representation of the Russian language in *Under Western Eyes* is consistent with Western Europeans' immediate response to it. Brandes notes that the most significant first impression of Russia is the language, which 'has not the least resemblance to any of the Western-European tongues' as well as an alphabet with characters that are novel to

Westerners.[31] Foregrounding the significance of language differences, Conrad goes further: not only representing the Russian language as incomprehensible and difficult, he suggests that it has no meaning and sounds almost inhuman:

> What must remain striking to a teacher of languages is the Russians' extraordinary love of words. They gather them up, they cherish them, but they do not hoard them in their breasts; on the contrary, they are always ready to pour them out by the hour or by the night with an enthusiasm, a sweeping abundance, with such an aptness of application sometimes that, as in the case of very accomplished parrots, one can't defend oneself from the suspicion that they understand what they say. (UWE 4)

The narrative device of an unreliable narrator, a Language Teacher with limited expertise in the Russian language who confesses that he has 'no comprehension of the Russian character' (UWE 4), may have appealed to the English reader, but it does not help the Russian reader make a connection with the narrative.

In contrast to Antipenko's translation, which does not deviate from the original and conveys its artistic merits in the best traditions of the Russian school of translation, other translators have tried to modify Conrad's text so as to make it acceptable to the Russian public. Conscious of the possible negative reception of the novel as it is, in his 1991 translation of selected chapters of *Under Western Eyes*, published under the title 'Betrayal' in the newspaper *Literaturnaya Rossia*, A. Malyshev presents an amended version of the novel. The selection contains the episode of throwing the bomb and Haldin's visit to Razumov's room, as well as other episodes from sections I and II from Part First. Malyshev's modifications consist exclusively in the excision of some passages that can be viewed as problematic for censorship and for the novel's reception by the Russian reader. Some cuts (like the short passage deleted from the parting scene between Razumov and Haldin) can be justified by the intention to save space, as the selection is published in a newspaper.

A passage describing Razumov's beating of Ziemianitch with a fork was deleted for its apparent cruelty, which portrays Russians as non-European barbarians. Other excisions, intended to prevent the Russian readers' negative reaction and make the novel appealing to the Russian audience, are related to criticism of the Russian political system. All mention of Russia's corrupt, despotic, oppressive regime, lack of freedom, injustice as an intrinsic feature of the society and lack of humanity are deleted. In the following particularly vivid example of excised material, Conrad describes Russia in terms of the moral corruption of an oppressed society where the noblest aspirations of humanity, the desire of freedom, an ardent patriotism, the love of justice, the sense of pity, and even the fidelity of simple minds are prostituted to the lusts of hate and fear, the inseparable companions of uneasy despotism. (*UWE* 7)

All statements of the superiority of Western thinking, ways of living and political organisation, which would no doubt make Russian readers feel as if they existed on the outskirts of history, are excised. The first instance is the passage suggesting that the events described could not have happened in the West. This passage might also have been excised because it is addressed to 'the Western reader' for whom the events might appear 'shocking, inappropriate, or even improper' (*UWE* 25). Similarly, conscious of the fact that Russian people might be offended by any suggestion that they are non-European barbarians, the translator eliminates Conrad's comments on Russian politics and its effect on the individual. Conrad's insights into the far-reaching and destructive effects of autocracy on an individual would resonate with the late twentieth-century Russian reader, still living in a modified version of an autocratic social organisation. Malyshev's translation transforms the text by removing any suggestions that would allow the Russian reader to extrapolate by association that Russian political and social institutions are working against an individual relying on his or her natural abilities and willing to follow a legalistic path to move up in the social hierarchy. This kind of modification can be attributed to censorship.

All Conrad's references to the Western reader suggesting the novel's intended reader is a British audience are also removed. It would appear understandable that in the newspaper medium with its limited space the translator would have no choice but to exercise his judgement and excise certain passages out of considerations of economy. However, while it appears to be a minor issue compared to the significance of politics and a subtle statement of the uncivilised nature of Russian political organisation, the references to the foreign reader as intended audience are viewed as potentially detrimental for the novel's relationship with the Russian reader, and so have to be removed. Those references turn *Under Western Eyes* into a narrative explicitly written for a foreign audience that makes Russian people the object of Conrad's contemplation, criticism and analysis. English culture is presented as more civilised, more orderly, less chaotic, stable and living by established rules; all this is personified in Conrad's hypothetical young Englishman who, unlike Razumov, lives in a society that would respect his civil rights and would never abuse its power:

> He would not have a hereditary and personal knowledge of the means by which a historical autocracy represses ideas, guards its power, and defends its

existence. By an act of mental extravagance he might imagine himself arbitrarily thrown into prison, but it would never occur to him unless he were delirious (and perhaps not even then) that he could be beaten with whips as a practical measure either of investigation or of punishment. (*UWE* 25)

Descriptions representing everyday Russian life in terms of poverty are also omitted from Malyshev's translation. 'A mild-eyed, ragged tramp drinking tea' in the low eating-house where Razumov searches for Ziemianitch disappears, as does a 'horrible, non-descript, shaggy being with a black face like the muzzle of a bear' that 'grunted angrily', calling Ziemianitch the 'cursed driver of thieves' (*UWE* 27–8).

Some excised passages describe Russian people as uncivilised drunkards and the Russian lifestyle as a weak patriarchy. When the owner of the vile den enlightens Razumov as to the details of the private life of Ziemianitch, whose woman had run away from him, Conrad makes comments on the general nature of the Russian character, representing drunkenness as a national feature:

> They [women] were always running away from that driver of the devil – and he sixty years old too; could never get used to it. But each heart knows sorrow after its own kind, and Ziemianitch was a born fool all his days. And then he would fly to the bottle. 'Who could bear life in our land without a bottle?' he says. A proper Russian man – the little pig . . . (*UWE* 28)

Ziemianich is portrayed as a Russian everyman, and therefore for a Russian reader the description of his habits and lifestyle and character becomes a comment on Russians per se. By excising phrases and passages representing ordinary Russian people in a negative light, Malyshev removed any causes for Russian readers' adverse visceral responses to the novel. These modifications leave a tight, dramatic, plot-driven, non-controversial narrative by an author with acceptable political views.

### London in *The Secret Agent*

Antipenko's translation of *The Secret Agent* provides a very different emphasis, in part enabled by the comparative strangeness of the novel's British setting. Antipenko is at pains to recreate the atmosphere of Conrad's London with the utmost attention to the original. In turn, Tolmachev's accompanying Notes convey the character of *fin de siècle* London and help the Russian reader understand the details of English culture. Tolmachev points out that *fin de siècle* Belgravia combined luxurious mansions and unsightly buildings.[32] To help convey the full extent of Winnie's family's social descent, as well as the surprisingly 'mean aspect of the shop' and 'the change from Belgravia Square to the narrow streets of Soho', Tolmachev explains that Soho, where Winnie settled with Verloc, in the 1890s was a rather poor area of London. He describes the other sights of Conrad's London, such as Rotten Row, Hyde Park, Knightsbridge, Green Park, Tottenham Court Road, Romney Road, Park Place, Charing Cross, Victoria and Waterloo stations, Maze Hill, Sloane Square, Whitehall, Islington and Kensington Gardens, with similar attention to detail. These meticulous topographical clarifications allow the Russian reader not only to visualise London but to understand the characters' places in the social hierarchy.

For the novel to be appreciated fully by the Russian reader, a number of places in London mentioned by Conrad indirectly also require clarification, and Tolmachev's notes serve their purpose in this regard. Conrad's reference to Millbank Prison, 'the great blind pile of bricks near a river, sinister and ugly like a colossal mortuary for the socially drowned', invites explanation.[33] Tolmachev provides more information than is needed by mentioning that it presently houses the Tate Gallery, and thus allows the reader to navigate *fin de siècle* London by contemporary landmarks. The translation eliminates Conrad's metaphor by replacing 'pile of bricks' with 'building' (*zdanie*). This transformation, simplifying Conrad's artistic style for the sake of clarity, may be considered unjustified, particularly given that this passage is accompanied by an extensive note. Conrad's reference to 'the walls of St Stephen's, with its towers and pinnacles' requires similar special clarification, as the Russian reader would not be able to connect the building with Westminster Abbey and the British Parliament (*SA* 116). The same applies to Conrad's reference to the towers of the Abbey and the Cheshire Cheese tavern (*SA* 219, 170). Tolmachev's notes often read like encyclopedia entries on English history. For example, in his explanation of Conrad's reference to the Palace Yard, Tolmachev points out the existence of two Palace Yards: Old and New. The detailed history of the Old Yard as the place where participants in the Gunpowder Plot were executed, and the New Yard as a protected territory with a five-level underground parking lot built in 1972–4 for members of Parliament, is hardly related to *The Secret Agent*. As useful as this information is for the Russian reader's education on the details of English life and culture, its excess displays a broader Anglophile tendency.

The names of London sights are conveyed either through translation of common nouns contained in them or by transliteration. For the names of sights that contain a noun of common etymology or a noun that has become an established borrowing from English, Antipenko uses translation. Russian *парк*, which like the English 'park' originates from the Latin *parricus*, and may have travelled into Russian through the Western European languages, is phonetically identical to its English counterpart; therefore Green Park in translation sounds like the original. Similarly, the translated London squares (such as Sloane Square and Chesham Square) sound similar to the original, as Russian сквер originated from the English 'square'. However, sights containing common names that are different in Russian are transliterated. Translating them using Russian equivalents takes away the English aura of mystery, as they become merely streets and roads. Russian улица and дорога do not share a common etymology with English, so when transliterated, Tottenham Court Road, Brett Street, Romney Road and Vauxhall Bridge Road add to the mystery of London in the Russian readers' collective imagination. Kensington Gardens is also transliterated, since Russian сад ('garden') is only used for areas planted with fruit trees.

A number of transliterated English, culturally specific objects that have not been established as familiar borrowings in Russian require further explanation. Tolmachev clarifies the meaning of Gladstone ('a shallow, light, leather travel bag named after British prime minister William Ewart Gladstone'); havelock coat ('a coat with a big turndown hood worn by Sherlock Holmes'); hobgoblin ('English folklore spirit similar to the Russian домовой'). Again, Antipenko strives to preserve the air of 'Englishness' and convey the flavour of turn-of-the-century London culture by transliterating various English carriages, such as brougham, victorias and hansoms; similarly, they all are accompanied by Tolmachev's explanation. Antipenko's transliteration of the English word 'coroner' exemplifies the difference between English common law and Russian civil law legal systems. The use of the long Russian descriptive translation of the term, судмедэксперт or следователь производящий дознание в случаях насильственной смерти ('a forensic scientist or investigator conducting interrogations in cases of violent death'), would have raised additional questions about the Chief Inspector's statement, 'The coroner's jury will have a treat' (SA 73), as the Russian судмедэксперт and следователь do not work with a jury. Given the difference in legal systems, this term is explained in the notes: 'an officer in common law countries who investigates cases of sudden deaths or deaths under extraordinary circumstances and determines the cause of death, often after conducting an investigation and questioning of witnesses'.[34] All transliterations of English words complicate the process of reading, as they require the reader to consult the Notes. In a number of cases they are inevitable, as there are no Russian equivalents, and by painting a picture of *fin de siècle* London, they accentuate cultural differences and help convey the atmosphere of authentic British culture.

A number of references to London landmarks require transformations. For example, Conrad's 'There's a constable stuck by every lamppost, and every second person we meet between this and Palace Yard is an obvious tec' (*SA* 106) cannot be translated verbatim. The translator would have to make a reference to the characters' exact location (for 'this'), which would involve changing the original without a compelling reason. The translator's answer to this predicament is to turn 'between this and Palace Yard' into 'on the way from the palace' (*на пути от дворца*). The only plausible explanation for this changing of direction is Antipenko's desire to preserve the flow of Conrad's style. The correct Russian translation, *k dvortsu*, sounds less fluid than Antipenko's *ot dvorca* because of the combination of three consecutive consonants (k, d, v), which starts with a voiceless plosive (k), and two consonants in the middle, one of which is a fricative sibilant (*ц*) [ts]. The preposition *ot* ('to') provides a vowel before the three-consonant cluster, and although it replaces one voiceless plosive, (k), with another, (t), it provides a seamless transition, as a 't' followed by the dental consonant (d) loses its plosion. Last but not least, the final vowel 'a' [a] in the translation is more melodious than 'u' [y]. This desire to convey the essence of Conrad's poetic style suggests that Antipenko is not only a skilled professional but a Conrad aficionado.

A number of transformations are predicated on idiomatic differences between English and Russian. For example, the translator uses the Russian saying *sdelannogo nie vorotish* (*сделанного не воротишь*), translated verbatim as 'what is done cannot be returned', since this is a semantic equivalent of the English 'what's done can't be undone' (*SA* 177). Conrad's 'lie low for a bit' (*SA* 184) is translated as '*tikhon'ko polezhat' na dnie* (*тихонько полежать на дне*), literally 'to lie quietly on the bottom', as this is an established Russian idiom conveying the same idea of keeping out of sight to avoid attention or detection. 'You are looking more like yourself' (*SA* 185) is translated through the Russian idiom *ty nachinaesh prikhodit' v sebia* (*ты начинаешь приходить в себя*), literally 'you are beginning to come to yourself', conveying the idea of appearing to be normal in health or spirits. Conrad's 'My heart went into my boots' (*SA* 22) becomes *u menia dusha ushla v piatki*, or 'my soul went into my heels', to provide the equivalent idiom. Likewise, the translation of 'Greenwich Meridian' as *nulevoj meridian* (*нулевой меридиан*), 'zero meridian', reflects the Russian cartographic convention. However, this transformation, a departure from Antipenko's tendency to preserve the authenticity of British culture, cannot be justified as necessary, since 'Greenwich Meridian' is also used in Russian, albeit not as an official topographic notion. Given that the Greenwich

Observatory is conceptually central to the overall design of *The Secret Agent*, 'Greenwich Meridian' might more accurately have been transliterated as *grinvichskij meridian*, particularly since it is accompanied by an extensive explanation in the Notes.

Conrad's narrative is intended for an English audience, so his oblique references to British cultural conventions require clarification. Russian readers do not understand Conrad's mention of 'the empire on which the sun never sets', or of '*the* House, *par excellence*, in the minds of many millions of men' (*SA* 157). The most challenging aspect of translation is to provide adequate equivalents to culturally specific notions that do not exist in the target language. A good example is 'panjandrum' (*SA* 23). Antipenko translates the word as *istukan* ('idol, statue') since there is no Russian equivalent of an artificially created lexical unit ironically referring to a person who has or claims to have a great deal of authority or influence. Titles of newspapers, the *Torch* and the *Gong*, are translated, contrary to the convention of transliterating periodicals. Given that one of them, the *Gong*, is made up by Conrad, and the other one, the *Torch*, requires an extensive explanation as it is a reference to *The Torch of Anarchy*, the translator chooses economy of the reader's effort over translation rules.

## Conclusion

Overall, Antipenko's translations of both *The Secret Agent* and *Under Western Eyes* follow the best traditions of the Russian academic school of translation. They are exceptionally well researched, precise, masterful, careful towards the original, attentive to details and imaginative. Their publication in the academic series Literary Monuments marks a new era in Conradian studies in Russia as it makes Conrad's political novels available in a new, high-quality translation. Moreover, in contrast to previous translations that tended to ignore all traces of anything beyond the translated page, including the facts of the writer's biography, the historical conditions that provided a temporal matrix for the work, and the immediate psychological circumstances that moved the individual author to arrogate or invent specific means of literary production, this translation provides valuable context that humanises Conrad and foregrounds his achievements in the world of literature. This publication sends a powerful signal to Russian readers, particularly to academics, that Conrad is no longer *persona non grata* in the Russian version of the English canon. It invites Russian critics whose opinion of Conrad has been shaped by criticism pointing to his lack of first-hand knowledge of Russian life and culture, his personal visceral hatred towards Russia, albeit justifiable, and his crass opportunism in response to the 'Russian vogue' in Europe, to recognise that there is value in Conrad's strength of conviction and his personal honesty.

## Notes

1. M. T. Choldin, 'Censorship via Translation: Soviet Treatment of Western Political Writing', in M. T. Choldin and M. Friedberg (eds), *The Red Pencil: Artists, Scholars and Censors in the USSR* (Boston: Unwin Hynan, 1989), pp. 29–51 at p. 30. (Initials rather than full forenames are given in author names in this chapter since this is the standard way of citing Russian authors.)
2. Y. I. Kagarlitsky and I. M. Katarsky, 'Joseph Conrad', in *Istoriya Anglijskoj Literatury*, Vol. 3 (Moscow: Academy of Sciences of the USSR, 1958), p. 97.
3. Dzhosef Konrad, *Tajnyj Agent: Na Vzglyad Zapada*, trans. A. Antipenko (Moscow: Nauka, 2012).
4. Joseph Conrad, 'Author's Note', in *Under Western Eyes* (London: J. M. Dent and Sons, 1923), pp. vii–x at p. viii. Subsequent references are cited in the text as *UWE*.
5. 'Novye Knigi ['New Books']: Dzhozef Konrad. "Na vzglyad zapada"', *Russkoe Bogatstvo* 9 (1912), p. 211. My translation.
6. Elsewhere Conrad uses the correct construction, for example for Peter Ivanovitch and Victor Victorovitch Haldin. Ivanovitch, with a 't', is a French transliteration of Russian patronymics, demonstrating the influence of French on Conrad's English. The English transliteration is Ivanovich. The same applies to Zemianitch.
7. Dimitry Urnov, *Joseph Conrad* (Moscow: Nauka, 1977), p. 82.
8. This might be Conrad misremembering what his father said. However, Apollo Korzeniowski, who was proficient in Russian, knew the difference between the way words with unstressed 'o' are pronounced and spelled. Conrad, who never had a formal education in Russian, would not know the difference, and since his contact with Russian, whatever it might have been, was in the oral mode, his spelling reflects that.
9. V. M. Tolmachev, 'Joseph Conrad I Ego "Russkie Romany"', in Konrad, *Tajnyj Agent: Na Vzglyad Zapada*, p. 524.
10. Ibid. pp. 524–5.
11. Ibid. p. 525.
12. Ibid. p. 478.
13. Urnov, *Joseph Conrad*, p. 80.
14. I. Kashkin, 'Dzhozef Konrad', in *Dlya Chitalelya-Sovremennika* (Moscow: Sovetskij Pisatel, 1977), pp. 71–5 at p. 74.
15. Georg Brandes, *Impressions of Russia*, trans. Samuel C. Eastman (London: Walter Scott, 1888), p. 17.
16. Ibid. p. 14.
17. Ibid. p. 7.

18. Ibid. p. 353.
19. Ibid. p. 25.
20. Ibid. p. 26.
21. Ibid. p. 18.
22. Ibid. p. 21.
23. Ibid. p. 42.
24. Ibid. p. 49.
25. Ibid. p. 11.
26. Ibid. p. 49.
27. Ibid. pp. 58–9.
28. E. E. Soloviova, 'Obraz Russkoj Prirody v Tvorchestve D. Konrada', *Vestnik Helqbinskogo gosudarstvennogo universiteta: Filologia. Iskusstvovedenie* 30.10 (148, 2009), pp. 138–42 at p. 138.
29. Quoted in Oksana Bulgakowa, 'The "Russian Vogue" in Europe and Hollywood: The Transformation of Russian Stereotypes through the 1920s', *Russian Review* 64.2 (April 2005), pp. 211–35 at p. 211.
30. Ibid. p. 212.
31. Brandes, *Impressions*, p. 6.
32. V. M. Tolmachev, 'Notes', in Konrad, *Tajnyj Agent: Na Vzglyad Zapada*, pp. 535–67 at p. 538.
33. Joseph Conrad, *The Secret Agent* (Oxford: Oxford University Press, 2008), p. 33. Subsequent references are cited in the text as *SA*.
34. Tolmachev, 'Notes', p. 542.

# Afterword
*Laurence Davies*

The chapters in this timely volume consider many junctures, many differences – not so much polarities as swirls of literary energy between and among spoken and unspoken, spoken and written, articulate and inarticulate, multinational and domestic; terms of art and terms of common discourse, heteroglossia and polyglossia, frankness and evasion, ontology and epistemology, the locutionary or illocutionary and the perlocutionary, *Jawi* and *Rumi*, *Rumi* and Cyrillic, manuscript and print. At the risk of sounding like Polonius heralding the players, one could say that these studies of Conrad and language mix in various proportions the aesthetic, philosophical, ethnographic, historical, ethical, cultural and geographical with the linguistic. The volume is timely because it speaks to current – and urgent – debates about transnationalism, cosmopolitanism, modernity, migrant cultures, translation, borders, cultural privilege and the rights to being seen and heard and read. It also speaks at a time of remapping Anglophone literatures in the spirit of these debates, epitomised in the title of Wai Chee Dimock's *Through Other Continents: American Literature across Deep Time*,[1] exemplified in the tables of contents of English-language journals of modernist studies such as *Modernism/modernity* and *Modernist Cultures*,[2] and demonstrated at length in a major study by Christopher GoGwilt, a contributor to this volume, who reads Conrad side by side with Jean Rhys and the Indonesian novelist (and political prisoner under both colonial and postcolonial regimes) Pramoedya Ananta Toer.[3]

Why, in these various realignments and debates, is language so important? And why is Conrad so worth framing in these contexts? To begin with, there is the phenomenon of his linguistic formation. As other contributors note, he passed the first ten years of his life in the Russian Empire. Part of that time was spent in exile to Russia proper, but the rest was in, to give them their present-day names, Berdychiv, Zhytomyr and Chernihiv.[4] In these towns, at least four secular languages were spoken – Ukrainian (then known as Ruthenian), Russian (the language of authority), Yiddish and Polish; three sacred languages were in ritual use – Hebrew, Latin and Church Slavonic; and in the Korzeniowski family there were books to read and to translate in French and English. Although the Korzeniowskis left the district when Conrad was only two years old, if only to illustrate its linguistic richness it is worth noting that two other remarkable authors would come from Berdychiv: the novelist 'Der Nister' (Pinchus Kahanovich, 1884–1950), who wrote in Yiddish, and the novelist and war correspondent Vasily Grossman (1905–64), who wrote in Russian.[5] Perhaps the point to make is not that the very young Conrad, jackdaw-like, picked up a phrase here and a word there, but that he must have experienced language as a congeries both of sounds which came gradually to make sense and of sounds which stayed mysterious. Moreover, whether or not he saw anything of the Hebrew alphabet, he would certainly have seen both Roman and Cyrillic characters at an early age – a point relevant to Christopher GoGwilt's chapter in this volume and arguably an exposure to Russia as an empire of signs.[6]

As Katherine Isobel Baxter and Robert Hampson observe in the Introduction, Conrad went on acquiring languages, starting with German when he and his father went to live under Austro-Hungarian rule. Conrad's letters to Cunninghame Graham include long passages in French, and phrases from Spanish, Italian and Arabic. Writing to congratulate Graham's mother, the Hon. Mrs Bontine, on her son's *Mogreb-el-Acksa*, a narrative of travel and captivity in Morocco, Conrad calls his letter, which oscillates between English and French, 'macaronic' (CL2 225–6). The macaronic is a witty verse form, popular in the eighteenth century, which bounces merrily from one tongue to another, but Conrad's macaronic tendencies do not show themselves only in comic mode: witness Marlow's interview with Stein in chapter 20 of *Lord Jim*, which incorporates Stein's English, awkward, enigmatic, moving; Marlow's English, fluent and precise; English renderings of speech in at least two languages of the Malay Archipelago (Javanese and Buginese); German (including a two-line quotation from Goethe's *Torquato Tasso*); botanical Latin and the Latin motto of Conrad's Nałęcz ancestors.

Recent studies of Conrad's linguistic agility have emphasised both its kinship with such twentieth-century authors as James Joyce and 'Italo Svevo' (Aron Hector Schmitz) and its significance in understanding the troubled relationship of language to privilege, place, ethnicity and citizenship.[7] In the late nineteenth century, as Conrad was starting to write fiction, the internationalisation of language moved in two directions.

The polyglot L. L. Zamenhof (whose mother tongues were Polish and Yiddish) published his *Unua Libro*, a primer of the would-be universal language Esperanto, in 1887. In 1889, enthusiasts at a conference in Paris held their proceedings entirely in Volapük, another syncretic language. On the other tack, assuming an audience literate in multiple languages, Fernand Ortmans de Sénéchal, the editor of the monthly magazine *Cosmopolis*, launched in 1896 and published simultaneously in seven major cities, aimed for a balance in each issue of contributions in German, French and English and provided no translations. Among its contributors were Stéphane Mallarmé, Anatole France, Theodor Fontane, Lou Andreas-Salomé, Theodor Mommsen, Henry James and Joseph Conrad, whose 'An Outpost of Progress' appeared there in serial.[8]

Conrad's writings deal again and again with the hardships and challenges of linguistic incomprehension and displacement, especially when it comes to voluntary or involuntary exile, not least among the poor and persecuted. In 'Amy Foster', for instance, the pain of lacking the right words and the panic of not being able to make mutual sense afflicts both the title character and Yanko Goorall (whose name points to his origins in the Tatra Mountains): even before her pity for Yanko exposes her to the mysteries of his foreign tongue (and body language) and the bigotry of the other Kentish folk, Amy Foster suffers from a stammer.[9] In his tiny polity on the other side of the globe, Karain is a conquering incomer, but in his pursuit of revenge, he has also experienced the hardships of migrant labour across the Archipelago. The hold passengers in 'Typhoon' are coming home after years of similar work. Peyrol, returning to the scenes of his orphaned childhood from a lifetime spent on the Indian Ocean, must learn, and swiftly, the vocabulary of revolution.

Thus it is appropriate that several chapters in this volume dwell on the ethics of speech and writing. According to Josiane Paccaud-Huguet: 'If we admit that ethics concern our acts and their consequences, Conrad's dealing with the power of the written word, however weird the effect, is eminently ethical' (p. 91). He exposes 'the pseudo-magic function of the commodified signifier full of empty promises of enjoyment – whether it be by advertising, the press or politicians' (p. 92). Conrad's distaste for gassy politics and journalism is borne out in his correspondence: 'Confound these papers.... Those infernal scribblers are rank outsiders' (*CL2* 211).[10] Andrew Glazzard takes up the theme: 'Conrad's examination of political language implies a need for scepticism, vigilance and an awareness of context and contingency' (p. 41). So does Katherine Baxter: 'the disabled languages of silences and speech-out-of-place ... draw our attention to the prosthetic function of ideological discourse, whether the radical politics of Yundt and Peter Ivanovitch, the reformist politics of

Avellanos and Holroyd, or the reactionary politics of Vladimir, Guzman Bento and General T—' (p. 114). Again, considering affinities between Conrad's fiction and G. E. Moore's rigorous scrutiny of philosophical Idealism, John Attridge sees in Conrad a 'scepticism about some of the misleadingly abstract "ideals" that had regulated nineteenth-century political discourse' and a 'desire to refurbish this faded vocabulary' (p. 44). In earlier commentaries on morality and ethics in Conrad's fiction, the emphasis often fell on character, choice and motive. He was read and admired, for example, by members of the Polish Home Army during the Second World War because of the dilemmas and decisions and the urgency of action in almost impossible circumstances enacted in his work. 'Earlier' of course does not mean 'lesser'. The critique of language and the critique of conduct are complementary, all the stronger for depending on each other. Yael Levin combines both aspects in her call for 'distinct ontological articulations in the refashioning of plot, narrative voice and character' (p. 64).

The authors of the other six chapters reflect on linguistic communities in ways germane to what one could call the ethics of interpretation. Andrew Francis considers the 'turmoil of languages' spoken in the Malay Archipelago,[11] showing that '"broken" language and language dispossession, sometimes presented as impairments to language, are powerfully symptomatic in the Malay fiction of a confusion of cultural relations' and 'part of how Conrad gives the voiceless a voice' (p. 133). In other words, the many misspeakings and misprisions in his fiction are better read as neither grotesqueries nor picturesque local colour, but as revelations of social circumstance. Christopher GoGwilt draws attention to the visual aspects of language present in the Cyrillic alphabet, Polish diacriticals and *Jawi* (the Malay script based on Arabic and Farsi), and thus implicated in a multitude of Conradian passages, showing that in 'Conrad's English . . . transcription, transliteration and translation from other languages into . . . Romanised print' establish 'a hierarchy of hegemonic relations between languages' (p. 117). Ludmilla Voitkovska examines the reception of *The Secret Agent* and *Under Western Eyes* in Russia, paying close attention to problems of translation and implied readership, censorship in the past and painstaking scholarly work in the present. Robert Hampson's survey of maritime terms, rich in clues for the study of 'Typhoon', *Lord Jim* and *The Nigger of the 'Narcissus'*, suggests that even in a specialised vocabulary such as that of seafarers, the layperson will find not an impermeable barrier, but degrees of intelligibility.[12] Andrew Purssell also brings initiation to the fore: Conrad's initiation into the English-speaking world, the world of work at sea, and the world of writing, all as reflected in *A Personal Record*, which was in itself an initiation into autobiography for its author and an initiation into the story of his life for the reader. Conrad's memoirs look both back and forward, not only back to his early years as a sailor, but back to the world of his extended family, and forward to a struggle for acceptance in British literary society. Purssell, in fact, regards the memoirs as in part a retort to Robert Lynd's nasty review of *A Set of Six*, which, as Conrad put it, accused him of being 'a man without country and language' (*CL4* 107), in other words, a cosmopolitan.[13] In the culture wars of late nineteenth- and early twentieth-century Europe, that term was as often an insult as a compliment. If Conrad was in a much more positive sense a cosmopolitan, he was a man without a country only in his affiliation with a subjugated and dismembered Poland. In effect he was grounded in three countries and, for all his polyglossia, in three languages above all the rest. Claude Maisonnat contends that 'Polish was for him a kind of repressed language' whereas French had 'hidden implications related to the innermost libidinal forces of his creative power' and is constitutive of his art (p. 152). Whether or not one agrees with this ranking of Polish (one could point to the force of its rhythms and cadences in his prose, for instance), the virtue of this chapter lies in its going beyond the simple arithmetic of flagging the polonisms or gallicisms and then totting them up without much speculation about what their presence signifies. Maisonnat, in effect, is the equivalent of a North American river driver throwing precisely aimed sticks of dynamite into a logjam.

In this collection, there's no lack of such sticks. Taking just a few examples, we could cite the reading of *The Secret Agent* and *Under Western Eyes* by way of disability studies; the force of 'jabber', unarticulated sound and silence in Conrad's early works; the significance of Sulu as an unvoiced but vital presence in the 'Malay' fictions; or the mapping of the 'terroristic wilderness' in the political novels. But every one of the contributors has something new and challenging to say. What's more, their chapters reinforce each other. I have already pointed to the vein of ethical critique. Another shared element is the evocation not so much of absence as of incompleteness, loss and imperfection. We can see – and hear – this missingness in the letter to Cunninghame Graham of 14/15 January 1898, written as Jessie Conrad lay in childbed: 'thoughts vanish; words, once pronounced, die; and the memory of yesterday is as shadowy as the hope of to-morrow' (*CL2* 17). In other letters, the Italian phrase *tempi passati* ('times gone by') is a familiar motif. The elegiac note sounds again and again in Conrad's work – in the closing paragraphs of 'Karain', in *A Personal Record*, in the opening sequence of *The Rover*. Nostalgia and regret figure also in the preceding chapters of *Conrad and Language*, but here one emphasis falls on misprisions, the difficulties of speech and writing, the inadequacies of translation, the enemies of promise blocking the path to full expression. The other emphasis falls on how much and how often Conrad was moved by muteness and inarticulacy and suspicious of the glib.[14]

Conrad worked by contraries. In the final section of 'The Planter of Malata', the Editor, as he is called throughout, becomes caught up in the false tale of the lost fiancé who, in the best traditions of tragic romance, has died in Felicia Moorsom's arms at the very moment of their reunion. The Editor, who is a glutton for knowledge of the lives and people of the South Seas, longs to sniff out the story behind the story. 'From professional incontinence, he thirsted for a full cup of harrowing detail.'[15] Sardonic judgements like this, witty, unexpected, laconic, rich in signification, crop up all through Conrad's works. Another example is Marlow's vignette of the French man-of-war in 'Heart of Darkness': 'she was shelling the bush. It appears the French had one of their wars going on.'[16] In this case, Conrad knew the political context perfectly well but, to memorable effect, ignored it.[17] In the same novella, Marlow says of Kurtz's intoxicating report: 'The peroration was magnificent, though difficult to remember, you know' (*HD* 118). Professional continence, damning with faint praise and tactical forgetting are as much a part of Conrad's linguistic repertoire as the operatic set pieces in the final pages of *Almayer's Folly*, described in a letter to Marguerite Poradowska as a solo and a trio (*CL1* 146).

In *Portraits* (1931), the critic Desmond MacCarthy recalls a friend's opinion of *The Rover*: '"I have just finished listening to a performance on the Conrad."' MacCarthy 'saw what he meant ... All the famous Conrad stops are pulled out one after another.'[18] The friend's witticism is like a caricature by Max Beerbohm: fantastic, apt enough to treasure but not quite take as gospel. MacCarthy himself seems to go along with his friend, but as it turns out, MacCarthy has in mind only 'the tremendous set pieces of storms and long breathless tropic night' found in Conrad's fiction rather than 'the familiar scene of passion, almost mystically imaginative and supersensual, tinctured perhaps with melodrama but never with a drop of sentiment' or 'the scene of tempted and exalted honour'. Yet, although the scenes might be familiar, the narrative tactics aren't. MacCarthy alludes to 'the curt, mild-spoken English sailor' as a recurrent type, but 'Youth', 'Heart of Darkness', *Lord Jim* and *Chance* each presents a different version. Rather than being performances on the Conrad, they are performances on the Marlow. Likewise, the characters that don't recur are marvellously voiced: the Intended, Flora de Barral, Emilia Gould, Gentleman Brown, Mister Jones, Peyrol and many, many more.

The musical metaphor is apt because Conrad needs to be heard as well as read. Ivan Kreilkamp's article on 'phonographic logic' in 'Heart of Darkness', which teases out the significance of Kurtz's disembodied voice, and on a larger scale Michael Greaney's *Conrad, Language, and Narrative*, with its discussion of oral communities, are two resounding additions to the scanty literature on oral and aural elements in Conrad's work.[19] Although in the 'Preface' to *The Nigger of the 'Narcissus'* seeing trumps listening, listening is still vital, represented by 'the shape and ring of sentences', 'the magical suggestiveness of music – which is the art of arts'.[20] The aural quality of his work lives in the rhythms and cadences of the narrative passages as much as in the dialogue. When a copy of Ford's *The Good Soldier* arrived, Conrad put off reading it because he was at work on *The Shadow-Line*. 'With a writer like you (and a couple of others) it's merely a matter of prudence. Your cadences get into my head till I can't hear anything of mine and become paralysed for days' (*CL5* 340). There are exceptions to this prudence, but the principle is telling.

Whatever other conscious or unconscious drives governed Conrad's writing, we can hear and see a determination to reinvigorate the language of fiction and to challenge clichés and abstractions uttered in bad faith. He inherited these imperatives from Flaubert and shared them with Ford during the ten or so years of their close friendship.[21] In any case, Conrad's hostility to dullness, grandiloquence and lies is akin to that of many other twentieth-century authors.[22] A theorist creating a category of author-response criticism – that is, the response of authors to their earlier work – might point to a moment right at the beginning of his literary career when Conrad tells Edward Garnett that 'The Lagoon' has 'lots of secondhand Conradese in it' (*CL1* 301). The just words to frame his working habits are in Elizabeth Bishop's 'North Haven', an elegy for Robert Lowell:[23]

> *repeat, repeat, repeat: revise*
> *revise, revise*

## Notes

1. Wai Chee Dimock, *Through Other Continents: American Literature across Deep Time* (Princeton: Princeton University Press, 2008).
2. Just as one example, the September 2014 issue of *Modernism/modernity* (21.3) includes essays on Virginia Woolf, Ford Madox Ford, Henry Roth, W. B. Yeats, Henry Green and 'George Egerton' (Mary Chavelita Dunn Bright), but also on Fernando Pessoa, Emile Zola, Rainer Maria Rilke and Paula Moderson-Becker.

3. Christopher GoGwilt, *The Passage of Literature: Genealogies of Modernism in Conrad, Rhys, and Pramoedya* (Oxford: Oxford University Press, 2011).
4. In Polish, Berdyczów, Żytomierz and Czernichów.
5. Adding to the evidence that, contrary to its proverbial reputation as a backwater, Berdychiv was in a literary sense no such thing, Balzac married the Polish aristocrat Ewelina Hańska there in 1850.
6. Borrowing the title of Roland Barthes's book on his encounter with Japan, *L'Empire des signes* (1970). He experienced the country in a cloud of blissful unknowing. Conrad's experience with Russia was anything but blissful; he often refers to it as a blankness, a negation; see, for instance CL4 489, and *Under Western Eyes* (New York: Doubleday, Page, 1926), p. 33. Ludmilla Voitkovska's chapter in this volume gives a nuanced account of his attitudes.
7. See the special issue of *Studia Neophilogica* on 'Transnational Conrad', ed. Stephen Donovan (85, Supplement 1, 2013), in particular the essays by Richard Ambrosini, 'Reconceptualizing Conrad as a Transnational Novelist: A Research Programme', and Katherine Isobel Baxter, 'Speaking Foreign: Conrad and Modernist Multilingualism'.
8. There was also a Russian supplement, with work by Tolstoy and Chekhov. The English-language prospectus expressed the hope that the magazine would 'bring about a sense of closer fellowship between the nations'. For a fuller discussion, see Laurence Davies, '"Don't you think I am a lost soul?": Conrad's Early Stories in the Magazines', in Stephen Donovan, Linda Dryden and Robert Hampson (eds), 'Conrad and Serialization', *Conradiana* 41.1 (Spring 2009), pp. 18–23.
9. For a vigorous discussion of bigotry and fear in this story, see Amar Acheraïou, *Joseph Conrad and the Reader* (Basingstoke: Palgrave Macmillan, 2009), pp. 63–5; see also Katherine Isobel Baxter, '"Senseless speech" and Inaudibility in Conrad's "Amy Foster": Rethinking Trauma and the Unspeakable in Fiction', *Textual Practice* (October 2015), pp. 1–17.
10. Letter to E. L. Sanderson. The context is the Second Anglo-Boer War.
11. The phrase itself has been subject to many definitions and some objections. As used in this chapter, the area includes present-day Malaysia, Singapore, Indonesia and the Philippines. The Philippines are frequently ignored in discussions of *Almayer's Folly*, though, as Francis shows, Sulu history and language are important aspects of the novel. Likewise, Karain's miniature sultanate is in Mindanao, at the time of Conrad's story part of the Spanish empire and soon to be annexed by the United States.
12. Many trades of course do have their secrets, but as Hampson shows, Conrad had good aesthetic reasons for striking a balance between mystery and illumination.
13. Lynd was an Irish cultural nationalist who sometimes wrote under the name Robeard Ua Flionn; his continued residence in England and steady employment as a columnist suggest that some circles, at least, of literary London were rather tolerant.
14. In these paradoxes, he has much in common with Shakespeare: with, for instance, the presentation of Cordelia in the first act of *King Lear* or Octavia in the third act of *Antony and Cleopatra*.

15. Joseph Conrad, *Within the Tides* (New York: Doubleday, Page, 1926), p. 84.
16. Joseph Conrad, *Youth* (New York: Doubleday, Page, 1926), p. 61. Subsequent references are cited in the text as *HD*.
17. 'C'était pendant la guerre (!) du Dahomey' (*CL3* 93).
18. Quoted in Norman Sherry (ed.), *Conrad: The Critical Heritage* (London: Routledge and Kegan Paul, 1973), p. 361.
19. Michael Greaney, *Conrad, Language, and Narrative* (Cambridge: Cambridge University Press, 2002); Ivan Kreilkamp, 'A Voice without a Body: The Phonographic Logic of "Heart of Darkness"', *Victorian Studies*, 40.2 (Winter 1997), pp. 211–44; see also Kreilkamp's *Voice and the Victorian Storyteller* (Cambridge: Cambridge University Press, 2005).
20. Joseph Conrad, 'Preface' to *The Nigger of the 'Narcissus'* (New York: Doubleday, Page, 1926), pp. xi–xvi at p. xiii.
21. Scholars differ about the veracity of Ford's *Joseph Conrad: A Personal Remembrance* (London: Duckworth, 1924), but at the very least, there's reason to believe that Ford and Conrad discussed the language of fiction often and at length.
22. Out of many, one can cite the ethical scorn and mockery in Virginia Woolf's comparisons of male and female sentences, Ernest Hemingway's dismissal of military abstractions in *A Farewell to Arms*, and Karl Kraus's insistent yoking of linguistic and political corruption after the First World War; or the reaction against fascist language by Primo Levi and Natalia Ginzburg after the Second; or the satires on Communist terminology by Stanisław Lem and Wisława Szymbórska; or the parodic rants of generals and other tyrants in Wole Soyinka.
23. Elizabeth Bishop, *The Complete Poems, 1927–1979* (New York: Farrar, Straus and Giroux, 1979), p. 188.

# Contributors

**John Attridge** is Senior Lecturer in English at UNSW, Australia. His essays on Conrad, Ford Madox Ford, Henry James and Flann O'Brien have appeared in journals such as *Modernism/modernity*, *ELH*, the *Henry James Review* and *Modern Fiction Studies*, and he is the editor, with Rod Rosenquist, of *Incredible Modernism: Literature, Trust and Deception* (Ashgate, 2013).

**Katherine Isobel Baxter** is Reader in English Literature at Northumbria University, UK. She has published widely on Conrad in the *Conradian*, *Conradiana*, *Critical Survey*, *L'Epoque Conradienne*, *Studia Neophilologica* and *Textual Practice*. Her books include *Joseph Conrad and the Swan Song of Romance* (Ashgate, 2010), *Joseph Conrad: The Contemporary Reviews* Volume 4, coedited with Mary Burgoyne (Cambridge University Press, 2012), and *Joseph Conrad and the Performing Arts*, coedited with Richard J. Hand (Ashgate, 2009). She is currently editing, with Richard J. Hand *The Plays*, for the Cambridge Edition of the Works of Joseph Conrad.

**Laurence Davies** is Honorary Senior Research Fellow in the School of Modern Languages and Cultures at the University of Glasgow, UK, and President of the Joseph Conrad Society (UK). He succeeded Frederick R. Karl as General Editor of *The Collected Letters of Joseph Conrad* (Cambridge University Press, 1983–2008), and is advisory editor to the *Conradian*, *Conrad Studies* (Amsterdam) and the *Polish Yearbook of Conrad Studies*. His *Selected Letters of Joseph Conrad* appeared in 2015. He also serves on the editorial boards of the Cambridge Edition of the Works of Joseph Conrad and the Oxford Edition of the Works of Ford Madox Ford. He has published widely on Conrad, Cunninghame Graham and their contemporaries and on speculative fiction.

**Andrew Francis,** following a career in commerce, received his PhD from the University of Cambridge, UK, in 2010. He has published in the *Conradian* and contributed a chapter on 'Post-Colonial Conrad' to *The New Cambridge Companion to Joseph Conrad* (2015). His *Culture and Commerce in Conrad's Asian Fiction* (Cambridge University Press) was published in 2015.

**Andrew Glazzard** is a Senior Research Fellow at the Royal United Service Institute, UK, and the author of *Conrad's Popular Fictions: Secret Histories and Sensational Novels* (Palgrave Macmillan, 2016). In addition to numerous articles and book chapters on Conrad, he has written on the Victorian dynamite novel, Arthur Conan Doyle, H. G. Wells and Arnold Bennett.

**Christopher GoGwilt** is Professor of English and Comparative Literature at Fordham University, USA. His most recent book, *The Passage of Literature: Genealogies of Modernism in Conrad, Rhys, and Pramoedya* (Oxford University Press, 2011), won the Modernist Studies Association book prize for 2012. He is also the author of *The Invention of the West: Joseph Conrad and the Double-Mapping of Europe and Empire* (Stanford University Press, 1995) and *The Fiction of Geopolitics: Afterimages of Culture from Wilkie Collins to Alfred Hitchcock* (Stanford University Press, 2000).

**Robert Hampson** is Professor of Modern Literature in the English Department at Royal Holloway, University of London, UK, and Chairman of the Joseph Conrad Society (UK). He is the author of three monographs on Conrad, all published by Palgrave Macmillan: *Joseph Conrad: Betrayal and Identity* (1992), *Cross-Cultural Encounters in Joseph Conrad's Malay Fiction* (2000) and *Conrad's Secrets* (2012). He is a former editor of the *Conradian*, and he has coedited *Conrad and Theory* (1998) with Andrew Gibson and a triple issue of *Conradiana* on 'Conrad and Serialization' (2009) with Stephen Donovan and Linda Dryden. He also sits on the editorial board of the Cambridge Edition of the Works of Joseph Conrad.

**Yael Levin** is a Senior Lecturer in English Literature at the Hebrew University of Jerusalem, Israel. Her work has been published in *Conradiana*, the *Conradian*, *Partial Answers*, *Twentieth-Century Literature*, *Secret Sharers* (M-Studio, 2011), *Each Other's Yarns* (Novus Press, 2013) and her book *Tracing the Aesthetic Principle in Conrad's Novels* (Palgrave Macmillan, 2008). She is currently working on *The*

*Interruption of Writing*, a book that traces the evolution of models of textual production and creative agency from Romanticism to the digital age.

**Claude Maisonnat** is Emeritus Professor of English Literature at the Université Lumière-Lyon2, France. He has published more than thirty articles both in English and in French in such journals as *Conradiana*, the *Conradian* and *L'Epoque Conradienne* and has written two books on Conrad: *Lord Jim: Joseph Conrad* (Hachette, 2003) and a monograph entitled *Joseph Conrad and the Voicing of Textuality* (Columbia University Press, forthcoming) in the Conrad: Eastern and Western Perspectives series. He was Chairman of the French Conrad Society from 2006 to 2013. He has recently edited (in collaboration with Josiane Paccaud-Huguet) a volume on Conrad for the series Les Cahiers de l'Herne (2014).

**Josiane Paccaud-Huguet** is Professor of Modern English Literature and Literary Theory at Université Lumière-Lyon 2, France. She has published extensively on modernist and contemporary authors. A regular contributor to Conradian journals, she has been President of the Société Conradienne Française (1996–2008) and the invited editor of *Conrad in France*, a volume dedicated to the reception of Conrad's works in France (Columbia University Press, 2007). She has recently edited (in collaboration with Claude Maisonnat) a volume on Conrad for the series Les Cahiers de l'Herne (2014).

**Andrew Purssell** is an Assistant Editor of the *Conradian*. He has published widely on Conrad, including contributions to the Cambridge Edition of the Works of Joseph Conrad and *The New Cambridge Companion to Joseph Conrad* (2015). He is the co-author (with Richard J. Hand) of a study of Graham Greene and film, *Adapting Graham Greene* (Palgrave Macmillan, 2015).

**Ludmilla Voitkovska** is Associate Professor of English at the University of Saskatchewan, Canada. She has published on Conrad, translation and cultural reception, including a recent chapter, 'A View from the East: The Russian Reception of *Under Western Eyes*', in *Under Western Eyes: Centennial Essays* edited by Allan H. Simmons, J. H. Stape and Jeremy Hawthorn (Rodopi, 2011), and articles in *L'Epoque Conradienne*, *Conradiana* and the *Conradian*.

# Index

abstract language, 41, 44, 50–4, 56, 59–61
Acheräiou, Amar, 211
affect, 82–4, 86–7, 90
Allen, Jerry, 134–5
alterity, 161, 164
Althusser, Louis, 172
Anderson, Benedict, 120, 126, 129
Arabic, 138, 142, 205
Arabic script, 121, 128–9, 136, 144, 147n, 207
Austin, J. L., 7, 83, 85

Bakhtin, Mikhail, 118, 164
Baldwin, Debra Romanick, 127
Barthes, Roland, 75–6, 211n
Baxter, Katherine Isobel, 99–116, 182n, 211n
Beckett, Samuel, 7, 64–9, 71–3, 76–8
Benjamin, Walter, 65, 79n
Berthoud, Jacques, 139
Bhabha, Homi, 118, 129
Buginese, 129, 141–2, 205
Burke, Edmund, 30
Busza, Andrzej, 124

Carabine, Keith, 27, 124
cartography, 132, 135, 169
Chinese (language), 129, 142
Clemens, Florence, 135
Coleridge, S. T., 75
colonial attitudes, 139–40, 143
colonisation, 132–3, 135, 141–5
comparative linguistics, 2–3
concrete language, 44, 50, 52, 54, 59, 61, 83
Conrad, Borys, 2, 33
Conrad, Joseph

*Almayer's Folly*, 10, 117–21, 128–9, 133, 134, 141–4, 160, 172, 180–1, 209, 211n
'Amy Foster', 100, 206
'Anarchist, An', 40–1
'Autocracy and War', 52, 54, 59
*Chance*, 60, 74, 82, 86–7, 88, 91–3, 95–6
*Congo Diary*, 2
'Crime of Partition, The', 169
'End of the Tether, The', 24–5, 141, 145
'Falk', 146n
'Freya of the Seven Isles', 141
'Geography and Some Explorers', 169
'Heart of Darkness', 11, 40, 51–3, 68, 73–4, 75, 83, 89, 90–1, 93–4, 127, 209
'Karain: A Memory', 84–5, 141
*Lord Jim*, 14–16, 20–2, 64–5, 67–8, 69–79, 84, 85–6, 95, 120, 138–41, 146n, 149n, 154, 159–60, 205
*Mirror of the Sea, The*, 48–50, 59, 61
*Nigger of the 'Narcissus', The*, 11–14, 16–19, 65–6
*Nigger of the 'Narcissus', The* (Preface), 48, 50, 53, 59, 61, 83
*Nostromo*, 54–61, 101, 106–10, 152
*Outcast of the Islands, An*, 139–40, 142
'Outpost of Progress, An', 87, 206
'Outside Literature', 6, 61–2
'Partner, The', 25–6
*Personal Record, A*, 1, 166, 168–85
'Planter of Malata, The', 209
'Prince Roman', 124–6

*Rescue, The*, 141, 142, 149n
*Rover, The*, 31–5, 100, 155–60
*Secret Agent, The*, 31, 35–7, 101–6, 186–8, 197–201
*Shadow Line, The*, 146n
'Silence of the Sea, The', 49–50
'Typhoon', 11, 19–20, 22–4, 25
*Under Western Eyes*, 37–40, 53, 87–8, 89–90, 97n, 99, 100, 110–14, 121–3, 127–8, 186–97
*Victory*, 70–2, 141, 142
*Within the Tides*, 53
'Youth', 14, 22, 74, 88–9
*Cosmopolis*, 206
cosmopolitanism, 108, 161, 180, 208
covert plot, 119–20
Cunningham, Valentine, 185n
Cunninghame Graham, Robert, 4, 51–2, 59, 205
Cyrillic script, 118–19, 121–3, 127, 205, 207

Darwin, Charles, 3
Davidson, Michael, 114
Davies, Laurence, 204–12
Davis, Lennard J., 99–100, 112, 114
de Saussure, Ferdinand, 3–4, 83
'delayed decoding', 52–3, 64, 88–9, 108, 117, 120
Derrida, Jacques, 126, 129, 161, 162
disability studies, 7, 99–114
Donovan, Stephen, 50
doubling, 67–8, 127
Dutch (language), 2, 133, 141, 142, 145

Eagleton, Terry, 174
Eco, Umberto, 163
Eliot, T. S., 4
eloquence, 37, 51, 54–5, 58–9, 61
Enderwitz, Anne, 82
English (language), 1, 117, 139–42, 171
Englishness, 118, 139, 177, 180
epistemological uncertainty, 64
Erdinast Vulcan, Daphna, 69, 159–60
Esperanto, 206

Fleishman, Avrom, 160
Ford, Ford Madox, 43n, 161, 166, 168, 173, 177–8, 180, 210
France, Anatole, 157, 180
Francis, Andrew, 132–50

Frege, Gottlob, 3–4
French (language), 1–2, 5, 7, 118, 146n, 151–67, 202n
French Revolution, 30–5
Freud, Sigmund, 34

Gallicisms, 133, 151–67
German (language), 2, 8n
Glazzard, Andrew, 28–43
Godwin, William, 30
GoGwilt, Christopher, 117–31, 204
Gokulsing, Tanya, 118
Graham, Kenneth, 80n
Gray, John, 43n
Greaney, Michael, 210
Greenblatt, Stephen, 173, 181

Hampson, Robert, 10–27, 33, 173
Harpham, Geoffrey Galt, 165
Hawthorn, Jeremy, 5–6, 63n, 89, 97n
Heidegger, Martin, 69
Henricksen, Bruce, 66
Hervouet, Yves, 5, 154, 157
Houston, Amy, 135, 148n
hybrid English, 140–1, 176

Idealism (philosophical), 44–8, 50, 60–1
ideals, idealisation, 51–62, 107
implicit translation, 148–9n
impressionism, 44, 48, 49, 52, 54, 64
international English, 139, 176
Italian (language), 2

Jameson, Fredric, 174
Javanese, 141, 205
*Jawi*, 121, 128, 136, 204, 207
journalism, 48–52, 108–9

Kagarlitsky, Y. I., 186
Karl, Frederick, 134, 174
Kashkin, I., 191
Katarsky, I. M., 186
Kerr, Douglas, 70, 80n
Keynes, John Maynard, 4, 45
Kipling, Rudyard, 14, 158
Koc, Barbara, 133
Korzeniowski, Apollo, 1, 8n, 123, 169, 191, 202n, 205
Kreilkamp, Ivan, 210

Lacan, Jacques, 85, 88, 90
language as event, 65, 74–9
language loss, 138

# 218 Index

language of the other, 64, 70–3, 74, 79
language-switching, 151, 154, 205
Latin (language), 2, 124–6, 176, 205
Leavis, F. R., 95, 175–6
Levenson, Michael, 53
Levin, Yael, 64–81
Lindskog, Anika, J., 90
linguistic nationalism, 174–6, 179
'linguistic turn', 82
Lucas, Michael, 158
Lynd, Robert, 175

macaronic, 151, 205
McHale, Brian, 67, 69
Maisonnat, Claude, 93, 94, 151–67
Malay, 2, 7, 10, 117, 119–21, 128–9, 132–3, 134–9, 141–2, 144–5, 147n
'material interests', 54, 59, 60
Maugham, Somerset, 16, 138, 186
'metaleptic leaps', 94
metaphor, 39–40, 50, 103–5
Miller, J. Hillis, 52
Mitchell, David T., 99, 100
modernism, 44, 64–79, 80n, 118, 176, 180, 204
modernist subject, 65, 69–74, 76–9
Moore, G. E., 4, 7, 44–8, 50, 59–62
Morf, Gustav, 154
Morzinski, Mary, 5, 154
Most, Johann, 31, 36, 42–3
multilingualism, 1–2, 134, 151–3, 204–5

Najder, Zdzisław, 124, 154, 173, 174–5
Nakai, Asako, 118
'naturalistic fallacy', 46
'New Realism' *see* Realism
Niland, Richard, 54, 57

objects of consciousness, 47
oral communities, 210
Orwell, George, 41, 151, 158, 160, 176
Orzeszkowa, Eliza, 179

Paccaud-Huguet, Josiane, 82–98
Pedersen, Lene, 65
perlocutionary, 83–7, 90, 94–5
phenomenology, 47–8
pidgin, 138, 142
Polish (language), 2, 5, 118, 119, 124–6, 153
Polish nationalism, 124–6, 169

Polonisms, 118, 133, 208
polyglossia, 164–5, 208
polyphony, 72
Poradowska, Marguerite, 5, 151–2, 154, 209
postcolonial criticism, 70, 118
post-modernism, 67
post-structural theories of language, 71, 74
pronouns, 65–6
psychopathology, 34–5, 38–9
Pulc, Irmina, 5
Purssell, Andrew, 168–85

Quayson, Ato, 100

Rapin, René, 5, 153, 154
Ray, Martin, 6–7, 48, 134, 146n
Realism (philosophical), 45–7
restricted code, 141
Roberts, Andrew Michael, 174
Roman alphabet, 144, 147n, 205
Romanised print form, 117–31
Rubery, Matthew, 51
*Rumi*, 121, 128, 204
Russell, Bertrand, 4, 44–5
Russian (language), 1–2, 7–8, 119, 121–3, 186–203
Ryle, Gilbert, 44–5

Said, Edward, 173
scepticism, 39, 41, 60–1
Schleicher, August, 3
seamanship, 34, 118
Senn, Werner, 5
Sherry, Norman, 36
silence, 110–13
Simmons, Allan H., 170
Skouen, Tina, 96n
Smith, David R., 123
Snyder, Sharon L., 99, 100
Spanish (language), 2
speaking subject, 66, 74, 89–90
speech, 65, 82–91
speech acts, 83–5, 87–8, 92–4, 95
Stape, J. H., 173
Stepniak (Sergei Kravchinsky), 31, 37–8, 42n
subjectivity, 53–4, 64–79
Sulu (language), 132, 136, 142–4, 146n, 149n
swearing, 16–22
Swift, Jonathan, 10–11
Szczypien, Jean, 124

technical language, 10–16, 48–50, 54, 59, 61
terrorism, 28–43, 190–1
  critical terrorism studies, 29, 40
Thomson, Rosemarie Garland, 113
translation, 119, 186–90, 195–9, 200–1
transliteration, 119, 144, 198–9
trauma, 33–4, 87, 90, 91, 94, 95

Valente, Joseph, 102
van Marle, Hans, 183n

violence, 28, 31–3, 35, 36, 38, 39
Voitkovska, Ludmilla, 185–203
Volapük, 206

Watt, Ian, 52–3, 117
Watts, Cedric, 85, 119, 174
Wells, H. G., 151, 180, 186
White, Andrea, 171
Wittgenstein, Ludwig, 4
Wollaeger, Mark, 53, 60
Woolf, Virginia, 155, 175
World War I, 33

EU representative:
Easy Access System Europe
Mustamäe tee 50, 10621 Tallinn, Estonia
Gpsr.requests@easproject.com

www.ingramcontent.com/pod-product-compliance
Lightning Source LLC
Chambersburg PA
CBHW051057230426
43667CB00013B/2331